THE FUTURE OF
AN ILLUSION

FILM, FEMINISM, AND PSYCHOANALYSIS

Media & Society

Richard Bolton, series editor

Simon Watney *Policing Desire: Pornography, AIDS, and the Media*

THE FUTURE OF AN ILLUSION

FILM, FEMINISM, AND PSYCHOANALYSIS

Constance Penley

University of Minnesota Press, Minneapolis

Published by the University of Minnesota Press
2037 University Avenue Southeast, Minneapolis MN 55414.
Printed in the United States of America.
Book and cover design by Lois Stanfield.

Library of Congress Cataloging-in-Publication Data

Penley, Constance, 1948-
    The future of an illusion: film, feminism, and psychoanalysis /
    Constance Penley.
        p.   cm. — (Media and society)
        Bibliography: p.
        Includes index.
        ISBN 0-8166-1771-6. — ISBN 0-8166-1772-4 (pbk.)
        1. Feminism and motion pictures.   2. Women and psychoanalysis.
3. Experimental films.   4. Psychoanalysis and motion pictures.   5. Motion
pictures—Philosophy.
I. Title.   II. Series.
PN1995.9.W6P46   1989   88-36664
791.43'088042—dc19   CIP

Earlier versions of these chapters originally appeared in the following publications:
Chapter 1: The Avant-Garde and Its Imaginary, *Camera Obscura*/2, Fall 1977; Chapter
2: The Avant-Garde: Histories and Theories, *Screen*, Autumn 1978, vol. 19, no. 3;
Chapter 3: "A Certain Refusal of Difference": Feminisim and Film Theory, *Art after
Modernism: Rethinking Representation*, ed. Brian Wallis (Boston: David R. Godine,
1985); Chapter 4: Feminism, Film Theory, and the Bachelor Machines, *m/f*
(London), no. 10, 1985; Chapter 5: Pornography, Eroticism (on *Every Man for
Himself*), *Camera Obscura*/8-9-10, Fall 1982; Chapter 6: Les Enfants de la Patrie (on
France/Tour/Detour/Two Children), *Camera Obscura*/8-9-10, Fall 1982; Chapter 7: Time
Travel, Primal Scene, and the Critical Dystopia (on *The Terminator* and *La Jetée*),
Camera Obscura/15, Fall 1986; Chapter 8: The Cabinet of Dr. Pee-wee: Consumerism
and Sexual Terror, *Camera Obscura*/17, May 1988; Chapter 9: Teaching in Your Sleep:
Feminism and Psychoanalysis, *Theory in the Classroom*, ed. Cary Nelson (Urbana:
University of Illinois Press, 1986).

The University of Minnesota is an equal-opportunity educator and employer.

For Janet Bergstrom and Elisabeth Lyon

Contents

Feminism and Pedagogy

Acknowledgments

*I*T IS ALMOST IMPOSSIBLE to thank all those who have contributed to my thinking on these essays written over the last twelve years. First, of course, I am indebted to Janet Bergstrom and Elisabeth Lyon, with whom I have worked for almost fifteen years now, on *Women and Film* and then *Camera Obscura*. Ideas, critique, and friendship have come from Jacqueline Rose, Abigail Solomon-Godeau, Elizabeth Cowie, Parveen Adams, Connie Hatch, Jim Pomeroy, Ben Brewster, Nancy Wood, Steve Fagin, Sandy Flitterman, Terrel Seltzer, Mary Kelly, Sam Kinser, Stephen Grosz, Malcolm Le Grice, Michael Covino, and Victor Burgin. To my teachers, who were even then my friends, go many thanks: Christian Metz, Thierry Kuntzel, Bertrand Augst, and Seymour Chatman. The ideas and help generously given by Raymond Bellour over the years have been invaluable. I want also to thank my comrades in the Unit for Criticism and Interpretive Theory at the University of Illinois, Urbana-Champaign, especially Paula Treichler, Cary Nelson, Richard Wheeler, Larry Grossberg, and Stanley Gray; and the members of the Susan B. Anthony Research Seminar at the University of Rochester, especially Sharon Willis, Susan Kent, and Bette London. For the last five years I have greatly benefited from the ideas and enthusiasm of the associate editors of *Camera Obscura*, Lea Jacobs, Denise Mann, Lynn Spigel, and Janet Walker. I couldn't have done any of it without the practical help I have had from the Pacific Film Archive (Edith Kramer and Nancy Rosales), Zoetrope Studios (Tom Luddy, Linda Reisman, Sara Strom, and Francis Coppola), and the British Film Institute (Ian Christie, Geoffrey Nowell-Smith, John Stewart, and Erich Sargeant).

And finally, thanks to Andrew Ross, who, although he shudders at hearing the word "support," gave that and much more.

Preface

*Having recognized religious doctrines as illusions, we are
at once faced by a further question: may not other
cultural assets of which we hold a high opinion and by which
we let our lives be ruled be of a similar nature? Must not the
assumptions that determine our political regulations be called
illusions as well? And is it not the case that in our civilization
the relations between the sexes are disturbed by an erotic
illusion or a number of such illusions?*

Sigmund Freud, *The Future of an Illusion*, 34

The essays collected here were written over a period of twelve years,
on topics ranging from avant-garde art and film to popular culture and
television. To present the sequence of these essays as a natural or characteristic evolution of feminist thinking over more than a decade
would be to give a too tidy account of their emergence. Rather, they
can best be seen as a series of provisional responses to specific and often very fraught debates in contemporary feminism, debates about
representation and sexual difference, feminism and the avant-garde,
the place of woman in classical Hollywood cinema, the feminist critique of film theory, pornography and eroticism, feminism and popular culture, and feminism in the academy. If not characteristic then,
they are at least symptomatic of a certain kind of theoretical approach—feminist and psychoanalytic—to the work on women and
the media that began in the early seventies.

Although the tone and style of the essays vary greatly, they were all
written in a utilitarian vein ("Someone *has* to say something right now
about the feminist relation to . . . "). Or at least I needed to believe
that my motive was one of feminist utility. Everyone needs a reason to

write, and that was my own working illusion. I am proud to say that none of the essays appeared in "refereed" academic journals. They were all written on demand, because they were "needed," at specific times and in specific circumstances, by small, political, even marginal journals like *Camera Obscura, Screen,* or *m/f,* or for edited collections aimed at making a particular intervention in, for example, art world practices or radical pedagogy. Fortunately for the reader of these essays now, I generally tried in each to be explicit in laying out what I took to be the issues to which I was responding. There are no hidden agendas here, or if there were, I can no longer remember them.

Because these essays are appearing now, I would like to say a few words about my use of "sexual difference" as a working term throughout the book. This seems all the more pertinent since many feminist theorists are now claiming that we have "gone beyond" sexual difference and necessarily so, they say, since theorizing around this term serves only to limit or even subvert feminist theory and practice. In its place they propose to substitute "gender" as a more capacious and less loaded term, one that could better describe and explain how human subjects come to take up their sexual roles in a system whose logic determines that they be either male or female. Certain claims have been made about the shortcomings of theories of sexual difference, along with proposals for ways in which theories of gender will resolve those deficiencies. In what follows, I will briefly examine these claims to show why I think it was and still is important to think in terms of sexual difference.

Beginning in the early seventies "sexual difference" rapidly established itself as an important analytical category for many feminist theorists. In an initial bifurcation that invariably led to misunderstandings, sexual difference became both the watchword for "New French Feminism," with its emphasis on, and celebration of, essential differences between men and women, and also the working notion for feminists looking to Jacques Lacan's rereading of Freud for a more complex account of subjectivity and sexual identity than any then available. My adoption of the term is taken from the latter usage. On the other hand, the term gender, for the most part, came into feminist theory from the social sciences. Joan Scott here summarizes the specific emphasis of gender as an analytical category:

> It is a way of referring to the exclusively social origins of the subjective identities of men and women. Gender is, in this definition, a social

category imposed on a sexed body . . . The use of gender emphasizes an
entire system of relationships that may include sex, but is not directly
determined by sex or directly determining of sexuality.[1]

Gender is thus defined as an exclusively social set of effects imposed
on a body that is already sexed. In *Technologies of Gender*[2] Teresa de
Lauretis understands gender in much the same way. In the introduction to her book she describes the gendered subject as constituted
"across languages and cultural representations; a subject engendered in
the experiencing of race and class, as well as sexual, relations; a subject
therefore not unified but rather multiple, and not so much divided as
contradicted" (2). De Lauretis's emphasis on "engendering" as an active process of taking on an identity contrasts with Scott's purely sociological notion of gender as imposed on an already sexed body, but
her call for a theory of a "multiple" subject (based upon her reading of
Foucault), rather than the split subject of psychoanalysis, resocializes
sexual difference by eliminating the effects of the unconscious from
the processes of "engenderment." Finally, like Scott, she conceives of
sexual difference as only one strand among many in a pluralistic array
of (purely social) differences.

The move to relativize and even deemphasize sexual difference by
feminists like Scott, de Lauretis, or Michèle Barrett,[3] for example,
arises from the perceived need for a theory of the subject that could
account for a range of differences, which, it is argued, are necessarily
neglected in any approach that *starts* from a theory of sexual difference.
(It has even been argued that the work on sexual difference over the
last ten to fifteen years has retarded work on other kinds of differences, like those of race, class, and ethnicity, a damning political
charge, if true.)[4] Feminist work on sexual difference is seen as having
reached an impasse because it, and the psychoanalytic theory to which
it is indebted, lacks the kind of social or historical "positivity" needed
to align it with other differences in a comprehensive feminist theory of
subjectivity.

What does it mean to say that theories of sexual difference lack
"positivity"? Perhaps it could be put this way: theories of sexual difference concern themselves with the construction of subjectivity but
not in a way that is seen as constructive. In other words, such theories
do not always contribute to the *reconstruction* of a new feminine or feminist subject. It is true that psychoanalytically based theories of sexual
difference lack "positivity" in that they offer neither instructions nor

prescriptions for reeducating the psyche along more progressive lines. This is because these theories take as their primary focus the role of the unconscious in the constitution of sexual difference. The psyche is not utopian: in fact, it is quite conservative. For Freud, the ego's motives are dubious at best, but for Lacan the ego is fundamentally narcissistic, constituted as it is through the mirrored image of itself. Thus the ego is a trap, only ever an illusion, and a rather destructive one at that. So too, because the subject is founded in a doubling of itself, Lacan claimed that its most characteristic feature is paranoia: whatever I do to that image in the mirror can come back at me. And as for sexual difference in psychoanalytic theory, that difference is seen to be imposed upon the subject (who is originally polymorphously perverse, then bisexual, with a strong homosexual tendency). But because that imposition is only ever more or less successful, never totally so, the subject will always be in conflict with its own ill-fitting, "authorized" sexual identity. Another "non-positive" emphasis arises from the attention psychoanalysis gives to the variety and vagaries of desire. In a psychoanalytic perspective feminists would have to consider their relation to their own aggressivity (not just that which comes from outside) and their complicity with desires (both their own and that of others) that cannot be described as politically "correct."

The picture of human subjectivity that emerges from psychoanalysis is not easily compatible with that espoused by American feminism, in particular, which is grounded in idealism, voluntarism of the will, and a traditional American strain of utopianism (its equal commitment to pragmatism notwithstanding). No political movement or ideology could generate itself without an idealistic sense of political will and a vision of a better future. But American feminists have often been reluctant to confront theoretical evidence about the limitations of those idealist and utopian ideas which are fundamental to feminist ideology and practice. This is true not only for those who present the best arguments against sexual difference but also for those who argue for a non-psychoanalytic theory of gender. In Joan Scott's rigorously argued essay "Gender: A Useful Category of Historical Analysis"[5] she admits to her own "hopeless utopianism" (1064) when faced with a theory that posits permanent psychical conflict and permanent (unconscious) antagonism between the sexes. In addition Scott confesses that she is uncomfortable with an analysis that is so universalizing. Although she believes that the psychoanalytic emphasis on psychical conflict and instability is an important one for feminist theory, she does not think it should be posed in a way that suggests the timelessness of conflict and instability, and their imperviousness to historical change.

Scott, like many feminists, is correct to mistrust the "universalizing" of psychic categories and to feel uneasy with the prospect that sexual antagonism and psychical conflict will never be resolved. Marxists have long felt the same way about the recalcitrance of "ideology." Although Louis Althusser's claims about the value of science over ideology and the determination of the economic "in the last instance" have been roundly criticized over the last ten years, at least one of his ideas still retains a great deal of force—ideology will never disappear, not even in a hypothetically classless society. In other words, humans will never have a nonimaginary relation to the lived world. It is not by coincidence that this formulation is very close to a psychoanalytic way of thinking, since it was precisely to psychoanalysis that Althusser turned in his attempt to rearticulate the Marxist theory of ideology. Ideology, then, in this sense, could be said to be "universal." Its structure, function, and contents will change according to historical circumstances, but humans will always have to negotiate their lived experience to real social conditions through the ways they imagine that experience, never directly. A similarly "universal" law or mechanism in psychoanalysis would be that of repression, the outcome of the splitting of the subject and the requirement that one take up a sexual position in relation to the dictates of symbolic law. Although the conditions under which its effects are manifest will vary in different times and places, this rule is "universal" insofar as it is impossible to foresee a culture in which it would not be the case that one must give up something to become socialized. Perhaps then it is not the feminist theoretical task to do away with ideology or repression, since it is not possible anyway, but to see how those terms might be historicized. Indeed, Scott argues for "a genuine historicization and deconstruction" of the terms of the binary opposition male and female, but only in order to refuse their "fixed and permanent quality" (1064). There may be, however, a certain *theoretical* fixity and permanence we will have to live with if we are not to fall into a wishful "utopianism of the psyche."[6]

Feminist theories have always relied heavily on utopianism as a guide to their commitment to reform. To argue, for example, that it is possible to change the functioning of the Oedipal complex by requiring men to do half the nurturing, one must posit the short-term refor-

mability of the psyche. Although there are many good reasons for
having men take on half the labor of raising children, the prospect of
changing fundamental psychical structures in the near future is not one
of them. However, if Marxists can accept Althusser's argument for the
relative autonomy of superstructural forces like ideology, then feminists should be able at this point to give theoretical credence to the
proposition that the unconscious has its own time and its own structures and modes of functioning that are not coextensive with those of
the social world. Whether we like it or not, that is the consequence of
taking the unconscious seriously, a theoretical habit that feminism needs
to retain, despite, or because of, the difficulties it poses for constructing a feminine or feminist political subject. Feminist theory is not homogeneous, and not every one of its contributing theories should be
judged by the degree and number of positive prescriptions it can offer.
To rewrite Gramsci, perhaps what feminist theory needs to consider is
the pessimism of the unconscious at the same time as it touts the op-
timism of the (feminist) will.

What would we stand to lose, in theory and practice, by doing otherwise? Feminism would have to give up the possibility of understanding that there is a part of each of us that does not always do what
we (think we) want it to do. So too, we would have to ignore the
mechanisms of denial, wish-fulfillment, resistance, and complicity
that suffuse all our personal and political life. (Psychoanalysis shows
us that the other side of "the personal is political" is true as well: the
political is personal.) Feminism would also have to relinquish a theory
of sexuality that demonstrates the difficulty of taking up a sexual position and the instability of that position (what a girl must go through
to become a woman, if indeed she ever does so).[7] Finally, feminist theory would have to abandon the idea of psychical life and its effects altogether since these would now be seen as no more than the simple
internalization of sociological or biological imperatives (gender as
"imprinting").

Can psychoanalytic feminism be charged with promoting a monolithic discourse, one that pretends to offer a universal description
about how one comes to take up a sexual role? On the contrary, I think
its claims are necessarily very modest ones. Precisely because psychoanalysis insists on the radical otherness of the unconscious to conscious life, it can offer no ready description of the direct relation of one
to the other; it does not assert that to change the one is to change the
other. Because it lays emphasis on the conservatism of the psyche and

the instability of sexual identity, it explains why the psyche can never be made the basis of a progressive politics, feminist or otherwise. It is precisely because psychoanalysis does not preach any such positivity that its insights are crucial to any version of feminism that wants to move beyond idealism, utopianism, or a political practice that would have its basis in wish-fulfilling desires.

In an essay for a volume on the politics of postmodernism, Laura Kipnis claims that feminists escaped into "academic" psychoanalytic theory when feminism as a political movement fell apart, which is another version of the charge that psychoanalytic criticism is a symptom or even a source of the fragmentation within the women's movement.[8] But to say that the women's movement has fragmented to the point of disintegration, one would have to be more specific about the nature of that original "unity" and about where one locates different kinds of feminist activity today. It is important to remember the real reasons why feminist theory turned to psychoanalysis. One of the most urgent was the need to develop a critique of the view that patriarchy is a force that oppresses all women, at all times and in the same way. This critique drew heavily upon the psychoanalytic understanding of the split subject and the complicated forms of the subject's resistance to, and complicity with, the imposition of symbolic law. Today we find that feminist historical research has been amplifying this critique by drawing attention to the uneven effects of male oppression with accounts of specific moments when the hegemonic imbalance between oppression, resistance, and complicity was especially complex.[9] Also crucial to the breakup of the notion of patriarchy as a monolithic force (and of women as universally oppressed) was the psychoanalytic claim that men do not possess the phallus any more than women do. Although history has appeared to favor those with a penis in its conferral of phallic powers, those powers must in fact be acquired and negotiated; they are not automatically given or unproblematically held.

A similar response could be made to the charge that psychoanalytic feminism, in its stress on the division and instability of subjectivity, makes it impossible to theorize a feminist subject. The emphasis on instability is sometimes interpreted as an uncritical reflection of a feminist movement in trouble, one that does not know if it is post-, neo-, or simply defunct. From this perspective, theories of sexual difference are seen as *directly* responsible for the fragmentation of a feminist movement already in sad disarray. As Rosalind Delmar puts it in her title essay in *What Is Feminism?*, "To deconstruct the subject 'woman', to question whether 'woman' is a coherent identity, is also to imply the question of whether 'woman' is a coherent political identity, and therefore whether women can unite politically, culturally, and socially as 'women' for other than very specific reasons. It raises questions about the feminist project at a very fundamental level."[10] Delmar finds the political implications of such an approach "alarm[ing]" and "potentially subversive" (28) of feminism as a political movement. One could only reply that theories of sexual difference have indeed asked whether the feminist project, "at a very fundamental level," is unified and whether it needs such a unity to exist at all. For many, this has been the most difficult line of questioning posed by theories of sexual difference, precisely because of its political implications. But in what respect do theories of sexual difference subvert a necessary political unity? Although the subject of the unconscious is divided, this does not mean that the social subject (which functions at a different level) cannot be cohesive, or at least cohesive enough to be able to enter into political groupings as a result of (more or less) conscious decision-making. So too, if we have learned from psychoanalysis to question the presumed unity of any given subjectivity, why should we feel obliged to drop this critique when it comes to the question of social configurations? "Conscious daily life" is hardly immune to the operations of the unconscious. To be faithful to this critique one would indeed have to say that women can "unite politically, culturally and socially as 'women' for [only] very specific reasons." The task therefore is not to seek the sameness that can unite women as women but to see how that unity can be forged and alliances created, *while always staying alert to the bases on which they are being made.* In such a way we might also, for example, be able to *avoid* such horrible alliances as that of the anti-pornography feminists and the right-wing moral reformers, who came together around the shared idea that women need to be protected from the victimization of pornography. The basis for such a unity was a presumed quality of all women (their victimization and need for protection), but it was a presumption that suppressed the considerable differences between each group's notion of the ideal status of modern women. It was a political embarrassment because the basis of the unity was not fully examined.[11]

There is, however, no doubt that theories of sexual difference, in their emphasis on splitting, the divided subject and fragmentation, do not make the task of a common articulation with other differences any easier. Gender-based theories appear to offer a much easier articulation of sex, race, class, ethnicity, and so on. But this is at the price of re-defining sexual difference as a social difference ("Gender is . . . a social category imposed on a sexed body [Scott 1056–57]). The "gendered" body, unlike the body described by psychoanalysis, is either already (unproblematically) sexed or its sexual identity is the result of a number of discourses and representations imposed on that body. Recast in this way as a social difference, sexual difference is then put on a level with other differences. It is no surprise, then, that American feminist historians and sociologists have turned to newer psychoanalytic theories, Nancy Chodorow's for example, that are fundamentally sociological. The result is a very economical theory of difference(s). One does not have to shift levels of analysis in order to account for the entire range of differences: they are now all seen to be historically determined *social* differences, and therefore answerable to the methods of empiricism and behaviorism. But what if these differences are theoretically incommensurable? What if there are different kinds of differences, each working at different levels, each requiring its own specific methods of analysis? This is not at all to say that the various differences have no relation to each other—one can look at any popular text—*Rocky* or *Cagney and Lacey*—to see how ideas, for example, about national identity are fundamentally dependent on interlocking ideas about sex, race, class, and ethnicity. And while each difference demands its own methods of analysis, one would not want to confine any method, like psychoanalytic theory, to the study of sexual difference alone. Psychoanalytic ideas, for example, have been profitably used to make sense of fantasies of racial difference.[12] Feminist theory today is mature enough to prove capable of formulating theories that acknowledge different levels of analysis, different temporalities, and different kinds of difference. At this point we do not need a new totalizing theory of differences, one in which each difference is perfectly articulable with all others. On the contrary, we need theories of difference(s) that are to be constructed, argued about, negotiated, linked, yes, but with an understanding of how those links need to be forged, not discovered.

I hope I have shown that there is a great deal at stake in how we define "gender" and how we use it as an analytical category today. It is precisely because feminist accounts of the cultural construction of gender cannot afford to lose sight of the role of the unconscious in that construction that I want to insist on retaining the ideas associated with the term sexual difference. So too, all of the essays collected here assume that the work on sexual difference is not simply a negative project of "deconstruction" (in the broadest sense of the term). Although psychoanalytic theory is attentive to the instability of subjective formations, it argues that subjectivity exists and that it emerges in real women and men. Not only does psychoanalysis show sexual identity to be a fiction, it also demonstrates how women and men resist that identity. It would be a mistake to celebrate those mechanisms of resistance (which, more often than not, bring a great deal of misery to the subject), but we do need to be able to explain how women and men negotiate symbolic laws about social and sexual identity that seem to be too rigid for modern life. If the essays that follow demonstrate that need, I will be content.

FEMINISM AND THE
AVANT-GARDE

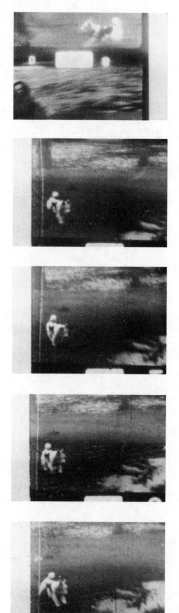

Little Dog for Roger *(Malcolm Le Grice, 1967)*.

The Avant-Garde and Its Imaginary

*T*HE NEW METAPSYCHOLOGICAL approaches to film and cinema can help us to think about the interest of certain recent avant-garde strategies to a feminist filmmaking practice. Any encounter of an avant-garde practice with an avowedly political one is, and has been, historically problematic. I would like to look at some of the presuppositions of one contemporary avant-garde movement from the point of view of these new approaches based on Freudian and Lacanian theory because I think they can illuminate some of the difficulties often found in the meeting of political and avant-garde practice. In the English Co-op movement we find a provocative attempt to bring these two practices together. The movement is described by its theoretician-filmmakers as a "structural/materialist" cinema aiming toward a "politics of perception." It sees its political effectiveness in its capacity to offer a cinematic experience completely outside of and against the effects and strategies of dominant classical cinema, especially the kind of identification with characters and diegesis that renders the spectator unconscious of his or her own experiences in watching the film.

A crucial starting point for these new metapsychological approaches is Christian Metz's claim that the cinematic signifier is by its very nature linked to the imaginary. He argues too that the cinematic institution constructs a fetishistic relation for the spectator to the frame, the characters, the story, and even the cinematic institution itself. Next, taking the Freudian notion of "dream-work" to an analysis of the progressive engenderment of the filmic text, Thierry Kuntzel describes the operations of dream processes like condensation and displacement at work in the spectator's unconscious reading of the film — the "other film" that takes place only in the mind. Jean-Louis Baudry goes even further in proposing that the entire cinematographic apparatus is taken in a wish inherent to the human psyche whose roots can already be seen in the time of Plato, a wish for a return to that "other scene," a movement that creates "a fantasmatization of the subject" by simulating a subject-effect that is an artificial state of regression. And finally, the recent work of Raymond Bellour on cinema and hypnosis attempts to describe filmic fascination and identification by showing the ways in which the film and the apparatus work together to produce hypnotic effects on the spectator. He also tries to show that both cinema and psychoanalysis had their origin in hypnosis, thus opening a discussion of their collusion on a particularly twentieth-century concern: the relation of subject to image, of the subject as a function *of* image.[1]

Given these recent theses on the psychical roots of the cinematic institution, the degree of "imaginariness" of the cinematic signifier, and the levels of regression, fascination, and identification involved in the spectator/screen relation, what is the place of a modernist practice like the Co-op movement that explicitly and militantly disavows any relation to "illusionism," the imaginary, identification, and even fiction? In what ways does it offer solutions to those problems basic to any attempt to formulate a filmmaking practice that would not reenact the illusions and manipulations of dominant cinema?

I will focus my discussion, for several reasons, on the theoretical writings that have come out of the English Co-op movement, mainly those of Malcolm Le Grice and Peter Gidal.[2] First, as I have already mentioned, this movement brings together more explicitly and more militantly than any other the problematic of a simultaneous political and formal avant-garde practice.[3] Many of the questions asked by these filmmakers and their films are posed implicitly in the work and writings of other experimental filmmakers, even in the United States where the two practices are almost unthinkable together. But for now I will take up the work of the structural/materialists as the most evident and articulated example of such a conjunction. Also, as theoretical writings, the work of Le Grice and Gidal offers an already secondarized and rationalized version of their own activity, thus making very apparent their manner of thinking about film.[4] Le Grice's writings, moreover, offer an account of both his and his contemporaries' filmmaking practice across a history of the abstract, formal avant-garde, thus opening the way for a discussion of the historical placement of this avant-garde, of its *historical imaginary*, that is, its own conception of its origins and influences, its relation to the other arts and to the history of art.

The theoretical writings of Malcolm Le Grice and Peter Gidal are highly complementary, one often citing the work of the other to help support an argument. They differ, however, in that Le Grice speaks from within a concerned historical reconstruction of the same movement for which Gidal polemically agitates, with wide-ranging references to much recent French theoretical work, including that of Jacques Derrida, Louis Althusser, and Julia Kristeva. Le Grice and Gidal are two of the most active filmmakers in the very movement they are attempting to describe in terms of its historical, political, aesthetic, and philosophical premises. In order not to collapse the specifics of the two arguments into each other, I will take them separately; in the course of my discussion their similarities should become evident and their differences remain distinct.

Abstract Film and Beyond (Malcolm Le Grice)

Malcolm Le Grice locates the roots of the filmic evolution he traces in the pre-cinematic painting of the Impressionist era, comparing the

---

Painting's mistake is the subject. Cinema's mistake is the scenario. Freed from this negative weight, the cinema can become a gigantic microscope of things never before seen and felt.

Fernand Léger, *L'Art du cinéma*, 1923

---

single brush-mark style of the Impressionists to the grain of the photographic image, and seeing the most significant philosophical parallels between painting and photography in their shared movement away from a religious view of the world to a scientific materialism based upon "observation, experiment and technological determination"(9). In citing Cezanne for creating an awareness of the relativistic nature of perception, he establishes the beginning of a historical line of artists who "make us aware of the flux of perception through process"(10). Quoting from Hans Richter, he also describes an evolution from one medium into another: "Problems of modern art led directly into film . . . Cubism, Expressionism, Dadaism, abstract art, Surrealism found not only their expression in films, but a new fulfillment on a new level" (20). Cinema thus emerged from, and improved upon, Dadaist poetry, modernist writing like that seen in *Finnegans Wake*, avant-garde music (Schoenberg), and Cubist and Futurist painting. From the very beginning of his argument Le Grice therefore establishes a cinematic essence prior even to the debut of film as a medium, and describes the movement of its progressive refinement through the abstract experiments of the twenties up to the present minimalist-influenced "structuralist" avant-garde. Because his argument sticks very closely to his own definition, this often results in eliminating films, filmmakers, and movements that do not fit neatly into the framework of "abstract" cinema; as he readily admits, this was a political decision. He sees the first work on abstraction (Cubism, Impressionism) as "opening up two significant possibilities: the first stems from considering painterly form as diagrammatic rather than pictorial representation, the second from direct perceptual response to the material and form of the work as an object itself" (15). And the result of this: "Art, instead of representing the world, could now be a model for it, functioning as analogy rather than imitation" (16). Among the many artistic experiments he describes in this reconstruction of the abstract movement is Viking Eggeling's attempt to create a universal language of visual composition, a complete syntax of form-relationships. Eggeling called for a "strict discipline of the elements" (21) and said, "Art is not the subjective explosion of the individual, but becomes the organic language of mankind, which must be basically free of misconceptions, clear-cut, so that it can become a vehicle for communication" (21). But accompanying this systematic, almost "scientific" abstraction is a tendency that paradoxically haunts the entire history of the abstract avant-garde movement, a tendency toward a strong metaphysical component. Le Grice notes the profound influence of Kandinsky and his *Concerning the Spiritual in Art* (1910) on the early formal filmmakers but has no answers for the similar collusion of science and mysticism in the first formal avant-gardists to use the most technologically advanced equipment ever available to filmmakers: John Whitney used computers to generate meditative mandala imagery, while Jordan Belson put to work his sophisticated, homemade, optical printer to create cosmic images of his inner religious experiences. For Le Grice it was crucial that the abstract movement broke away from the dominance of Kandinsky and moved toward an aesthetic of the "finite and physical" (84). While charting the history of this "intrinsic" movement toward abstraction, Le Grice offers both a normative definition of what new form cinema should seek—one that is "essentially 'cinematic'—not dominated by literature or theater, nor for that matter by painting or music" (32). But in each case, both in trying to describe the movement inherent in the medium and arguing for cinematic specificity, he must eliminate as not properly within that definition some of the very films which have been considered *the* cinematic avant-garde (*Un Chien Andalou, L'Age D'or, La Coquille et le Clergyman,* etc.). He sees fit to eliminate these films (either partially or wholly) from this evolution because they use "associative," "symbolic" imagery and narrative—elements always susceptible to being recuperated by dominant cinema in its efforts to construct and manipulate a passive spectator. The only films allowed to be progressive in his definition are those which use "procedure as the basis of content," that is, films which "draw attention to the material nature of the film itself and the images on it as a photochemical reality" (35). Le Grice speaks several times of the filmmakers' lack of awareness of their own evolutionary direction, and also of their techniques as being "beyond the full grasp of the artists at that time," (48) "a kind of path of the early filmmakers which can only be known to us now," (48) thus reinforcing the teleology of his historical description and the omniscience of his own point of view.

Providing some of the most crucial articulations of Le Grice's argument is the work of Dziga Vertov, which he sees as an exemplary solution to the question of how "radicalism in the formal aspect of cinema can be related to radical politics . . . the link between politics and the mode of perception engendered in the film audience" (52). Since one of the aims of the book is to demonstrate the intrinsic political thrust of formal cinema, the "politics of perception" (135), he insistently refers to Vertov's strategies, comparing them to those of the formal avant-garde. He praises Vertov for having presented a revolutionary critique of dominant cinema and for having rejected narrative and fiction in his attempt to depict post-revolutionary daily life. For Le Grice all of Vertov's work stresses the relation of perception and consciousness, and the need to create a new revolutionary consciousness through extending the possibilities of perception. Vertov's most important aim was to create a conscious spectator: "the conscious alone can fight against magical suggestions of every kind" ("Consciousness or Subconsciousness," 56). The Kino-Eye can accomplish this because it is not a substitute for the human eye but "a machine in its own terms capable of extending or creating a new perception" (58). Vertov's editing makes impossible the "passive, cathartic, emotionally manipulated mode which is normal in the popular cinema culture." And, "this is further reinforced by the direct reference to the machinery"

Consciousness or Subconsciousness

We rise against the collusion between the "director-enchanter" and the public which is submitted to the enchantment. The conscious alone can fight against magical suggestions of every kind. The conscious alone can form a man of firm convictions and opinions. We need a conscious people, not an unconscious mass ready to yield to any suggestion.

---

(60). *The Man with a Movie Camera* is thus seen as a forerunner of recent films that explore self-referential structures: seeing the camera, the projector, the screen, *in* the film can recall to the spectator the fact that s/he is watching a film and thus foregrounds the spectator's own perceptual processes. Le Grice believes the post-war European avant-garde took up Vertov's materialism because it was "strongly anti-romantic and clearly based in the psycho-physical as material phenomena" (87), and then, since 1966, "the formal aspect of avant-garde film has exploded to become its mainstream" (105), culminating in "an implicit search for a film which can function essentially on the psychophysical rather than the psycho-interpretive level" (106). The aim of these films is thus to create an experience in which "action on the autonomic nervous system seeks to create a nervous response which is largely preconscious, the psychological reactions sought being a direct consequence of physical function" (106). These films, which Le Grice refers to as "perception training films," contain only one kind of information, that which concerns filmic processes. The films, however, are not concerned with the *intellection* of these processes, a mental act involving a semantic dimension, but a direct apprehension: "the primacy of current experience over the illusory or retrospective." As one of the most effective strategies in this attempt, Le Grice cites what can be learned from information theory: by reducing the information within the film to an extreme degree, the spectator's awareness can be focused solely onto his or her own perceptual responses. Finally, Le Grice states the aim of all this deliberate and didactic reflexivity, this complete attention to the material processes of film and the changing perceptual responses of the spectator: "to give the spectator an affirmation of his own reality." Thus this strategy, seen as entirely counteractive to the mode of popular cinema, represents "the most advanced and radical state of cinematic language and convention" (153).

Theory and Definition of Structural Materialist Film (Peter Gidal)

The polemicism of Peter Gidal at the same time narrows into more precise definitions and expands into a set of philosophical presuppositions the historical descriptions and conclusions of Malcolm Le Grice. Gidal's argument resolves itself into a series of dichotomies that can be schematized as follows:

idealism/materialism[5]	narrative/non–narrative
ideology/knowledge	illusionist time/real–time
reproduction/production	signified/signifier

Each step of the argument pits one half of the dichotomy against the other as its polar opposite, both philosophically and politically. Just as for Le Grice, Gidal's argument turns around an analysis of the functioning of classical film to posit certain avant–garde strategies as completely counter to the classical model. Here too the political effectiveness of these films lies in the construction of a self-conscious, perceptually aware spectator as the result of self-reflexive strategies. The first tactic of the structural/materialist film is to empty the cinematic signifier of all semantic, associative, symbolic, representational significance. Gidal argues that any kind of representation is always susceptible to being naturalized by the dominant ideology and used to

---

All I want anyone to get out of my paintings, and all I ever get out of them, is the fact that you can see the whole idea without any confusion . . . what you see is what you see.

Frank Stella quoted by Peter Gidal, 19

---

manipulate the spectator. The only images not susceptible to such recuperation are images of actual filmic processes; Gidal emphasizes not *representations or reproductions* of these processes but the actual experience of the production process inscribed in the film. The viewing activity of the spectator is the deciphering, anticipation, correction, clarification, and analysis of this material process: "Thus viewing such a film is at once viewing a film and viewing the 'coming into presence' of the film, i.e. the system of consciousness that produces the work, that is produced by and in it" (2). The spectator is blocked from any sort of identification with these films insofar as they are non-narrative: "Narrative is authoritarian, manipulative and mystificatory" (4) because it represses the reality of material space and time; therefore its only function is illusionism. Instead of the illusionistic time of the narrative, Gidal offers the solution of "real-time," in which the duration of the processes depicted and the time of watching the film are one and the same. The basic unit of film will thus be duration: "Point 'a' to point 'b' in duration as opposed to narrative."[6]

Structural/materialist film is then at once object and procedure, a didactic aesthetic using reflexive strategies to ensure a conscious spectator: "A filmic practice in which one watches oneself watching. . . . Filmic reflexiveness is the presentation of consciousness to the self" (10).

The Imaginary Signifier (Christian Metz)

At the center of Christian Metz's discussion of the psychoanalytic constitution of the cinematic signifier, he warns that the film which would aim to be a film of intervention must take into consideration the cinematic signifier's higher degree of imaginariness in comparison to, for example, the theater. Since the main thrust of Le Grice and Gidal's arguments is that the structural/materialist film is constructed to eliminate the spectator's imaginary relation to the film and to prevent identification, largely through a disavowal of narrative and fiction, let

---

Thus as a beginning it is absolutely essential to tear the symbolic from its own imaginary and return to it as a look. To tear it from it, but not completely, or at least not in the sense of ignoring it and fleeing from it (fearing it): the imaginary is also what has to be rediscovered precisely in order to avoid being swallowed up by it: a never ending task.

Christian Metz, "The Imaginary Signifier," 16

---

us look at these specific claims in the light of the metapsychological points raised in the essay of Christian Metz that most directly addresses these problems.

Le Grice and Gidal note that both the represented content and the sequential organization of film have an effect on the viewer; if one can successfully eliminate a certain kind of imagery ("symbolic," "associative" images, ones that are "representations" or "reproductions") and a particular ordering of the images (editing that suppresses material space and time) then the spectator would be confronted with an image, a film, that would call forth a direct and conscious response, a response focused on the subject's own act of perception. But in "The Imaginary Signifier" Metz emphasizes that what is "characteristic of the cinema is not the imaginary that it may happen to represent, it is the imaginary that it is from the start" (48). Basic to the constitution of the cinematic signifier is that it is *absent*: unlike in the theater where real persons share the time and space of the spectator, the cinema screen is always the "other scene"; it is a recording and what it records is not there at the moment of its projection. But even more fundamental is the way the cinematic signifier *combines* presence and absence—it is more "there" than almost any other medium (because of its density of perceptual registers) and less "there" at the same time (because it is always only a replica of what is no longer there). This combination of presence and absence exactly describes the characteristic functioning of the Imaginary[7] according to Lacan: the ego is constituted by an image, that is, something that is a reflection (which is there) of the body (which is not really there "in" the mirror). The question that arises

---

The image is the strict reflection of reality, and its objectivity is contradictory to imaginary extravagance. But at the very same time, this reflection is a "double." The image is already imbued with subjective powers that displace it, deform it, project it into fantasy and dream. The imaginary enchants the image because the image is already a potential sorcerer. The imaginary proliferates on the image like its own natural cancer. It crystallizes and deploys human needs, but always in images. The image is the common place of the image and imagination.

Edgar Morin, *Le cinéma ou l'homme imaginaire* (1956)[8]

---

then is whether presenting an image of a filmic process, even the process of the "coming into presence" of the very film we are watching, is a way of making that process, the image of that process, more "there," less imaginary (because truly "present"), more directly apprehendable by perception. If the cinematic signifier shares the characteristic structuration of the Imaginary, then to insist on the *presence*, the "materiality" of the image, would that not be to simultaneously (if unconsciously) insist on its *absence?* Indeed, would it not risk moving the imaginary quotient up another notch? To show the film in its materiality—for example to film a strip of film, or to emphasize the screen as surface through projecting not images, but clear light onto the screen—is to show the film in its "materiality" at the very moment that it is no longer film. The piece of film footage that we see is not the film; the film exists only when it is projected. The empty, white screen is also not the film, for the film exists in a dialectic of image and screen—when we see a screen, even in all its "materiality," we are just seeing a screen. And the same for the structural/materialist approach to demonstrating film *processes*: to show film in its stages of becoming a film or disintegrating as film is a little like the *fort-da* game described by Freud in which the child plays out obsessively, repetitively the experience of separation, of loss. (Another reading of this could be that of Melanie Klein in relation to the handling of the fetish-object: it is sometimes quasi-venerated, sometimes destroyed in a constant alternation of destruction and reparation.[9]) Material "possession" of the film is always at the price of losing the instance in which it is film as such. This is not to say that these strategies involving the demonstration of filmic material processes are not instructive; it is just to say that no matter how "scientific" these experiments may be, they have psychoanalytic roots in a play of possession and loss. Such "materialization" strategies refuse or disavow any knowledge of the imaginary inherent to the cinematic signifier itself. The imaginary can only be endlessly played out; its infinite metonymy can only be stopped into *fictions* of materiality, never materiality itself.

Thus the cinematic signifier is imaginary in its very constitution as a signifier. It is also imaginary, Metz argues, because the screen reactivates the mirror stage described by Jacques Lacan (or at least the images have their power of fascination because the subject has already undergone the mirror stage). Any relation to an image is imaginary; that is, since the ego itself is constituted by images (the first being the image of the subject in the mirror) and all the rest of the images being doubles of this double, then it is impossible to separate images from this fundamental imaginary operation. (We will see later that this operation also involves the work of desire.)

In specifying the imaginariness of the cinematic signifier, Metz shifts the grounds of all previous discussions of the processes of identification in film, maintaining that the primary identification (primary in terms of its relative importance to the subject-effect, that is) is not with the characters on the screen but with the subject's own activity of looking. The spectator is the constitutive instance of the film, of the cinematic signifier; the film would not exist without the sight (and hearing) of the spectator. "In other words, the spectator *identifies with himself*, with himself as a pure act of perception: as condition of possibility of the perceived and hence as a kind of transcendental subject, anterior to every *there is*" (51). If the primary identification is with the subject's own act of perceiving, then the primary identification in film is with the camera and not with the characters or the depicted events. It also follows from Metz's claim that the act of seeing is itself the primary cinematic identification, that the images themselves, that is, what the images depict (even what filmic processes they present) do not have that much to do with the fundamental form of cinematic identification, the identification that establishes the spectator as transcendental subject. Thus the avant-gardists' program of eliminating "associative," "symbolic," extra-referential significance from filmic images (we will take up later the question of whether this is even possible)—Peter Gidal's example of an image-moment of a leaf that is only a leaf and nothing more—would have relatively little effect in terms of subverting this most fundamental identification.

As for Le Grice and Gidal's argument that narrative must be eliminated because it constructs and manipulates an unconscious spectator, it is not completely sure that even the least "montaged" avant-garde films escape the fundamental structures of narrative. In another text ("Métaphore/Métonymie ou le référent imaginaire"),[10] Metz has noted that even though avant-garde films do not use the typical metonymic discursive operation of classical film, they do not completely escape this regime because they have (among other things) a *point-of-view* in relation to a contiguous organization of images. (See also Stephen Heath's "Narrative Space" on the primary narrative function of cinema as the suturing of the look into a metonymy of images.)[11]

Le Grice and Gidal also maintain that identification is eliminated in their films because, along with getting rid of narrative, fiction too is eliminated. "Fiction" here is taken to mean a series of images that refer the spectator to an illusory elsewhere, an imaginary space rather than the material reality of the spectator's own space and time. When Metz says that "every film is a fiction film" (47), he is not trying to say that every film, no matter how abstract, has the functional equivalent of a "character" or that all films, at bottom, have a "story." Again, Metz is pointing to the imaginariness of the cinematic signifier, whose referent is always imaginary insofar as what it represents is not there and thus fictive. Is it therefore possible to avoid the construction of an "else-where"? Isn't any art object, art process, exactly that, no matter how minimal, no matter how little the conceptualizations structured to happen in that space resemble a story? Even when the metonymic con-tiguity of the images is designed to construct a "specifically cine-matic" space, as opposed to the illusionistic scene of classical represen-tation, this space is never "there" in any material way, and as soon as it is "elsewhere," there is no way of controlling the interactions of the film with the processes of memory and fantasy (always fictional) of the perceiving subject. The work of Thierry Kuntzel (especially "Savoir, pouvoir, voir" and "Le travail du film, 2")[12] describes the structuring function of certain basic fantasies in the vision of the spec-tator, the most important being perversion (especially fetishism) and the primal scene. Fetishism and the primal scene are notable for their particular imbrication of vision and fiction since both the perversion and the primal fantasy function across the scopophilic drive. Both the fetishistic ritual and the primal-scene fantasy serve the subject exactly as fictions, fictions that are fabricated in order for the subject to work through/defend himself against questions of sexual knowledge. Al-though Kuntzel's two articles address themselves to the effect of these fantasies on the vision of the spectator of classical film, we will see later how these psychical structures that fictionalize the subject to himself may be inherent in the act of vision. Thus, several times over, at several levels, "Every film is a fiction film" (47).

At the level of cinema as a social institution Metz speaks of the role of the cinema spectator as essentially voyeuristic: participating in a form of scopophilia not normally sanctioned by society, we sit in the theater in darkness and solitude looking toward the framed screen as through a keyhole. This is one of the reasons why it is so startling when a character looks at us from the screen, catching us in our own voyeuristic activity. As Metz points out, the cinema as an institution functions to sanction this activity, thereby making film-viewing au-thorized scopophilia, legalized voyeurism, desire within the limits of the law. The social situation of the spectator of, say, Malcolm Le Grice's *Little Dog for Roger* or Peter Gidal's *Room Film, 1973* would, of course, be different from that of the spectator in a commercial cinema. The films are presented as near-scientific investigations of perceptual processes. We come to them in a more active manner, knowing they will be difficult, challenging, and that we are coming to learn something, to be productive not passive spectators (Peter Gidal would say for knowledge and not for ideology). Here it is not a matter of being temporarily authorized to exercise our scopophilic pleasure, legally yet still furtively, in the manner of classical cinema. Instead we are asked by the films and the viewing situation to *investigate*, and we are even promised the sanction of science. As valuable as these strategies might be on one level, they also tend to suppress a knowledge of the imaginary of the image by asserting the objectivity of those images and the rationality of our relation to them.

The Apparatus (Jean-Louis Baudry)

The previous discussion concerned recent work on the imaginary status of the cinematic signifier. Jean-Louis Baudry's work,[13] on the other hand, considers the imaginary status of the entire apparatus, that is the cinema "machine" that includes not only the instrumental base (camera, lens, projector, etc.) but also the subject, most important being the subject of the unconscious, the subject as a desiring machine without which the cinematic institution could not (would have no reason to) function. Baudry's article gives the sketch for a historical reconsideration of the cinema not as a machine that came into existence

---

> . . . *And here*
> *the painting becomes*
> *this enormous*
> *thing which*
> *moves*
> *The wheel*
> *Life*
> *The machine*
> *The human soul.* . . .
>
> Blaise Cendrars,
> "Constructions" (1919),
> dedicated to Fernand Léger

---

because of the state of technology at the end of the nineteenth century, but as the most perfected material realization of an unconscious goal perhaps basic to the psychical functioning of the human mind—the wish to return, by simulation, to that "other scene." And it is especially through artistic practice that the unconscious tries to represent itself. For Baudry all the other arts were merely "dry runs" in this

---

We need Cinema in order to create the total art towards which all the others, since the beginning, have tended.

Ricciotto Canudo, "La théorie des septs arts"

---

unconscious historical experiment to devise an apparatus that could simulate not "reality" but a subject-effect or state. This state would be an artificial state of regression that would return the subject to an earlier phase of development, with its own forms of satisfaction, a relative narcissism in which desire could be "satisfied" through confusing real perceptions (filmic images) with representations (the subject's own endogenous images) and then taking them for perceptions (something existing "in reality"). In dream, however, there are no real perceptions coming from the exterior, only the subject's own representations hallucinated as perceptions. The impression of reality particular to this state would be closest to that of the dream-effect and would therefore have the same possibilities for figuration and refiguration of the form of desire inherent to it. The impression of reality that the spectator has in the cinema, and the consequent form of identification, thus has less to do with a successful rendering of the real than with the reproduction and repetition of a specific condition, a "fantasmatization of the subject."

Metz, as we have seen, displaces the primary cinematic identification from an identification with the signified contents appearing on the screen to the act of perception itself; Baudry, however, displaces the question of identification from the degree of reality of the images on the screen to a more fundamental identification with the entire apparatus. (A basic difference between these positions is the more Lacanian emphasis of Metz on identification across the specular regime as opposed to Baudry's primarily Freudian emphasis on satisfaction through regression as the basis for primary identification. However, as Baudry points out in his essay, the form of archaic regression that he isolates "does not exclude other processes of identification which derive from the specular regime of the ego, from its constitution as imaginary," 112.)

Le Grice's book offers necessary historical background that could tend to support Baudry's thesis. He does so in tracing the evolution of an urge to cinematic representation that preexisted cinema and found its greatest perfection in cinema. Both authors would therefore be able to say, "there was never any first invention of cinema" (Baudry 113). Le Grice documents both the ecstasy of visual artists at the time, the Futurists, Dadaists, and Surrealists, in discovering a medium that offered possibilities beyond what they had been able to achieve in painting, and also charts this "natural evolution" from the concerns of modern painting to film. (However, it must be remembered that although Le Grice documents this movement, he is also a part of it and has a tendency to force the idea of a natural evolution; his is a strategic reconstruction of art history according to the need to justify a certain kind of filmmaking practice as the "natural" culmination of an evolution intrinsic and inevitable to the medium itself.) Therefore, both Baudry and Le Grice would trace an evolutionary movement from painting to film and within film itself: Le Grice's logic offers a formalist and idealist description of inevitable aesthetic progress in the resolution of a series of formal problems posed by the medium itself (see Clement Greenberg); Baudry's logic is that of the unconscious in its successive attempts to represent itself.

Several questions can now be posed about avant-garde strategies in relation to the functioning of the apparatus as outlined by Baudry:

1. If the entire cinematic institution is taken in this grand historical wish-fulfilling fantasy, that is, if the apparatus is always already a function of the archaic mode of identification that "created" it and permits its functioning, then what is the specific aspect of this wish fulfilled by structural/materialist film?

2. In what ways, and to what degree, do the experiments of the structural/materialist filmmakers subvert this archaic form of identification?

Further on in this paper I will attempt to answer the first question about the specific psychical function filled by structural/materialist film by looking at what kind of "fantasmatization of the subject" it creates. I will argue that rather than fulfilling a role of giving cinematic *pleasure* or *satisfaction* (the argument of most metapsychological studies of film, however they might differ in defining these terms), this kind of filmmaking represents an extreme form of cinema's capacity for serving a *defensive* function for the spectator/subject. But for the moment I would like to undertake a discussion of the second question, the degree to which the theoretical presuppositions of these filmmakers could provide strategies for subverting the overall functioning of the apparatus.

In *The Interpretation of Dreams* Freud offers an answer to the enigma of critical feelings in dreams, that is, the moment when the thought "this is only a dream" occurs in a dream.[14] Freud claims that this moment of critical judgment, this instance of "reality" intruding into the dream, is only a strategy to ensure that the anxiety arising in the dream is sufficiently suppressed to enable the person to continue sleeping and dreaming. Baudry, as we have seen, makes the equation *apparatus = dream-state*. This therefore leaves open the possibility that, like the "rational" and "critical" thoughts that occur in dreams, everything that occurs within the apparatus, for example the images and sounds of the film, are susceptible to being "desecondarized," "derationalized," and even used to contribute to maintaining the dream-state. And the most perfect strategy for maintaining this state?: that moment of *the most extreme self-reflexivity*, that moment of insistence on the material and rational. The use of self-reflexive aesthetic strategies is, of course, almost the definition of avant-garde practice. Le Grice cites Vertov's exemplary practice of showing every stage of the production of a film, of demystifying the machinery and process, to reinforce the consciousness of the spectator (59). Throughout *Abstract Film and Beyond*, films are included or excluded to the degree to which they are properly materialist and self-reflexive, that is, whether or not the images show the functioning of the camera, projector, editing equipment or use "filmic material processes" as subject matter: celluloid scratches, splicing tape marks, processing stains, fingerprints, image slip, etc. Both Le Grice and Gidal repeatedly emphasize that this kind of imagery should not be used for expressive ends but should be used only to demonstrate "an awareness of the implications of changing forms of visual/kinetic information" (Le Grice, 115). But if we take Metz's thesis that the primary identification is with the camera, then we must immediately question the "objectivity" of the strategy of showing the spectator these "protheses" of his own body, of his own vision, because it is quite likely that this could *reinforce* the primary identification, which, as Metz argues, is the basis of the construction of a transcendental subject.

At a more sociological level, we can look back into cinema history (and its prehistory) to see the perpetual fascination with machines that record and project images. Beaumont Newhall's *The History of Photography*[15] describes the frenzy surrounding the first public presentations of photographic equipment and the first demonstrations of "how-it-works." This high pitch of excitement was seen again at each innovation in film technology: the invention of sound, color, 3-D, CinemaScope, etc. Films that demonstrate the possibilities of perception, in no matter how "scientific" a framework, cannot help but play on this fascination. The following section will suggest, following Jean-Louis Baudry, some theses on the psychical roots of this exuberance.

Side by side with the axiom of self-reflexivity is the emphasis on these films as epistemological enterprise. "Knowledge" and "investigation" are the positive terms opposed to the negative ones, "ideology" and "passivity." However, the desire to know and to investigate are not entirely unproblematic: when an intellectual process is shown and examined it enters immediately into the sexual fantasy of infantile sexual investigation. (From a more Lacanian perspective, one could say, with Piera Aulagnier-Spairani, "Knowledge has the narrowest relation to desire and to the unveiling of that which is the cause of it.")[16] In its extreme form the desire to know slips from epistemology into epistemophilia, the perversion of the desire to know. This perversion involves the attempted mastery of knowledge and the demonstration of the all-powerfulness of the subject. Such attempted mastery of knowledge (or of desire) traps the subject in an imaginary relation, an endless circle of trying to *know*. And since the object of all knowing is a knowledge of desire, there is no end and no way out, especially if the subject's aim is *full knowledge*. It is only in accepting the limits, the loss of the possibility of total mastery, that some symbolizing advances through this imaginary web are possible.[17]

The strategies of this avant-garde cannot hope to offer the means of subverting the apparatus if they ignore these levels of unconscious functioning, choosing instead to work on the codes of "conscious" reception of the film. The "expanded cinema" experiments of Le Grice, Annabel Nicolson, William Raban, and others could appear to offer a rethinking of the problem of the place of the subject in (of) the apparatus. In their work the entire space of the viewing situation is altered through multi-screen projection, sometimes of several different films at once. Often the artists place themselves between the space of the screen and the projector, interacting with both. But once again all of this effort is aimed toward constructing a subject "affirmed in his own reality," a situation in which "one watches oneself watching": a construction of a conscious subject, unified and affirmed as the place of

the synthesis of all perceptions. Given the level of address in these expanded cinema experiments, it could therefore be asked whether they
offer anything more than a *multiplication of effects*, all striving toward a
new recentering of the subject, this time not in a transcendental elsewhere but in the body of the subject himself (a "materialist" transcendental subject?).

   In both Baudry's earlier essay, "Ideological Effects of the Basic Cinematographic Apparatus," and in "The Apparatus: Metapsychological Approaches to the Impression of Reality," he argues the profound link of cinema and idealism. Both construct a subject whose
function as perceiver and synthesizer makes that subject the center of a
universe (because the place through which all signification must pass),
which he then believes to have created himself, and over which he believes he has ultimate control. (Too, it is a philosophy of consciousness: if the subject is the origin of all vision and knowledge then there
is nothing hidden from the subject, no possibility for a part of him to
function in a way unknown and inaccessible to him — see Thierry
Kuntzel's "Savoir, pouvoir, voir" on the relations of seeing and knowing in the idealist version of vision reenacted by the classical film). In
both essays, but especially in "The Apparatus," idealism is presented
as a psychoanalytic as well as philosophical phenomenon, idealism
having a great deal to do with the desire of the subject. As a response
to the shortcomings of reality, the subject wants to be able to change it
according to his desire. The cinematic apparatus structures for (with)
the spectator a sensation of full vision ("Ideological Effects of the Basic Cinematographic Apparatus": Renaissance perspective inscribed in
the instrumental base itself) and ensures a confounding of the order of
satisfaction of desire with the order of reality ("The Apparatus": simulation of the dream-effect in which representation can no longer be
distinguished from perception). Much of the historical material cited
in *Abstract Film and Beyond* gives support to Baudry's thesis of the inherent idealism of the cinematographic apparatus. What is most important for our interests, however, is that the formal film movement
in its own self-description appears as *the most extreme expression of this
inherent idealism*. Jacques Lacan's essay "Du regard comme objet petit
a"[18] (which we will look at more closely in the next section) stands as
one of the most important psychoanalytic critiques of the idealist (specifically phenomenological) notion of vision. Lacan describes the
world as "omnivoyeuristic": "We are looked-at beings in the spectacle
of the world" ("Nous sommes des êtres regardés, dans le spectacle du

monde," 71). We can see only from one place, through our own eyes: we can never see ourselves from the place where others see us and our vision is thus always affected by the field of the other, the imagined look. The fantasy that we find in the Platonic perspective inverts this relation: here we find an absolute being to whom is transferred the quality of all-seeing. The ability to reshape space and time in the "cineplastics" of Elie Faure, the Kino-Eye of Dziga Vertov, which is more perfect than the human eye because it can go everywhere and see everything, the cinema philosophy of the Futurists: "This is how we decompose and recompose the universe according to our marvelous whims"—to document the avant-garde film movement, even the most "abstract" strains of it, is to cite the exuberance of artists who had at last found a perfect supplement to their vision, a machine-eye capable of "remaking the very figuration of life" (Ricciotto Canudo).[19] Popular cinema only chained vision to outworn theatrical and novelistic forms, but "pure cinema," "abstract cinema," was to be the liberation and joyful education of vision to create the "new man" of the twentieth century.

The rhetoric of the inheritors of this enterprise, the structural/materialist filmmakers, differs a great deal, of course, from this romantic idealism. Le Grice, for example, documents a movement away from the idealism of the early avant-gardists to the present "cool" experiments and didactic exercises on human perception. But some striking similarities remain, particularly the attempt to expand the capacities of vision and knowledge of a spectator "affirmed in his own reality," a spectator completely conscious of his own activities in "producing" the film. The subject constituted by the early avant-gardists and the structural/materialists is essentially the same, even if one constructs its subject in the name of a romantic idealism and the other in the name of science and "materialism." Both play on an infantile wish to shape the real to the measure of the subject's own boundless desire.

Like almost all the other writers on experimental film (David Curtis, Standish Lawder, Gene Youngblood, etc.) Le Grice emphasizes the close dependence of the avant-garde aesthetic on technological development. More so than with popular cinema, all the advances in avant-garde "film thought" have depended upon the refinement and expansion of the technological possibilities: computers, color processing, optical printers, improved quality of film stock. The idealist tendency of the avant-garde could be in part determined by this close dependency on technology for many of its advances. In "Ideological

Effects of the Basic Cinematographic Apparatus" Baudry opens the questioning of "the privileged position which optical instruments

---

Using war surplus anti-aircraft gun directors . . . began the construction of an animation table, which allowed sections to rotate according to pre-programmed patterns, transforming very simple forms into complex movements similar to oscilloscope or pendulum-pantograph figures.

John Whitney, cited by Malcolm Le Grice, 80

---

seem to occupy on the line of intersection of science and ideological products." That is, the cinema, based as it is on optical equipment derived from science, tends to treat its own technology as neutral or free from ideological inscription. But Baudry argues that the idealist spectator is in large part a construction of the Renaissance perspective of the lens itself.

It is true that the majority of the structural/materialist films work against the centering of the spectator that results from the Renaissance perspective inscribed in the physical construction of the lens. However, after making this (by now, automatic) critique of Renaissance representational space, the machine is often unquestioningly reabsorbed into the project to "expand" vision. Le Grice vitriolically rejects the mystical tendency in filmmakers like Jordan Belson and Scott Bartlett who use highly sophisticated technology to create the blend of spiritualism and science particular to their work. He criticizes their work as regressive in relation to the larger tendency toward nonpsychological abstraction. It could be, however, that this mystical tendency is only the logical extreme of the "materialist" avant-garde's own unconscious direction; it is for this reason that they must be rejected so violently.

The recent work of Raymond Bellour on cinema and hypnosis[20] examines the place of the camera in the imaginary and symbolic of the late nineteenth and twentieth centuries. He argues that machines (and particularly image-making machines) came to have the function of an ideal ego (*moi idéal*), that is, an extended and perfected model of our own capacities, which we then introject as an ego ideal (*idéal du moi*). In cinema, as in hypnosis, the introjection of the ego ideal takes over the function of reality testing, permitting external stimuli to be perceived as originating in the subject. Cinematic identification becomes a rhythm of projection and introjection, a constant dialectic of ideal ego and ego ideal. For Bellour, as well as Metz, the unconscious identification with the camera creates the primary subject-effect and filmic "fascination" in general. No matter how "aware" we are, then, of the functioning of the camera/projector in our perceptual functioning, this helps us very little in thinking about our unconscious relation to images, to the technological apparatus, and to the fundamental connection of the two. The structural/materialist movement seems to have taken up and synthesized both an idealism embedded in photographic

---

We have married Science and Art, I mean the discoveries and not the givens of Science, and the Ideal of Art, applying them to each other in order to capture and fix the rhythms of light.

Ricciotto Canudo, "L'usine aux images"

---

and cinematographic technology itself and an idealism inherited from its art-historical tradition, this last seen in their continuation of the rhetoric of "expanding" consciousness through expanding vision of the earlier abstract filmmakers, and in their Greenbergian notion of progress-in-art as a series of solutions to formal problems logically intrinsic to the medium.

The look as small object o (Jacques Lacan)

One of the most important theoretical bases for the recent metapsychological studies of film is the work of Jacques Lacan on the imaginary constitution of the subject, first formulated in "The Mirror Phase as Formative of the Function of the I")[21] and continued in his more recent work on the specular regime ("Du regard comme objet petit a").[22] This work looks at the ways subjectivity functions at the level of the scopic drive. The four seminars grouped under the heading "The look as small object o" offer a critique of the idealist notion of vision and project onto the act of vision itself the same dialectic of desire and lack at work in the unconscious.

For the structural/materialist filmmakers perception operates at a conscious or perhaps "pre-conscious" level; Malcolm Le Grice states that the aim of these films is to create an experience in which "action on the autonomic nervous system seeks to create a nervous response which is largely preconscious, the psychological reactions sought being a direct consequence of physical function" (106).[23] Except for the complicated physiological exigencies, these filmmaker/theorists think of perception as a fairly unproblematic act and their aim is its knowledge and mastery. For Lacan, however, the scopic drive is quite different from the other drives and the most problematic. He first makes a distinction between the *eye* and the *look*: the eye refers to the organ and its physical functioning, and the look is a matter of that which is "always to some degree eluded" in vision (70). The look is exactly that which escapes from philosophy's notion of the plenitude met by the

---

The function of the blot and the look is, at one and the same time, that which commands the most secretly, and that which always escapes the grip of that form of vision which finds its contentment in imagining itself as consciousness.

Jacques Lacan, *Les quatre concepts fondamentaux de la psychanalyse*, 71

My body simultaneously sees and is seen. That which looks at all things can also look at itself and recognize in what it sees the "other side" of its power of looking. It sees itself seeing; it touches itself touching; it is visible and sensitive for itself . . . a self that is caught up in things, that has a front and a back, a past and a future.

Maurice Merleau-Ponty, The Essential Writings of Merleau-Ponty

---

contemplative subject, the unified and all-seeing subject; the look is the very inverse of consciousness. When Lacan says that "in the domain of vision small object o is the look" (97), he is attempting to describe the functioning of lack at the level of the scopic drive. "Small object o" in the Lacanian algebra stands not for the object of desire itself, but for the experience of separation, separation from all the things that have been lost from the body (for example, the mother's breast, which was once experienced as part of the infant's body).[24] The imaginary relation itself, through which the subject becomes a subject for himself, occurs only at the price of the subject seeing his own body as *other* in the mirror; that is, the moment of the constitution of the ego is also a moment of separation.[25] Thus Lacan can say, in relation to the domain of vision integrated into the field of desire: "In the dialectic of the eye and the look, there is no point of coincidence, only basic lure" (94). The look is not a look that can be seen, but rather a look imagined by the subject in the field of the other: the look is no more than the presence of the other as such. That is, the important look is not our own (as in the phenomenological notion of the intentionality of perception and the subject as master of the visual field) but the one from outside; this look pre-exists the subject in the same way that the symbolic and the "real" pre-exist the subject's constitution through the imaginary. We think of ourselves as the subject of repre-

sentation but within the always reciprocal (yet nonsymmetrical) structure of the look we are, virtually, the object of representation also. Lacan even speaks of the subject being "*photo-graphed*" by the incarnated
and returned light of its own look (98). There is, then, something in
vision nowhere mastered by the subject: the look of the other pre-exists the subject's look; the subject's visual field is always organized in
relation to the other's look that it is not (what Lacan calls the "blot" [*la
tache*]); and the relation of the look to what one wants to see is always
a relation of lure. Certainly the subject here is not an objective subject,
nor the one of reflecting consciousness, but the subject of unconscious
desire.

One could argue that it is wrong to criticize the structural/mate-
rialist filmmakers for failing to consider the unconscious level of vision. It is not, say, the area they are "interested in." However, one of
the largest claims of these filmmaker/theorists is that their films offer
a relation to vision completely counter to that of dominant cinema;
this is the very ground of their argument that their films can be politically effective in a struggle against bourgeois ideology. Christian
Metz has discussed the close links of phenomenology and cinema (that
is why, he says, up to a point, a phenomenological description of cinema can be useful.)[26] Both phenomenology and cinema posit the subject as a pure instance of perception, a subject with full mastery of vision, a subject of consciousness. From this perspective it appears that
the premises of Le Grice and Gidal, based as they are on a denial of
unconscious processes at the level of vision, image, and the apparatus,
extend, reinforce, and finally erect into a set of theoretical presuppositions the idealist and phenomenological bases of dominant cinema.

The two dangers lying in wait for the subject-in-process of poetic
language are psychosis and fetishism.

Julia Kristeva[27]

In taking up again the question of what sort of fantasmatization of the
subject the minimalist work constructs, let us first look at what fetishism in the work of art represents in Kristeva's statement. She sees it as
"the constant screening, concealment (la dérobade) of the symbolic,
paternal, sacrificial function, producing an objectification of the pure
signifier, more and more empty of meaning, insipid formalism."[28]
Here "fetishism" is not being used in the commonly accepted sense of
the sexual overvaluation of an object separated from the body, but in

the sense of it as a psychical mechanism for transforming signification, the reworking of the fact of castration, that is, the attempt to fantasize a whole and unified body (a basic narcissistic wish).[29] Thus, the fetish is not related to a *thing*, but involves a *process*, a refusal of signification brought about by a constant oscillation of meaning. The fetishistic disavowal rephallizes the mother to ensure the subject of the integrity of his own body: if the mother has the phallus, then she has always had it and the question of castration "disappears." These minimalist efforts, in their attempt to strip away all problematic significations and replace them with a hyperrational and conscious knowledge, identify this enterprise as the cinema of the lack *par excellence*: it constructs emptiness and insufficiency only in order to fill it. Other theorists have discussed the fetishistic structuration of classical film (Metz, Rose, Bellour, Kuntzel), and others have gone so far as to equate the basic processes of aesthetic elaboration with fetishistic operations like disavowal, doubling, condensation, displacement, and metaphorical and metonymical movements (Kristeva, Heath, Rosolato). Guy Rosolato, for example, says that the work of art fascinates by keeping in play oscillations of signification (simultaneously establishing and effacing meaning), generating for the subject a self-representation that would be a totality offered as inexhaustible.[30] But even if fetishism is basic to art-making, there are still degrees of it and the minimalist enterprise seems to offer a particularly pure and extreme example of the quest for an unproblematic core of meaning, a unified and coherent subject, a position of pure mastery, a phallus which is not decomposable. And it is through the look, that is, across the specular regime, that the subject assures himself of the integrity of the object and thus of his own body. The minimalist film-work, then, can be seen to serve a defensive function for the spectator, assuring the subject control over his own body through an identification with the camera (as carrier of his look), which then reorganizes space, time, and signification according to the needs of his own narcissism.[31]

A metapsychology of film must be able to account for the subject's relation to the film in terms of both the activity and the passivity of the sexual drives. The defenses against the drives are as important as the activity of the drives themselves, and the description of cinematic "pleasure" will therefore have to be made more complicated through analyzing the possibilities of defense offered by cinema. We can now say that cinema, like perversion, *eroticizes* the mechanisms of defense against the drives, the object of desire and the means of attaining it.

To say that minimalist film is the extreme example of the fetishism inherent in cinema is to recall at the same time the ambivalent position of fetishism in relation to the Law. (Christian Metz has said that the Law, at the level of the cinematic signifier, is the codes.)[32] The fetishist attempts to substitute the rules of his own desire for the culturally predominant ones; the minimalist artist wants an easily manipulable abstract set of rules completely devoid of cultural signification. In each case the totality of the denial of signification tends to affirm the potency of the paternal function, thus exhibiting a very strong identification with the Law. This is the risk with any aesthetic of transgression.

In terms of a political filmmaking practice, a practice that emphasizes transformation rather than transgression, is there any way to eliminate the imaginary relation between spectator and screen? Is it possible to systematically subvert this relation without ending up in the fetishistic impasse described above? Barthes (who, like Brecht, has always been suspicious of cinema) believes that the only solution is in "complicating a relation with a situation."[33] There is perhaps only one way to complicate this particular (imaginary) relation: language can offer us an oblique route through the image; it can "unstick" us a little from the screen, as Barthes puts it. The films of Godard have consistently taken into account this work of language on image, as have those of Straub and Huillet, and Mulvey and Wollen. These filmmakers realize that images have very little analytical power in themselves because their effects of fascination and identification are too strong. This is why there must always be a commentary *on* the images simultaneously with the commentary *of* and *with* them.

Stephen Heath has argued that "deconstruction is clearly the impasse of the formal device" and that a socio-historically more urgent practice would be a work not on "codes" but on the operations of narrativization, that is, "the constructions and relations of meaning and subject in a specific signifying practice." We have one example of a politically motivated avant-garde practice that addresses itself exactly to this task. The recent work of several women filmmakers focusing on feminist concerns is less a work on "codes" and "perceptual processes" than it is on narrative, fiction, and the construction of another subject-relation to the screen. It is not the modernist pressure toward finding the most "advanced" solution to formal problems that motivates filmmakers like Chantal Akerman, Marguerite Duras, Yvonne Rainer, Babette Mangolte, Jackie Raynal, and others, to make films involving "an action at the limits of narrative within the narrative film, at the limits of its fictions of unity" (Stephen Heath).[34] Rather, it is the pressure of a specific socio-historical situation that demands this response, a situation in which narrative and the subject placement it involves is dominant; that is, narrative which reunifies and rephallizes a spectator posed by the film as coherent and all-powerful. The strategies of these feminist filmmakers point to a manner of reworking subjectivity within an analysis of social/sexual relations that avoids the kinds of transgressions of the symbolic paternal function that risk ending in an identification with patriarchy. If filmic practice, like the fetishistic ritual, is an inscription of the look on the body of the mother, we must now begin to consider the possibilities and consequences of the mother returning the look.*

---

*Because the last line of this essay has received so much comment, especially from Stephen Heath ("Difference," *Screen* vol. 19, no. 3, pp. 97–98) and Peter Gidal (see exchange between me and Gidal described by Stephen Heath, also in "Difference," pp. 97–98), I would like to say how I intended it to be read since it so obviously failed to make the point I wanted it to make. Both Heath and Gidal thought I was suggesting that the typical relations of filmic fetishism can be undermined by substituting the figure of the mother or woman for the boy child or man who looks. Stephen Heath states his objection to my conclusion in this way: "to invert, the mother returning the look, is not radically to transform [but] is to return as well the same economy, the same dialectic of phallic castration, the same imaginary . . . the difference inverted is also the difference maintained." I could not agree more, but a simple inversion was not what I meant to propose (the mother instead of the father or the little boy). As I was writing this last line what I had in mind was Guy Rosolato's emphasis, throughout *Essais sur le symbolique* (see note 29), on a description of the fetishistic scenario that fully acknowledges its relation to the Oedipus complex and thus its tripartite structure: child, mother, father. Such a description stresses the presence or agency of the mother and the father in that scenario and the consequent effects for the look of the child onto the body of the mother. This notion of fetishism offers a more complex account of vision and desire than the stripped-down version of it that is usually imported into film theory to describe the spectator's unconscious relation to the image, a version in which the only look that counts is that of the little boy/man. What my last line thus represents is an early attempt to break out of the confines of this too-simple model. Such an attempt was of course much more successfully realized in later work in feminist film theory, particularly when feminist theorists took up the Freudian account of fantasy to give a better description of the multiple possibilities of identification in film spectatorship, possibilities that involve more positions than just the masculine one.

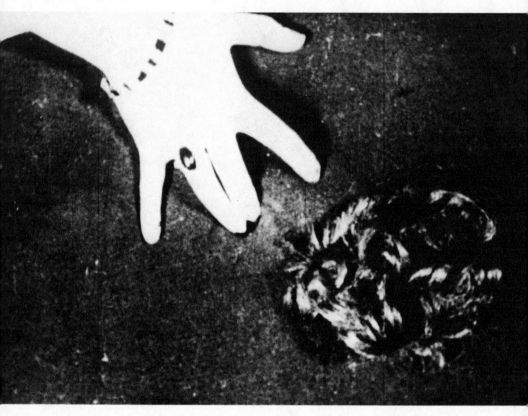

L'Age d'Or *(Luis Buñuel, 1930)*.

TWO

The Avant-Garde:
Histories and Theories

*I*N THE INTRODUCTION TO *A History of the American Avant-Garde Cinema*,[1] one of several scholarly treatments of avant-garde film published in the last three or four years, Marilyn Singer emphasizes that avant-garde film requires both a new criticism and a new way of looking at film. There is now enough American critical work on experimental film to enable us to ask if and to what degree it indeed represents a new kind of criticism and a new way of looking at film.

Whether known as "underground," "independent," "experimental," or "avant-garde," this kind of film, produced outside the industry, usually by a single person, almost always on a very low budget, offers a distinct challenge to a film criticism that has for the most part concentrated either on Hollywood commercial cinema or on "art house" films like those of Fellini, Antonioni, or Bergman. The sixties marked a consolidation of American avant-garde film activity. The success of the film co-ops helped regularize distribution, and the growth of film studies in the university ensured a large and serious audience. Anthology Film Archives, devoted exclusively to avant-garde film, established itself in New York, and the work of the filmmakers came to be powerful enough to demand consideration in the context

---

This is the first part of a two–part essay that originally appeared in *Screen* vol. 19, no. 3. The second part was written by Janet Bergstrom and discusses the definition of "avant-garde" found in *The American Avant-Garde Cinema* and *The Essential Cinema*. She also discusses the critical and institutional politics of Anthology Film Archives. P. Adams Sitney wrote a lengthy reply to our essay in *Screen* vol. 20, nos. 3–4 (Winter 1979–80) and we replied to him in the same issue.

of other American modernist art. Filmmakers like Michael Snow, Hollis Frampton, Paul Sharits, Ernie Gehr, Joyce Wieland, and Barry Gerson developed an international reputation, and experimental film, itself influenced by minimalism and post-minimalism, began to influence the other arts.

The recent critical work is a direct response to this flourishing of American independent film, and, even though quite scholarly in tone and method, sees itself as having an active function in supporting this kind of filmmaking activity and in making the films more widely accessible, both physically and intellectually. Within the formal rigor of this new criticism one thus finds a necessary and important promotional tone. The desire to legitimize the critical object is, however, bound to insinuate itself into the methodology—something that up to now has not been sufficiently recognized by even the most theoretical of the new approaches to avant-garde film. This is not at all to say that active public support for this kind of film, and theoretical work on it, should be kept separate. But the desire to "prove," for example, that these films are as sophisticated as other modernist art, that they have irrevocably changed the face of *all* art, and that they are the most successful form for twentieth-century epistemological inquiry, is bound to inflect any presentation of these films' conceptual strategies and material realizations. As Christian Metz points out in his self-ironic analysis of the metapsychology of the film analyst,[2] any critical discourse attempting to valorize the object cannot address the *properties* of cinematic language; these properties are instead presented to us as "resources," "riches," "means of expression," such a vocabulary revealing a very different project from that of an analysis of how film functions.

We can see this problem most clearly in *The Essential Cinema: Essays on the Films in the Collection of Anthology Film Archives.*[3] Can a project involving definitively establishing "the monuments of cinematic art" (introduction, v), a project whose stated criteria, determined in advance, are that the films be "sublime achievements," and exhibit "wholeness" and "unity" (introduction, *passim*), be compatible with evolving a theory of film, or even a new kind of criticism? *The Essential Cinema* allows any critical approach as long as it serves to substantiate the quality of its chosen monument: Seymour Stern's passionate anecdotal account of the making of Griffith's *Intolerance*, in which he offers the remarkable argument that "*Intolerance*, like *The Birth of a*

Nation, was produced and exhibited in entire independence of the Hollywood film industry; although made in Hollywood, it was not of Hollywood" (37); Ken Kelman's thematic readings of Buñuel, Vigo, and Bresson, in which he makes his controversial claim that Buñuel's *L'Age d'Or* was neither "social criticism" nor "revolutionary," but that rather the seemingly "socially conscious" scenes are merely "counterpoint or background to the main theme and action of love" (122); P. Adams Sitney's rhetorical analysis of Bresson's *Pickpocket*, in which he catalogs the devices Bresson uses to present his metaphysics of predestination and acquisition of grace; and Annette Michelson's explicitly phenomenological approach in which she argues that the important shift in Dziga Vertov's work was from "the articulation of a comprehensive and dialectical view of the world to the exploration of the terrain of consciousness itself" (100), that is, his evolution from the attempt to forge a historical materialist analysis to a concern with phenomenology as epistemological enterprise: "That philosophical phantasm of the reflexive consciousness, the eye seeing, apprehending itself through its constitution of the world's visibility" (98).

A History of the American Avant-Garde Cinema, on the other hand, is much more homogeneous and coherent in its methodology, even though its primary function is also to present and explicate films that are almost all in the collection of Anthology Film Archives, that is, those films in the constellation of avant-garde masterpieces as determined by the board of Anthology Film Archives. But is it a new criticism? One can see immediately in these articles the important influence of the rigorous and thoroughgoing formalist art criticism of the sixties (such as appeared in *Artforum*) rather than that of literary criticism, which has up until now been the basis of film criticism. Not only the careful descriptive mode, but the categories themselves (when discussing the later "structural" films) are those of sixties criticism responding to minimalist and post-minimalist artwork: the function of repetition and other noncausal strategies, the devaluation of interpretation as a mode of viewing, the elimination of psychological interiority, the focus on the spectator's conscious relation to his or her own perceptual and logical activities, the shift of interest away from referential illusion, and an attention to the materials and processes specific to the medium.

To characterize this "new criticism," this "new way of looking at film," it is important to recall Annette Michelson's influence on the work of these critics, many of them either her colleagues or former students. Michelson's approach to film, whether in analyses of Vertov, Eisenstein, Brakhage, or Snow, has been explicitly phenomenological. She sees film as *the* twentieth-century medium for epistemological inquiry. For her, as a phenomenological critic, the power of film lies in its striking capacity to serve as a grand metaphor of vision used to trace out the essence of all the activities of consciousness. As she puts it, "Epistemological inquiry and cinematic experience converge, as it were, in reciprocal mimesis."[4] Let us take a specific example of her phenomenological method at work in her analysis of Michael Snow's *Wavelength*. She says of the 45-minute film that depicts the movement of a "zoom" toward a photograph on a far wall: "The film is a projection of a grand reduction; its 'plot' is the tracing of spatio-temporal *données*, its 'action' the movement of the camera as the movement of consciousness."[5]

In the work of Michelson, as well as that of Sitney, the phenomenological approach is not meant to be an explanatory model "applied" to the film; rather, it is both a description of the intentional efforts of the filmmakers and an analysis of the *nature* of film. In other words, their critical discourse finds its justification in the belief that the methodology mirrors filmic processes, thus making film the perfect phenomenological scene: Merleau-Ponty called film the "phenomenological art."[6] In *Visionary Film* Sitney finds a historical basis for this claim in the work of Maya Deren: "The potential for a phenomenology of cinema, which is implied in the notes on [Deren's] *Meditation on Violence*, later came to be realized by Stan Brakhage and Michael Snow, among others, whose achievements can, in part, be traced back to Maya Deren's vision" (29). Sitney refers to the American avant-garde filmmakers as "mythologists of consciousness" (332). About Sidney Peterson he says: "It is specifically his use of radical techniques as metaphors for perception and consciousness . . . that elaborates Deren's central contribution" (55); on Gregory Markopoulos: "The ultimate aspiration of Markopoulos's form has been the mimesis of the human mind. In different degrees and in different ways this might be the aim of the American avant-garde filmmaker in general" (142); on Snow: "In *Back and Forth* (1969) and *The Central Region* (1971) the filmmaker elaborates on the metaphor of the moving camera as an imitation of consciousness" (419).

Throughout *A History of the American Avant-Garde Cinema* we see

the same emphasis on film as phenomenology. Writing of Maya Deren's *A Study in Choreography for the Camera*, Lucy Fisher says: "Thus
the fluid transitions of Beatty's dance movements seem to stand as analogues for the movements of consciousness" (73); Stuart Liebman describes Brakhage's "great project" as "the representation of the movements of consciousness itself" (97); Fred Camper insists that Jordan
Belson's films are "not images at all, but forms of consciousness"
(125); Ellen Feldman claims that "the use of persistence of vision becomes the foundation for creating an analogy between the processes of
viewing film and that of consciousness" and that "the film structure
functions as both analogue and an instant of consciousness" (149). In
The Essential Cinema Ken Kelman adds his voice to those of Michelson
and Sitney in claiming that Buñuel's *Land Without Bread* "is a film concerned with consciousness" (125) and that the process of Bruce Conner's *Report* is "analogous to the process of thought" (241). Phenomenology thus permeating all the new writing on avant-garde film,
what consequences might this have for developing a methodology (or
methodologies) of film analysis? And further, how does this kind of
criticism relate to current developments in theoretical work on film?

A *History of the American Cinema* and *The Essential Cinema* consist
primarily of descriptions of films. Although these descriptions are often careful and even rigorous in their attempt to demonstrate that
these films are "analogues of consciousness," or subversive of filmic
illusionism through consciousness, they seldom go beyond that.[7] But
then methodology is not a problem in a phenomenological approach:
"It is a matter of describing and not of explaining or analyzing." Phenomenology aims at a "report [*compte rendu*] of space, time, of the
'lived' world. . . . It is also the attempt to describe directly our experience as it is, without respect to psychological genesis and causal
explanation."[8] Such an approach differs greatly from the recent work
in film theory, which focuses instead on the construction of abstract
systems in order to understand how the film works, systems like the
specific and nonspecific codes and their hierarchical arrangement in
the filmic system. Such an approach sees the "textual system" of the
film not as the reconstruction of *the* system of the film, but a construction by the analyst of *a* system of the film, according to the level and
purpose of the analysis. That this degree of abstraction is able to remain close to the film can be seen in the work of Thierry Kuntzel, for
example, in which semiological codes and psychoanalytic structures

are described in relation to the moment-by-moment unfolding of the filmic text.[9]

Much of the French and English theoretical work on film, which can best be characterized as a psychoanalytically informed semiotics, has also concerned itself with phenomenology and cinema, but from a very different perspective. Both Jean-Louis Baudry and Christian Metz, for example, have discussed the similarity between cinema and phenomenology. In "The Imaginary Signifier" Metz says that "the to-pographical apparatus of the cinema resembles the conceptual appara-tus of phenomenology, with the result that the latter can cast light on the former" (55).[10] While it is true that all film recalls "the conceptual apparatus of phenomenology," it is the tautological structure of exper-imental film that most closely mirrors the phenomenological *Gestalt*, in that the films themselves are "about" the spectator's spatio-tem-poral traversal of the film. According to Metz it is therefore "no acci-dent that the main form of idealism in cinematic theory has been phe-nomenology" (54). For both Baudry and Metz, then, it is not that cinema just happens miraculously to work like human perception (and like the psychical apparatus) but rather that a certain wish-fulfilling placement of the spectator is implicit in the structure of the cinematic "institution," the institution here seen to include the industry, the technological base, and the spectator's "desire to go to the cinema." Cinema replays unconscious wishes the structures of which are shared by phenomenology, particularly the illusion of perceptual mastery that results in the creation of a transcendental subject.

The critical approach discussed here takes for granted, both histor-ically and theoretically, the phenomenological *Gestalt* of cinema, and of avant-garde film in particular. It takes its critical cues from what it has determined in advance to be the nature of film and especially of these films. Thus, everyone is in agreement. The filmmakers write their *Metaphors on Vision* (Brakhage), Snow talks of his project of mak-ing a film (*Wavelength*) that would be "a definitive statement of pure film space and time . . . all about seeing,"[11] Warhol reminds us to "just look." And the films themselves will be seen as the exemplary phenomenological event by their very nature. Criticism's function will thus be to refine our seeing and affirm the modernist credo of knowledge through self-consciousness. The discourse about the ob-ject becomes (is the same thing as) the discourse of the object.

Such a narrow emphasis on film as phenomenology makes it difficult if not impossible to consider the spectator's unconscious relation to the film, the screen, and the entire viewing situation, the primary focus of French and British film theory. When the unconscious is discussed in the recent American work, it is either brought in as an example of one of the possible "states of consciousness" presented by the film, or is incorrectly referred to as the "subconscious," thus eliminating the radical sense of otherness in Freud's notion of it.

As a first step toward a theory of film a phenomenological approach can be essential. We are still getting to know this object "film" and any discipline must have a basis in careful description. Both books discussed here often do an excellent job of written re-presentation of the films, a tedious job requiring long hours of close work in the screening room and at the editing table. This "phenomenology of cinema," even though limited to a descriptive mode and an overly confining model of film as an "analogue of consciousness" can still serve an important first step, its mirroring exaltation of the film gradually giving way to a desire to develop critical tools going beyond description to an analysis of the aesthetic, psychical, and social functioning of cinema.

FEMINISM AND FILM THEORY

Psycho *(Alfred Hitchcock, 1960).*

THREE

"A Certain Refusal of Difference": Feminism and Film Theory

LOOKING BACK OVER ten years of feminist theoretical writing on film, it is possible to pick out one distinct and insistently polemical strain that has had pervasive effects on the ideas and methods of film theory, as well as on feminist filmmaking. While taking film theory on its own terms—semiology, psychoanalysis, textual analysis, theories of the cinematic apparatus—this is an approach which, nonetheless, questions those "terms of analysis" on one specific issue: the way in which each takes up the problem of sexual difference in the cinema. For, the feminist film theory that I am citing here has discerned in the work of film theory in general a "certain refusal of difference,"[1] a particular understanding of the functioning of women in film which prematurely closes off sexual difference as a problem or question for film and theory. To keep the issue of sexual difference problematic and questionable, feminists have reread some of the privileged objects of analysis of film theory and have begun to examine some of the working assumptions of the earlier semiological and psychoanalytic approaches to film.

Even in the pioneering work done in England in the mid-1970s by Pam Cook, Claire Johnston, and Laura Mulvey, there was a clearly polemical recognition that the classical film text had always been in trouble over the question of sexual difference. For Cook and Johnston[2] this discord took the form of a symptomatic instability in the text caused by the film's failure to resolve the female figure as simultaneously castrated and phallic, or because of that figure's inherent resistance to being reduced to the status of a "sign" exchanged by men. Although this textual disorder is apparent in the work of male directors like Raoul Walsh or Jacques Tourneur, they claimed that it

41

was even more pronounced in the case of a woman directing Holly-wood films—Dorothy Arzner. In Arzner's films, however, the dom-inant textual contradiction results from her attempt, as a woman, to locate and convey the "discourse of a woman" in a representational form that is entirely male. The discourse of the woman in Arzner films like *Christopher Strong* (1933) or *Dance, Girl, Dance* (1940) gives the fil-mic system its structural coherence, "while at the same time rendering the dominant discourse of the male fragmented and incoherent."[3]

A similar attention to the trouble caused in the classical film text by the female figure is seen in Laura Mulvey's "Visual Pleasure and Nar-rative Cinema,"[4] an essay that established the grounds of the feminist inquiry into sexual difference in relation to cinematic pleasure. A clear sexual dichotomy exists in looking: men look and women are to-be-looked-at. "The determining male gaze projects its phantasy on to the female figure which is styled accordingly" (11). A similar active/pas-sive division of labor controls the narrative structure because it is the man who makes the story happen at every textual level. Through identification with the male character, the spectator, then, is privileged both as the viewer of the woman exhibited as spectacle and as control-ler of those events on the screen which unfailingly lead to the male's possession of the female. But at the level of the spectator's uncon-scious, the female figure is associated with a potential danger. Al-though the woman in the film has been objectified by the male gaze, and is thus iconically secure as a full image, she also connotes "some-thing that the look continually circles around but disavows: her lack of a penis, implying a threat of castration and hence unpleasure" (13). The female figure as spectacle can therefore provoke the very anxiety it was intended to contain. Again, as with Cook and Johnston, we see the idea of a symptomatic turbulence that results from the presence of the woman in the film: "The structure of looking in narrative fiction film contains a contradiction in its own premises: the female image as a castration threat constantly endangers the unity of the diegesis and bursts through the world of illusion as an intrusive, static, one-dimen-sional fetish" (18).

This critique, however, thematizing femininity or female discourse as a disturbance in the film text, began to be challenged in a major way by significant work in the area of textual analysis of film by such the-orists as Raymond Bellour, Thierry Kuntzel, and Stephen Heath.[5] In their attempts to provide an increasingly more systematic description of the workings of classical film, they sought to shed some light on the extreme tendency of the classical film to incorporate repetition, over-determination, and redundancy, but, above all, on the necessity for that text to rupture and fissure itself in order to satisfy its intrinsic function of smoothing over division, splits, differences. Thus the contradictions and gaps that the feminists had been positivistically ascribing to the attempts to stage a feminine discourse in a patriarchal form or to the specific difficulty that the woman's image entails, were for the male theorists no more than necessary components of the classical film's illusionistic economy. In setting forth a description of the classical economy as one of rupture and resolution, textual analyses of films like *The Birds* (Bellour), *North by Northwest* (Bellour), and *Touch of Evil* (Heath)[6] also stressed the positive outcome of that economy— its formal success. Classical film aims toward homogeneity and closure and, for all practical purposes, attains it. According to the textual theorists, then, a feminine look, a female discourse, a woman's desire—everything that feminist film criticism had been concerned to establish and describe—exist in the film only to be annexed by the male character and hence the male spectator. As Janet Bergstrom said of Raymond Bellour's work on Hitchcock, his most "insidious" argument is that which proposes the female character's desire as crucial and pervasive to the logic of the enunciation of classical film.[7] And for the female spectator, Bellour offers a bleak interpretation of her narrow role: "I think that a woman can love, accept and give a positive value to these films only from her own masochism, and from a certain sadism that she can exercise in return on the masculine subject, within a system loaded with traps."[8] What sort of feminist reply or response would it be possible to make to this massively elaborate and detailed description of classical film that allows no place for a woman's desire or discourse, nor any position for the woman "outside" the film as spectator that is not an alienated one? If the response claims that the male privilege in the classical film cannot be as total as the textual theorists contend, then it must meet head on the warning that Freud, in his "Dostoevsky's knife" footnote in "Female Sexuality," issued to the defenders of women's interests: it is an argument that cuts both ways. That is, if feminists maintain that there is some masculine interest or prejudice at stake in the theoretical "fact" that female sexuality in the classical film serves only to mirror or be subsumed by that of the male, then opponents can say that this feminist objection is a natural one, that it has no basis other than an instinctive, feminine refusal of a view that is unflattering to them. This is a good point, and one that clearly has been taken to heart in the feminist writing on classical film. For, rather than repudiate the work of the textual theorists and the psychoanalytic theory on which it is largely based (the defense against the narcissistic wound), these feminists film theorists have chosen to work within those terms, while at the same time trying to understand why indeed a certain image of woman comes to serve as a guarantee of both textual system and film theory:

> What is central here is that cinema appears as an apparatus which tries to close itself off as a system of representation, but that there is always a certain refusal of difference, of any troubling of the system, an attempt to run away from that moment of difference, and to bind it back into the logic or perfection of the film system itself. . . . This is the crucial point within the theory. The system is constituted as system only as a function of what it is attempting to evade. . . . The psychoanalytic approach to these questions parallels or echoes those analyses of cinema which have addressed themselves to this question of the way the woman gets set up, not simply as a certain image (which can be very easily criticized sociologically or historically) but as a guarantee against the difficulties of the cinematic system itself. (Jacqueline Rose)[9]

A further problem posed for feminists writing about classical film, and one that had already suggested itself in the earlier work, was how to argue that there was a contradiction between the "feminine" and the classical system, without falling back on an essentialist notion of "femininity" or "Woman" as an eternal and naturally subversive element. There would be no feminist advantage to positing either a historically unchanging feminine essence or a monolithic patriarchal repression of that essence. The idea of an essence is ahistorical and asocial, and suggests a set of traits not amenable to change, while the "repression" thesis (visible in Cook and Johnston's work) fosters the belief that, once liberated from patriarchal constraints, femininity would finally assume its uncontaminated and naturally given forms. In the examples that follow, we will see various attempts to deal with this troublesome issue, one that is common to feminist theory in general.

In her study of *The Birds*, "Paranoia and the Film System,"[10] Jacqueline Rose offered one of the first feminist criticisms of semiological and psychoanalytical film theory by suggesting that the textual theorists had too hastily assimilated the structure of classical film to an orthodox psychoanalytic description of the male's negotiation of the Oedipus complex, in other words, his "integration into the Symbolic through a successful Oedipal trajectory" (85). When Rose points to Melanie Daniels's catatonic state at the end of *The Birds*, she does so to say something about the place of the woman in the Hitchcockian system, but also to emphasize the way contemporary film theory has understood and described that place. Her article is a direct response to Raymond Bellour's important study of *The Birds* ("*Les Oiseaux*: analyse d'une séquence"),[11] an essay which, in its rigorous attention to sets of binary oppositions within the text and their common pattern of alternation, repetition, and rhyming, established the terms for all future work on the textual operations of cinematic codes. It is equally a reply to "Le blocage symbolique,"[12] Bellour's exhaustive analysis of the effects of the Oedipal structuring of *North by Northwest*, from its smallest signifying elements to larger narrative and symbolic movements. While agreeing with Bellour that *North by Northwest* exhibits perfectly the ideal psychoanalytic scenario for the male character, Rose objects to extending this same analysis to a film like *The Birds* in which the Oedipal narrative closure is not as clearly and easily achieved as in *North by Northwest*, and in which that closure depends on relegating the woman either to catatonia or infantile speechlessness. In Bellour's version—that is, in his answer to the question "Why do the birds attack Bodega Bay/Melanie?"—he argues that the birds, as representatives of the men, and ultimately its director (as a figurative stand-in for all men in the culture), attack Melanie as a punishment for her sexual aggressiveness (bringing the love birds to Bodega Bay as a lure for Mitch). In Rose's reading of the film, however, the birds "emanate" from an inherent instability in the film's own system which releases an "aggressivity" that focuses around the woman, one that finally cannot be contained by the film. This systematic instability allows Mitch to resolve his Oedipal task "successfully" only at the cost of Melanie's sanity and sexuality.

Where does this aggressivity come from? For Rose, it originates in the point of view structure of the film, particularly in the system of shot/reverse-shot whose ubiquity in the film is a Hitchcockian signature. Bellour describes the shot/reverse-shot system in Melanie's motorboat trip out and back across Bodega Bay to show how her look appears to predominate, but is actually circumscribed and contained by the looks of the male characters (and Hitchcock's, and the male spectator's). What seems to be symmetry is actually dissymmetry: women look only to be looked at while looking. But Rose adds another element to the shot/reverse-shot structure of Mitch and Melanie's specular reciprocity. She reminds us that the Lacanian description of the mirror-phase not only accounts for this kind of structure but also characterizes it as paranoid and aggressive. Because it is a specular image, cause and effect are reversible (the gull attacks Melanie because she brought the love birds to Bodega Bay), while the reciprocity of the structure provides for mutual aggression (the attacking birds are associated with both Mitch and Melanie). The birds, then, are not representatives of Mitch and the other men in the film but the sign of the aggressivity released by the filmic reproduction of the Imaginary in the shot/reverse-shot system. Rose argues that the aggressivity focuses around the woman because of her privileged relation to the Imaginary, deriving from the strength of the pre-Oedipal bond between the mother and the girl. An important point being made here (albeit implicitly), and one vital to subsequent feminist work, is that the "disruption" of the text is not the result of a feminine essence rubbing against the patriarchal grain of the film, but rather the conflation of two separate elements: a contradiction or lack in the textual system of the film itself (e.g., the aggressivity released by the miming of the Imaginary in the shot/reverse-shot structure) and the traits of the female character (e.g., Melanie's sexual aggressiveness). The significance of Rose's argument is that the woman comes to represent through the textual work of the film both the difficulty of sexual difference and the problems of cinema as a representational form. This question of how and why the woman in the film comes to bear such a heavy representational load constitutes the focus of later feminist readings of classical film.

Rose's complaint against Bellour's reading of *The Birds* is twofold. On the one hand, she questions his application of the psychoanalytic model to classical film — *The Birds* does not represent a smooth, Oedipal outcome for the man. On the other hand, she questions the psychoanalytic model itself, or rather Bellour's understanding of that model. His is not only a wish-fulfilling version of psychoanalysis — one that assumes the possibility of a stable sexual identity, and thus a real "resolution" for the Oedipal male subject — but also a use of psychoanalysis that neglects the difficulties specific to feminine sexuality (for example, the greater strength of the pre-Oedipal bond of the girl to the mother). In a later article, on *Psycho* ("Psychosis, Neurosis, Perversion"),[13] Bellour took the opportunity to reply to Rose, presenting his case in even stronger terms. He agrees that the reciprocity of looks in the alternation of shot/reverse-shots evokes the "structure of the cinematographic apparatus, and thereby of the primitive apparatus it imitates, namely the mirror wherein the subject structures himself, through a mode of narcissistic identification of which aggressivity is an indelible component." However, he goes on to say that

> this reference only makes sense . . . within the global system in which it has been constructed (Hitchcock's films, classical American cinema in general), that is, a system in which the aggressive element can never be separated from the inflection it receives from sexual difference, and in the attribution of this difference to the signifier that governs it. In other words it is directed from the man towards the woman, and that difference which appears due to woman is nothing but the mirror-effect of the narcissistic doubling that makes possible the constitution of the male subject through the woman's body. (118–19)

Bellour supports his argument that cinema reduces femininity to the narcissistic mirroring of masculinity by taking up Luce Irigaray's similar observation about psychoanalysis, that it always collapses sexual difference into one, masculine sexuality:

> The American cinema is entirely dependent, as is psychoanalysis, on a system of representations in which the woman occupies a central place only to the extent that it's a place assigned to her by the logic of masculine desire.[14]

The feminist analyses of classical film that have followed this exchange between Bellour and Rose have dealt with the questions raised there in two ways. The first approach concentrates on psychoanalytic theory itself and offers another, more complicated, reading of it. Thus, in various articles discussed here, the writers have reexamined such crucial psychoanalytic concepts as identification, object relations, fetishism, voyeurism, fantasy, and the Imaginary, in order to understand the full complexity of their original theoretical application. This rereading is undertaken in the belief that psychoanalytic theory can help to give an account of the difficult path of cinematic sexual difference for both the man and the woman. The second approach deliberately selects for study films like *The Birds,* films which do not comfortably accommodate a male Oedipal scenario or ones in which the difficulties specific to feminine sexuality figure prominently. In actual practice, the two approaches overlap.

One of the ways in which the psychoanalytic model has been redefined in its application to film can be seen very strikingly in Janet Bergstrom's reading of another of Bellour's favored theoretical objects, *Psycho*.[15] Whereas Bellour argues that the woman is always the object of the man's look (and thereby adopts the basic Freudian fetishistic schema of the little boy's look onto the mother's body), Bergstrom's more complex counter-version of looking and identification in *Psycho* is taken from Freud's description of the structure of fantasy. For Bellour, the active male gaze (Norman's eye-phallus-camera) is directed toward Marion's body which passively receives it (her *jouissance* in the shower serving only to excite his desire), in exactly the same way that the little boy enacts a fetishistic disavowal around the mother's "penis" (he knows that it is not there, but believes it to be there nonetheless): the mother's body serving as the site of the little boy's narcissistic fantasy. In trying to move beyond this limited fetishistic interpretation, Bergstrom cites the multiple and successive identificatory positions found in fantasies like those reported to Freud, primarily by female patients, and which are summarily expressed in the words "A child is being beaten." In the analysis, the patient reveals the progressive stages of the fantasy. At first, she says, "My father is beating the child"; then, "behind" that scenario is a more masochistic one consisting of "I am being beaten by my father." Finally, she reports, "I am probably looking on." As Freud puts it, the situation of being beaten, "which was originally simple and monotonous ['a child is being beaten'], may go through the most complicated alterations and elaborations."[16] In this fantasy, then, the woman respectively identifies, during its three stages, with the adult doing the beating, the child being beaten, and with herself as a spectator viewing the beating. She can thus be both subject or object, or identify with the entire scene itself. In addition to pointing out the intricate subject/object permutations found in the structure of fantasy, Bergstrom also cites Freud's case studies of the Wolf Man and Dora to show just how complex "identification" can be. Dora, for example, can love Frau K. only through a masculine identification, thus demonstrating once again the bisexuality of the unconscious (and also considerably complicating our Freudian understanding of "woman's desire"). Perceiving the multiple unconscious possibilities for the exchange and doubling of roles in fantasy, Bergstrom offers the following alternative reading of *Psycho*:

> Wouldn't Norman's scenario have to read something like this? When he meets Marion, it is as the son to an available woman. When he watches her in the shower, Norman is the son watching the mother (Marion), imagining himself as the mother's lover ("the imaginary and ungraspable relation of the primal scene"). When Norman, impersonating his mother, kills Marion, it is as the mother killing a rival of her son's affection. . . . Each shift necessitates corresponding changes in the imaginary identifications of the other characters in the scenario.[17]

Bergstrom concludes by insisting that it is now "possible and absolutely necessary to complicate the question of identification as it functions in the classical film, first of all in terms of the realization that spectators are able to take up multiple identificatory positions, whether successively or simultaneously" (58).

Mary Ann Doane, in her study of the "women's films" or "woman's pictures" of the forties ("*Caught* and *Rebecca*: The Inscription of Femininity as Absence"),[18] films intended for a predominantly female audience, also argues against the theoretical assumption that the spectator is implicitly male and against the accompanying stress on psychical mechanisms related primarily to the male spectator—voyeurism, fetishism, and even identification. In the course of examining the specular and narrative problems of these films for women, she tries to show how the standard theoretical model cannot fully account for films explicitly constructed for a female spectator. If Hollywood narratives are analyzed simply as "compensatory structures designed to defend the male psyche against the threat offered by the image of the woman," and if classical cinema's appeal to male voyeurism or fetishism is infinite or exhaustive, then how are these "women's films" able to construct a position of female spectatorship (and how, theoretically, are we to make an argument for it)? Doane argues that the "women's films" nonetheless attempt to do so by basing themselves on an idea of female fantasy that they both "anticipate" and "construct" (75). As for the fantasies themselves, it is interesting that they are the very ones which have been typically associated with the female—masochism, hysteria, and paranoia. Although these films claim to deal directly with female subjectivity and desire, "certain contradictions within patriarchal ideology" become apparent within the film text because classical Hollywood film—in its forms and conventions—is intrinsically geared toward masculine fantasies and cannot sustain such an exploration.

Doane agrees, then, with the conclusion of film analysts like Mulvey and Bellour that the classical film is constructed with a male spectator in mind, that in Hollywood cinema, the "male protagonists (act) as relays in a complex process designed to ensure the ego-fortification of the male spectator" (75). But she believes that the "women's films" attempt to do the same with the female spectator, "obsessively centering and recentering a female protagonist." Because of their effort to mirror the structure of classical film by constructing the scene/the film for a woman to look at, the "women's films" offer a crucial counterexample to an analysis that insists on the passive specularity of the woman, her objectification as spectacle by and for the masculine gaze. When a woman looks in these films, she too is given an objectified image of a woman to look at: in Ophul's *Caught*, the image is that of a woman in a mink coat; in Hitchcock's *Rebecca*, that of "a woman of thirty-six dressed in black satin with a string of pearls" (each woman is seen looking at these images in a fashion magazine). Significantly, the woman in the film cannot keep her distance from the proffered image of objectified desire: in *Caught* Leonora makes the social leap from carhop to millionaire's wife in order to become the picture of the woman in the fur coat; the Joan Fontaine character in *Rebecca* transforms herself into the image of the woman she had promised Maxim she would never be: a woman "dressed in black satin with a string of pearls." Not only does the woman become the image that she desires (being it rather than having it), but her desiring look is interrupted in the film by a masculine gaze that recasts the image of her desire into a desire to be desired.

In common with Bellour, Doane assumes the extreme circumscription of the woman's point of view and desire in the classical film. She does, however, agree with Jacqueline Rose that this process is threatened by the latent paranoia activated by the shot/reverse-shot system; the relevant interest here is to show how this paranoia is exacerbated by the film's attempt to construct a female spectator. For the subject matter of the films — a woman's near-destruction at the hands of a deranged husband — accelerates the paranoiac collapse of subject and object positions of looking, and swallows up the distance between the woman (character and spectator) and the image presented to her. What consequences does this paranoiac structure have for the film? On the one hand, Doane, like Rose, argues that the film is driven to act out or represent its own contradictions. In each of her examples there is a scene of a film being projected (Leonora's husband's documentary of his business exploits, Maxim's home movie of their honeymoon) in which the "normal" viewing situation of classical film is recreated: controlling male auteur and spectator, alienated female spectator. Not only does the film within the film stand in marked contrast to the "impossible" project of the "women's film," it also manages to recuperate the image of feminine desire found in the larger film, returning the woman, by the end of the film, to the confines of an image and/or the standard couple.

Doane, like Bergstrom, is dissatisfied with the adoption of the fetishistic scenario as the basic model for cinematic looking and identification, and as the vindication of the division of the male look/female look into an active/passive dichotomy. For the woman, to possess the image (fashion magazine photograph) is to become it. Doane points out that in "becoming the image, the woman can no longer have it. For the female spectator, the image is too close—it cannot be projected far enough" (83). The heroines can either accept or reject the imaged offered to them; the scenario gives them no other choice. In other words, they do not partake of the fetishism of male spectators who can "have their cake and eat it too (as Laura Mulvey describes Sean Connery's position in *Marnie*). The male spectator does not have to choose between accepting or rejecting the image; only men can maintain the proper fetishistic distance. In another article, in which Doane characterizes the position of the female spectator, as a "masquerade,"[19] she emphasizes that it is not an essential trait of woman to lack distance, to be too close and present to herself, but that this nearness is the delimitation of a place culturally assigned to women (and especially so by films such as the women's pictures of the forties). Equally, Doane wants to argue that, even though the woman's gaze and desire is radically circumscribed and even staged by the films as "impossible," it is not repressed in the sense of no longer existing. She cites Michel Foucault's critique of the "repressive hypothesis," the idea that repression is always total and fully effective:

> [It] entails a very limited and simplistic notion of the working of power. . . . In theories of repression there is no sense of the productiveness and positivity of power. Femininity is produced very precisely as a position within a network of power relations. (87)

Doane makes her point about the resistant tendencies of classical film by taking up Foucault's hypothesis concerning repression and power. It can, however, be argued equally well from a psychoanalytic perspective which acknowledges that repression is never complete. For, in fact, we only know of repression through its failures; if repression were total, nothing would remain to make us aware of what had been repressed or the act of repression itself.

Although it is theoretically necessary to establish that these points of resistance are linked to the problem of sexual difference in the classical film, we must consider the possibility that, as far as the feminist interest in film is concerned, the most vital sites of opposition lie elsewhere. In fact, with the exception of the early work of Claire Johnston and Pam Cook, the feminist work on classical cinema did not seek to study Hollywood film either to legitimize its pleasures for feminism or to reform it. Rather, the movement has been away from the discussion of classical film's equivocal efforts to contain the discord of sexual difference and toward a polemical consideration of films made by women and men that attempt to do what classical film (and sometimes the theories of classical film) suggest or even insist is structurally impossible: run counter to the Oedipal structuring of Western narrative form and the imaginary and fetishistic imperatives of the cinematic apparatus. The movement away from classical film includes, however, a frequent and strategic return to it. Not only do the feminist critics discussed here[20] feel it necessary to write concurrently about both classical and more experimental forms of film, but the experimental films themselves often insist on their own critical and aesthetic relation to classical film, the necessity of understanding and acknowledging its powers and effects to more effectively displace them. Although a great deal of important and vital work is being done in the realm of "personal," even abstract, film which attempts to engage or depict a woman's consciousness or vision, the area of work of most concern here is exactly those films that try to rework or thwart what we have come to expect from classical film in terms of narrative organization, point of view, and identification. For if, as the feminist studies of classical cinema claim, woman in the textual system of classical film comes to represent both the difficulty of sexual difference and the problems of classical cinema as a representational form (its lacks and contradictions), then the newer, experimental work will have to address itself simultaneously to sexual difference as a psychical and social phenomenon, and to the specifically cinematic forms and ideas of that difference.

The films of Chantal Akerman furnish a prominent example. In *News from Home* (1976) or *Jeanne Dielman, 23 Quai du Commerce, 1080 Bruxelles* (1975) the absence of reverse shots coupled with the use of extremely long sequences serve to give an unusually strong emphasis to the positions of implied spectator and narrator. Here, for example, the spectator is not "included" in the film through a character's adoption and relay of his or her look. Both the spectator and the narrator (implied in *Jeanne Dielman*, an off-screen woman's voice in *News from Home*) are designated as being "outside" the scene, allowed to look at it with a controlled and fascinated gaze, one which is not caught up in or radically circumscribed by a masculine gaze or logic of desire.[21] Similarly, Yvonne Rainer's *Film About a Woman Who . . .* (1975) offers the viewer, including the female spectator, the possibility of a strategically distanced look at a woman's body, a body that is offered not as an icon of what the woman character or spectator should become, but a body to be looked at and thought about in relation to the "phenomenon of male dominance/female submission."[22] And even when Rainer's film begins to cut up both body and language, this fragmentation—"devices to break-up, slow-down, and de-intensify the narrative" (66)—leads not to the fetishistic comfort of the spectator but, rather, to a more concrete understanding of the vicissitudes of sexual hierarchy.

But it is perhaps Marguerite Duras's *India Song* (1974) that takes on the most "impossible" task of all when it attempts to accomplish what women "theoretically" and from the perspective of classical cinema cannot do: create a representation of lack, the precondition of all symbolic activity; the engagement with language and culture. Psychoanalysis, which along with semiotics is the founding theory of the textual analysis of classical film, suggests that women are not capable of representing lack because they have never possessed and then been threatened with the loss of that which allows one symbolically to depict lack—the penis. Classical film in its turn positions women characters (and, implicitly, female spectators) as being the image, and not as having it or not having it (as Mary Ann Doane says, the woman is too close to the image, she has no choice but to become it). *India Song*, nevertheless, through its deployment of off-screen voices and their ambivalent and impossibly desiring relation to the inaccessible image on the screen of Anne-Marie Stretter—a woman who, the film tells us, is already dead—stages a representation that is fundamentally about loss and distance. In enacting a fantasy of loss and distance, then, it is also, and necessarily so, a fantasy of desire, specifically a desire that cannot be satisfied, and finally a desire for an unsatisfied desire. *India Song*, as "the mise en scène of this impossibility,"[23] thus leaves open the question of desire, and of a feminine position in relation to it, refusing, in contrast to classical film, to "answer" it with an assured definition of the nature of both masculine and feminine desire, and of desire itself.

In offering these few brief and selective examples of films that have received a great deal of feminist critical interest, my intention is to suggest the necessary affinity or continuity of two projects: an analysis of constructions of sexual difference in classical cinema and the way those ideas have been taken up or elided in film theory, and alongside that, an equally polemical attention to films that experimentally seek to reorder the relations of power and difference at work in classical film and its theory.

*Paul, the Myth of Pygmalion, in
Kennie McDowd, "The Marble
Virgin,"* (Science Wonder
Stories 1, *1929). Reproduced in* Les
Machines Célibataires, *eds. Jean
Clair and Harald Szeeman (Venice:
Altieri, 1975).*

Feminism, Film Theory, and the Bachelor Machines

"BACHELOR MACHINE" is the term Marcel Duchamp used to designate the lower part of his "Large Glass: The Bride Stripped Bare by Her Bachelors, Even," a term aptly borrowed by Michel Carrouges to name a phenomenon that he describes in *Machines Célibataires*.[1] From about 1850 to 1925 numerous artists, writers, and scientists imaginatively or in reality constructed anthropomorphized machines to represent the relation of the body to the social, the relation of the sexes to each other, the structure of the psyche, or the workings of history. His spectacular inventory of literary and artistic bachelor machines lists Mary Shelley's *Frankenstein*, Edgar Allen Poe's *The Pit and the Pendulum*, Villiers de l'Isle Adam's *L'Eve Future*, almost everything of Jules Verne or Alfred Jarry, Raymond Roussel's *Impressions of Africa*, Franz Kafka's *The Penal Colony*, Fritz Lang and Thea von Harbou's *Metropolis*, and the machine–sculptures of Jean Tinguely. And as for more scientific bachelor machines, we find Freud exclaiming to Fliess of his work on the *Project for a Scientific Psychology*, "Everything fell into place, the cogs meshed, the thing really seemed to be a machine which would run of itself."[2] This "inexhaustible inventiveness and dream-like renewal of mechanical models"[3] is, however, circumscribed in a particular way. As Michel de Certeau says of the bachelor machine, "It does not tend to write the woman. . . . The machine's chief distinction is its being male."[4]

The bachelor machine is typically a closed, self–sufficient system. Its common themes include frictionless, sometimes perpetual motion, an ideal time and the magical possibility of its reversal (the time machine is an exemplary bachelor machine), electrification, voyeurism and masturbatory eroticism, the dream of the mechanical reproduction of art, and artificial birth or reanimation. But no matter how compli-

57

cated the machine becomes, the control over the sum of its parts rests with a knowing producer who therefore submits to a fantasy of closure, perfectibility, and mastery.

It is only fitting that these characteristics should remind us of another apparatus, one that can offer impeccable credentials with respect to the bachelor machine's strict requirements for perpetual motion, the reversibility of time, mechanicalness, electrification, animation, and voyeurism: the cinema. Indeed, it is around the metaphor of the cinema as an *apparatus* that much of the most energetic contemporary thinking about film has taken place. We have only to recall the conspicuous influence of Jean-Louis Baudry's two articles about the cinematographic apparatus and Christian Metz's "The Imaginary Signifier"[5] to recognize how forcefully the idea of cinema as a technological, institutional, and psychical "machine" has shaped our current ways of understanding film. Just as influential, however, has been the theory of classical film narrative as itself a machine, and an avowedly bachelor one. On the latter point, Raymond Bellour, for example, describes the narrative mechanism of Hollywood film ("a machine of great homogeneity, due to its mode of production which is both mechanical and industrial")[6] in terms of a "massive, imaginary reduction of sexual difference to a narcissistic doubling of the masculine subject."[7] And as for the infinitely sustaining and self-sufficient qualities of the machine model, Stephen Heath argues that the classical narrative system is programmed to carry out "a perpetual retotalisation of the imaginary."[8]

What are we to make, then, of Michel de Certeau's assertion that the bachelor machine "does not . . . write the woman"? Or, similarly, Freud's claim that "it is highly probable that all complicated machinery and apparatus occurring in dreams stand for the genitals — and as a rule the male ones"?[9] For feminists writing about film the question of the fitness of the apparatus metaphor has been a secondary one, that is, whether or not it provides an adequate descriptive model of the way classical film functions on the basis of and for masculine fantasy (most agree that this is largely the case). They have found it more productive to ask whether this description, with its own extreme bacheloresque emphasis on homogeneity and closure, does not itself subscribe to a theoretical systematicity, one that would close off those same questions of sexual difference that it claims are denied or disavowed in the narrative system of classical film. Thus in recent feminist writing about film it is clear that this critique of the theories of the apparatus

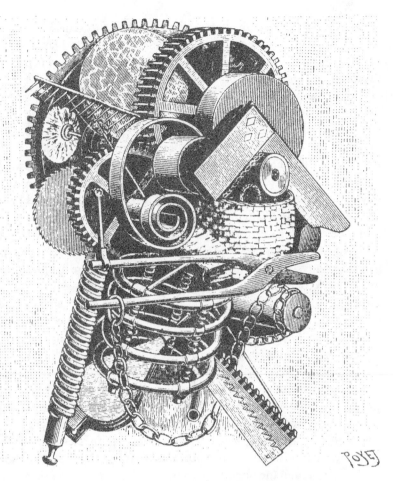

Poyet, The Inventor, *wood engraving, end of the nineteenth century. Reproduced in* Les Machines Célibataires.

parallels the feminist challenge to two other theoretical practices which also stand accused of keeping bachelor quarters: Marxism (its awkward dealings with the "woman question") and psychoanalysis (its negative construction of "feminine sexuality").[10]

In examining the model or metaphor of the cinematic apparatus, the most useful and successful feminist approaches have been those that take film theory on its own terms — semiology, psychoanalysis, textual analysis — while questioning the capacity of each to elide the difficulties specific to feminine sexuality, if not gendered subjectivity *tout court*. Another approach to the same apparatus question in its relation to ideas like the Imaginary, identification, and repetition, would be to reject, out of hand, all the work produced by film theory on the grounds of its manifest exclusion of the woman; and then strike out along the well-worn dissident paths of a reductive biologism, sociologism, or mysticism of the feminine, resurrecting once again the expressiveness of the woman's body or "women's experience," and summoning up such pale specters as the "Electra complex," archaic pulsionality, womb envy, and the feminine principle. All of these "alternatives" represent merely another version of the easily accepted (because narcissistically desired) or the already known (the comfort of repeating the same).

The metaphor of cinema as an apparatus arose from the need to account for several aspects of film, ranging from the uniquely powerful impression of reality provided by cinema and the way the subject is positioned as a spectator, to the desire intrinsic to cinema-going itself. In this metaphor the cinematic apparatus is not merely the technological base (although the popular perception of cinema's "scientific" and technological origins are fantasmatically crucial to its reality-effect), but the entire institution of cinema, its means of promoting and distributing itself and its administration of the social spaces in which films are viewed. Broadly speaking, the cinematic apparatus achieves its specific effects (the impression of reality, the creation of a fantasmatically unified spectator-subject, the production of the desire to return to the cinema) because of its success in re-enacting or mimicking the scene of the unconscious — the psychical apparatus — and duplicating its mechanisms by way of illusion. For both Metz and Baudry, the apparatus model is effective because, like Freud's *psychischer Apparat* (which, in *The Interpretation of Dreams*, he defines in comparison to an optical apparatus), it allows us to describe the coexistence of the different systems or agencies that make up the cinematic apparatus, allot them their various functions, and even assign them a temporal order. In the earliest Freudian model, the function of the psychical apparatus was to keep the internal energy of the organism at the lowest possible level in accord with the "constancy principle." The cinematic apparatus, like the psychical system, is therefore a homeostatic model, in which all circulating energy is regulated, balanced, controlled. (Stephen Heath similarly characterizes classical film narrative as functioning according to "the capture and regulation of energy."[11])

It is Baudry's work which most completely identifies the psychical apparatus and its topography with that of the cinematic apparatus. For Baudry, the cinema is not an extension or prothesis of the psyche (as it is for Metz) but a faultless technological simulacrum of the systems Ucs and Pcs-Cs and their interrelations. In a grand teleological gesture, Baudry claims that all the other art forms (drawing, painting, photography, and so on) are simply rehearsals of a primordially unconscious effort to recreate the scene of the unconscious, while cinema is its most successful achievement. Baudry agrees with Metz that the success of the apparatus in its production of cinematic pleasure is due to the fact that it was, after all, "built" in conformity to strictly wish-fulfilling requirements. Thus, in Baudry's Freudian terms, the apparatus induces (as a result of the immobility of the spectator, the darkness of the theater, and the projection of the images from a place behind the spectator's head) a total regression to an earlier developmental stage in which the subject hallucinates satisfaction; or, in Metz's more Lacanian scheme, the apparatus mimes the mirror stage and therefore structures for the spectator a completely imaginary relation to the screen in which the subject is given the seamless illusion of unity and totality, as well as an identificatory feeling of mastery over the visual field.

The initial problems posed by the theories of the cinematic apparatus for a feminist consideration of film are both theoretical and practical. Jean-Louis Baudry's psyche-machine-cinema model is not only ahistorical but also strongly teleological. The shackled prisoners fascinated by the shadows on the wall of Plato's cave are the first "cinema" spectators; the only historical changes in the apparatus since then have been little more than technological modifications. If the apparatus stages an eternal, universal, and primordial wish to create a simulacrum of the psyche, then Baudry's argument is blind to the economic, social, or political determinations of cinema as well as its basic difference from other art forms (painting and photography are merely less successful versions of the cinema–machine; they are all "metonymies . . . [of] the same metaphor").[12] A further problem is that Baudry's teleological argument asserts that cinema aims at pleasure alone, and that it unfailingly achieves it, an assertion, moreover, that is merely stated and not supported. *Why* does the subject necessarily seek only pleasure and its fulfillment? Surely psychoanalytic theory has offered us a more complex account of the vicissitudes of desire (the repetition compulsion and the death drive), let alone posited the desire for an un-satisfied desire (hysteria as the desire not to have one's desire satisfied). The question of pleasure has been a crucially troubling one for femi-nist film theory and filmmaking, and the theory of the apparatus ap-pears to answer the question before it is even raised.

A final difficulty is that neither Metz nor Baudry (in his second ar-ticle) mentions specific films. Are we then to conclude that every kind of film elicits the *same* labor in the apparatus and the same ruthlessly deterministic effects? Although it would seem important to describe the workings of the apparatus itself prior to specific inflections of it, doesn't this lead to an overwhelmingly negative and deterministic idea of the possibilities of radical experimentation in film? For if the effects of the apparatus are total, and always totally successful (for example, its creation of a unified, transcendental subject and of a completely imaginary relation of the spectator to the screen), then it begins to look like mere wish–fulfillment to imagine the kind of film that would subvert its power. There must be a way of recognizing the pervasive power of the apparatus without sacrificing this sense of acceptance on the altar of fatalism.

Beyond these general complaints about the apparatus as a model for cinema, feminists have also questioned its association with several in-terconnected ideas or psychic functions: the Imaginary and the mirror stage, identification, repetition, and homeostatic regulation. I want now to examine some of those specific criticisms of the apparatus the-ories and then point to possible ways of evicting the cinematic appa-ratus from its well-appointed bachelor residence.

> The imaginary, of which the cinema may well be the most privileged and efficient machine, is precisely a *machine*, an apparatus in which what is at stake is a repression or refusal of the problem or difficulty of sexuality.[13]
>
> Jacqueline Rose

From the evidence of the above quotation, it is clear that at least one feminist has found the machine or apparatus metaphor polemically useful or illuminating. But what is also obvious in these few lines is an attention to what is *at stake* in this configuration of sexual difference as a problem for both film and feminist theory. The psychoanalytic concept of the imaginary was formally introduced into film theory by way of Christian Metz's "The Imaginary Signifier," a lengthy essay exhaustively devoted to a discussion of the "imaginariness" of the cinematic signifier and, by extension, of the cinematic apparatus. For Metz, cinema is the art form of the imaginary par excellence, and for two reasons. First, because of its manipulation of five material components or channels of communication (analogical image, graphic image, sound, speech, dialogue) film is more sensorially *present* than any other medium. At the same time, however, that which it depicts is extremely *absent*. In contrast to theater, for example, where the actors physically share the time and space of the audience (although not necessarily in the fiction of the play, of course) film actors typically do their work far in advance of the moment of viewing and are not physically present in the same space as the cinema audience (they are on the screen but that space is, for example, a sound stage at Warner Bros). This combination of presence and absence is characteristic of the Imaginary, as exemplified in the mirror stage of Jacques Lacan. The infant, seeing itself in the mirror, has the sense of being "there" for the first time, existing as a separate and autonomous entity at exactly the moment when it is "not there" because what it in fact sees is an *image* of a separateness and independence that it has not yet achieved. For Metz, however, the mirror identification is not a primary but a secondary form of cinematic identification. Even more fundamental in its effects is the spectator's identification with his own act of vision as it is taken up and relayed by the camera. Primary identification, then, is with the camera, or rather with the spectator himself in his own act of perceiving. This primary identification is the basis for the formation of a transcendental subject, a spectator centered for absolute mastery over the visual domain. As for the spectator's belief in the reality of the cinematic images, Metz links this to the inherent lack or absence at the heart of the cinematic signifier. By a process of fetishistic disavowal, the spectator admits that what he is perceiving is not really there, but makes himself believe it to be there nonetheless (the fetishistic formula of "I know, but": "I know that she [the mother] does not really have a penis, but I believe it to be there all the same").

*Umbrella lightning-conductor, ca.
1800. Reproduced in* Les Machines
Célibataires.

In two essays on the use of the concept of the imaginary in psycho-analysis and film theory,[14] Jacqueline Rose argues that Metz makes his claims about the excessive imaginariness of the cinematic signifier on the basis of an overly schematized and reductive notion of the imaginary. What Metz disregards is that the imaginary is never purely imaginary just as the visual is never merely perceptual. In Lacan's later work on vision, particularly in the four seminars included under the heading "The Look as *objet petit a*,"[15] he stresses that the imaginary is always permeated by the desire of the Other, and that it is a triangular rather than a dual relation. This triangulation can be seen most vividly when the child in front of the mirror turns to the one who is holding it and appeals with its look for an affirmation of what it sees. This appeal places the imaginary relation in the register of demand and desire, thus pre-empting any theoretical use of the mirror stage as an absolute or exemplary instance of unity or completion. Similarly, Metz's conclusions about the spectator's primary identification and the formation of his transcendental subjectivity need to be qualified by a more subtle and intricate reading of the psychoanalytic insights into vision and subjectivity. In Lacanian thought, for example, the subject of vision is also an object of representation. Since vision always takes place in the field of the Other's vision and desire, the important look is the one that comes from outside ("What fundamentally determines me in the visible is the look which is outside").[16] The subject can be "seized by the object of its look";[17] moreover, the subject cannot see what it wants to see because the look is never a pure look (purely perceptual) but conditioned by the look (the desire) of the Other. As a third and final consideration, the subject can never see from the place from which it is seen. All of this colludes against any idea of a subject identifying with itself as a pure act of perception or that act leading to a mastery or transcendence at the level of vision. On the contrary, it suggests that the seeing subject (the subject of the unconscious) is in an extremely vulnerable position, that, if anything, the subject is more seen than seeing. Metz, in claiming that the cinema spectator is immediately and successfully positioned as a transcendental subject within a fantasy of omniscient perception and knowledge, confuses the actual effects of the apparatus with its aim. The apparatus may "aim" to construct a transcendental subject but it must necessarily always fail, subverted by the presence of desire in vision. This is not to discount the power of the illusionistic effects of the apparatus; it is merely to call into question the idea of an always successfully achieved subject construction that would be a purely imaginary one.

The bacheloresque cast of Metz's formulation lies in its overemphasis on the Imaginary at the expense of the Symbolic. Here, the subject, that is, the subject of the unconscious, is sexless or nongendered. As we have seen, however, the imaginary is not to be construed as a developmental "stage" that exists "before" symbolization or desire (the triangulation of the mirror situation through the demand made to the Other) or as a moment preceding the splitting of the subject, a moment which is inseparable from sexual division. But perhaps this theoretical elision of sexual difference can be seen even more strikingly in Metz's discussion of filmic fetishism where the spectator doubles up on his belief in the image to counter the perception that the image is not real or that the depicted object is not really present. As Rose points out, however, fetishism does not bear, finally, on the image or the object but rather on the structure of subjectivity. In the psychoanalytic scenario of fetishism the traumatic moment is the boy child's perception that the mother has no penis. However, the spectator's perception of the absence of the object and thus of the unreality of the image cannot be compared directly to this traumatic perception. First, the absent object of fetishism is not just any object but the maternal penis. Metz fails to account for the "context" of that look, a context in which the act of perception is irremediably bound up in a structure of sexual difference. His argument, moreover, conceives the moment of perception as a moment of realization or knowledge and its disavowal. It is questionable, however, whether that moment can have any meaning in itself; more probably the meaning comes only after the fact. For Freud, the meaning of that moment is delayed and only acquired after the subject has come to recognize the value of having a penis or not. Meaning, as Rose puts it, lies "elsewhere,"[18] and not in the immediacy of perception.

Another problem with Metz's account lies in its undue emphasis on the conscious nature of the spectator's belief in the moment of perceiving. For Metz, the spectator "doubles up"[19] his belief as a defense against the anxiety caused by recognizing the absence inherent to the cinematic signifier. The result amounts to an elision of any unconscious effect because it transforms that moment into a conscious "I know, but . . . "—"I know that it's not real, but I'll pretend while I'm here that it is."[20] Rose is quick to point to the feminist consequences of such a theoretical repression of the concept of the unconscious: disavowal (of the maternal penis) must be understood as an unconscious fantasy or else we are left with the theoretically unfeasible and politically unacceptable notion that the child has a real perception of a real feminine inferiority.[21]

Finally, then, the only notable consideration of "difference" in Metz's theory of the cinematic signifier is the difference of a given image from the real object. Disavowal turns upon the spectator's recognition that the image is really lacking (in relation to the real object which it is not) and his subsequent attempt to repress that knowledge; thus the only thing that could disturb the illusion of imaginary identity would be an image that is too unreal. "Any challenge to the imaginary remains within the terms of the imaginary itself."[22] The effects of the Symbolic (or the Real, for that matter), inasmuch as they inscribe *sexual* difference, are disregarded, and Metz's "imaginary signifier" begins to assume the familiar dimensions of a bachelor apparatus.

Rose's attempt to counter the bachelor tendencies of the apparatus looks to psychoanalysis as a source of more sophisticated readings than the theory of the apparatus has provided. By contrast, Joan Copjec ("The Anxiety of the Influencing Machine"),[23] in her comparison of Metz and Baudry's theories of the apparatus with the Tauskian machine constructed by schizophrenics to deny sexual difference, chooses to engage the Derridean critique as a way of raising questions of sexual difference. Copjec argues that the theory of the apparatus constructs an anthropomorphized machine that is a projection of a libidinalized body, a phallic machine producing only male spectators. She even suggests that the theory of the apparatus is paranoid, and claims that it arose as "*the delusional defense against the alienation that the elaboration of cinema as a language opened in theory.*"[24] In other words, the theory of the apparatus sprang up in the wake of Metz's *Langage et cinéma* as a way of denying that book's most important insights for cinema, particularly its insistence on the idea that subjectivity is a linguistic construction or effect.

In "Freud and the Scene of Writing," Derrida has, in fact, written a critique of those machine metaphors of the psychical system, a critique that closely parallels our concern here with the bacheloresque tendencies of the cinematic apparatus. His essay attempts to locate and follow in Freud's text (from the *Project for a Scientific Psychology* [1985] to the "Note Upon the Mystic Writing Pad" [1925]) the path of a metaphoric investment in writing or the scriptural "which will eventually invade the entirety of the psyche" (75). Derrida's interest lies in the progress of Freud's effort to find a model that could represent both the psychical system and its contents, beginning with the "neurological fable" of the *Project*, proceeding through the optical machines of the *Traumdeutung*, and concluding with the writing machine modeled on the Mystic Writing Pad. Derrida, however, is not so much concerned with the adequacy of the model (its mimetic accuracy) but rather with the question of representation itself:

> Psychical content will be *represented* by a text whose essence is irreducibly graphic. The structure of the psychical apparatus will be *represented* by a writing machine. What questions will those representations impose on us? We shall have to ask not if a writing apparatus—for example the one described in the "Note Upon the Mystic Writing Pad"—is a *good* metaphor for representing the work of the psyche; but rather what apparatus we must create in order to represent psychical writing, and what the imitation, projected and liberated in a machine, of something like psychical writing might mean. (76)

What questions, indeed, will those representations impose on us?

In *The Interpretation of Dreams* Freud proposed that we picture the instrument that carries out our mental functions as resembling a compound microscope, a telescope, or a photographic apparatus. With his optical machine metaphor he hoped to overcome several limitations that had become increasingly apparent in his earlier neuron model, one based on a mode of explanation borrowed from the natural sciences, in which psychical events are characterized as states quantitatively determined by distinct material particles. Freud wanted to move away from the biologistic idea that these events take place in specific anatomical areas of the brain. To distinguish psychical locality from anatomical place, he suggested that we understand that locality as corresponding to a place inside an optical instrument where a *virtual* image forms: "In the microscope and telescope, as we know, these occur in part at ideal points, regions in which no tangible component of the apparatus is situated."[25] Freud, to give a better account of the functioning of memory, needed a model that would emphasize the temporal order rather than the spatial distribution of psychical movements, and he felt that the optical model was better able to describe the regulated timing of movements as they were "caught and localized in the parts of the mechanism" (98). The shortcomings of the optical instrument metaphor were eventually to become obvious to Freud, not least because his better understanding of the workings of the psyche involved cer-

Harper's unicycle, 1894. Reproduced
in Les Machines Célibataires.

tain contradictions that the optical model could not properly represent. The psychical system, in fact, consists of two systems, one which will receive impressions and another system to permanently record those impressions. The optical machine, however, is too one-dimensional to incorporate this "double" register. Derrida notes that it was through the metaphor of the Mystic Writing Pad that Freud discovered a solution to all the cumulative problems encountered in this project. To begin with, the Mystic Pad can accommodate both systems: the top sheet (covered by a transparent protective layer) receives the impressions made by the stylus, but can be fully erased, leaving room for more marks, by simply lifting it away from the wax surface underneath; the wax layer permanently records all of the impressions made upon it. The act of writing itself solves other problems. Temporality, for example, is now inscribed in the process because of the seriality of steps involved: making the impression, lifting the second sheet to erase it, lowering the sheet, making new marks, etc. Also, the two-handed nature of the machine suggests a level of ambivalence about the agencies and origins of its *modus operandi*.

> This machine does not run by itself. It is less a machine than a tool. And it is not held with only one hand. . . . At least two hands are needed to make the apparatus function, as well as a system of movements, a coordination of independent initiatives, an organized multiplicity of origins. (112)

As Derrida reminds us, one always writes for someone and we must be several to write and to "perceive" (113). The subject of writing, then, is very different from the singular subject of the optical apparatus: "The subject of writing is a *system* of relations between strata: of the Mystic Pad, of the psyche, of society, of the world. Within that scene the punctual simplicity of the classical subject is not to be found" (113).

Joan Copjec calls into question the equally punctual simplicity of the subject of the cinematic apparatus by pointing out that a more complex idea of subjectivity, of subjectivity in language, is already at work in the notion of the *dispositif* as opposed to the *appareil*. The English translation of the titles of Baudry's two articles on the apparatus hides the fact that he uses two different words: *appareil* in the first and *dispositif* in the second. Copjec reminds us that *appareil* can be translated as "apparatus" but *dispositif* would be better translated as "arrangement." The apparatus, she argues, anthropomorphizes a social

construction which privileges the male, but by emphasizing the apparatus as something else, called an "arrangement," we can begin

> to question the anthropomorphic power it assumes, the functionalism it
> exhibits. Patriarchy can only be an effect of a particular arrangement of
> competing discourses, not an expressive totality which guarantees its
> own self-interests. . . . What must be analyzed is the way particular
> discourses inscribe sexual differences, different subject positions. . . .
> Woman produced as a category in various signifying practices . . . the
> multiformity of the construction of sexual differences. (58)

In another essay, on repetition or the compulsion to repeat in film
and film theory,[26] Copjec presents a second critique of the cinematic
apparatus, this time from the perspective of the ideas about repetition
and pleasure at work in the theories of the apparatus as well as current
narrative theory of film, particularly that of Raymond Bellour. She
cites Baudry's description of the apparatus as activated by a compulsion to repeat, a return to a former stage of satisfaction, and Metz's
insistence that cinema is motivated by the pleasure principle, which
entails the production of "good objects" only, that is, pleasurable
films. "Behind" this pleasure principle, moreover, is an *a priori* intention that Baudry and Metz ascribe to the apparatus. For Baudry, the
cinema *aims* to produce a hallucinated satisfaction because it is the embodiment of a primordial wish to reproduce that infantile pleasure.
And for Metz, it is the *intention* of the institution which defines the
success of the cinematic performance, "since the institution as a whole
has filmic pleasure alone as its aim."[27] Similarly, Raymond Bellour,
who, more than any other film theorist, has addressed himself to the
question of repetition in the cinema, says:

> Beyond any given film, what each film aims at through the apparatus
> that permits it is the regulated order of the spectacle, the return of an
> immemorial and everyday state which the subject experiences in his
> dreams and for which the cinematic apparatus renews the desire.[28]

"The cinematic apparatus renews the desire": a final feature of the apparatus is its ability to reproduce itself. As Metz says, "It is the specific
characteristic of every true institution that it takes charge of the mechanisms of its own reproduction."[29] Repetition, then, occurs at every
level of functioning of the apparatus: it repeats for the spectator a
former pleasure, and it repeats itself as it reproduces its own mechanism. In addition, at the level of classical narrative, the contradictions
of that narrative system are worked through and resolved in what Bel-

lour calls the "repetition-resolution effect" ("the fact that the film resolves itself, moves from its beginning to its end by means of differ-
ential repetition or the final integration of a certain number of
elements given at the beginning and in the course of the narrative").[30]
Faced with the marked emphasis of these theorists on the crucial role
of repetition in film, Copjec nevertheless maintains that, for all the
psychoanalytic references found in the theories of the apparatus, this is
not, in fact, a very psychoanalytic idea of repetition. For psychoanalysis moved itself beyond an early understanding of repetition as either
reproduction or restitution. Repetition does not reproduce past scenes,
as the analysis of the Wolf Man reveals in its elaboration of the structure of fantasy; it is not necessary for an event to have taken place for
it to have an existence in concrete, retrospective effects. Neither does
repetition restore a lost object or a lost relationship to an object; as
Freud observed of his nephew's fort/da game, mastery over the mother's absence is secondary to the primary feat of replaying the loss itself,
of "returning to the ever-open gap introduced by the absence,"[31] an
activity that situates itself distinctly beyond the constant, homeostatic
circuit of the pleasure principle. Above all, as Lacan has shown, repetition involves alienation because of its association with the splitting of
subjectivity. The mother's departure incites the infant to "mutilate
itself,"[32] to use a part of itself to signify her absence. This part will
eventually become the *objet petit a*, the cause of desire which, to remain
desire, must remain unattainable. Alienation, splitting, and the impossibility of satisfaction are a far cry from the version of repetition as
pleasure that we find in the theories of the apparatus.

Again, what is at stake for feminism in the superiority of one definition over the other? For Copjec, Baudry undermines his own effort
to account for the ideological determinations of cinema by attributing
an unconscious aim to the apparatus and ascribing to it a kind of transhistorical agency. Desire, in this light, would be an originating force
and its unquestionable aim would be satisfaction: "The cinematic apparatus becomes, once again, a tool that restores the integrity of the
subject, supplies the subject's demand" (50). Derrida, she says, follows Freud, and avoids this "incipient anthropomorphism" by substituting a writing machine for the optical apparatus. The Mystic Pad, as
we have seen, is a vastly more complex metaphor because (and this is
the problem of representation again) it can also represent the *insufficiency* of the psychical apparatus, its supplementary (rather than complementary) status: "The apparatus may be an ancient dream of man

but in Derrida's analysis this dream is itself a psychic supplement, the indication within the subject of its unfulfillment" (51). And to show that he, too, knows exactly what is at stake in the apparatus model, Derrida appropriately concludes "Freud and the Scene of Writing" with one of Freud's own conclusions (already cited above) concerning the dream-work: "It is highly probable that all complicated machinery and apparatus occurring in dreams stand for the genitals—and as a rule the male ones."

If, as Copjec claims, the theories of the apparatus constantly reproduce the same (that is, the male, as well as a male) point of view through their repeated emphasis on structures of masculine voyeurism, fetishism, and identification; and if, as Rose asserts, film theory's use of the concept of the imaginary tends to elide questions of sexual difference, is there any way in which the "excluded" woman can be reintroduced without falling back upon appeals to feminine identity and essence? Is it possible to dismantle, or rather debachelorize, the bachelor machine? Striking and, I would argue, symptomatically, two writers have each come to similar conclusions about ways of subverting the male narcissism of the apparatus theory. Both Mary Ann Doane[33] and Joan Copjec[34] have suggested substituting the "anaclitic" model of the drives for the account which bases itself on the fundamental importance of narcissism to the structuring of human subjectivity. The logical appeal of this is interesting not only because of the similarity of their conclusions, but also because it would seem to contradict other of their arguments, particularly those in which subjectivity is presented in terms of a linguistic or symbolic construction. I will suggest moreover that it is symptomatic because they introduce a model which ultimately risks (again) closing off questions of sexual difference.

Freud introduced the notion of anaclisis in *Three Essays on Sexuality* (1905) to describe the emergence of the sexual drives from the self-preservative instincts. In his 1915 essay, "On Narcissism," he contrasts anaclitic object-choice to narcissistic object-choice. Anaclitic choices are made along the lines of an initial attachment to the image of the parental figures, either to the woman who fed the infant or the man who protected it. In other words, the choice of love-object (the prototype of the sexually satisfying object) is determined with respect to the specific parental responsibilities for the child's feeding, care, and protection. The contrasting form of object-choice, the narcissistic one, was postulated by Freud to account for homosexual object-choice; it includes four possibilities, all of which are modeled on the subject's relation to himself rather than on a pre-existing relation to a parental figure. A narcissistic type can thus love: (1) what he himself is (i.e., himself), (2) what he himself was, (3) what he himself would like to be, (4) someone who was once part of himself. (Conventionally gendered language creates a confusion here: Freud in category 4 is actually describing a woman who narcissistically loves her child because it was once part of her body.) This points up some of the difficulties inherent in the distinction between anaclitic and narcissistic. Although Freud states that male object-choice is typically anaclitic while the female's is as a rule narcissistic, he points out that this distinction is only a schematic one and the "both kinds of object-choice are open to each individual."[35] The two types of object choice are thus purely ideal and can be alternated or combined in any actual individual case. Furthermore, in Freud's own examples, the antithesis between anaclitic and narcissistic object-choice does not always hold up. He describes as narcissistic, for example, the woman's choice of a man primarily for his love toward her, and not for her own love toward him. Here, however, the woman seems to be attempting to reproduce her relationship to the mother who fed and took care of her, which would thus be characteristic of anaclitic object-choice.

"Anaclisis" has by and large become an obsolete term, now used only descriptively or historically, because of our increased understanding of the fundamentally narcissistic nature of all object relations, even the very earliest ones. It is Lacan's mirror stage, of course, that has given us the metaphor of the narcissism underpinning all object relations: a child can only take another for an object once it has taken itself as an object. One's first love-object is oneself.

What would be the advantage then of substituting the anaclitic model of the drives for the narcissism of the apparatus, as Doane and Copjec have advocated? They each object to the central role cast for narcissism in the structuring of human subjectivity because this formula (the Lacanian account) requires both the man and the woman to define themselves in relation to a third term, a term which stands for the insufficiency or incompleteness of the subject—the phallus. They object above all to the fact that this formula supports the claim for a single libido, which Freud called masculine. Thus, in Doane's words, the narcissism/phallus model fails to provide a theory of woman's "autonomous symbolic representation" (33). While Copjec criticizes the apparatus theories for their exclusion of the feminine body, Doane goes even further, detecting what she interprets as tell-tale tendencies of bachelor thinking in those feminist anti-essentialist critiques which militate against any consideration of a "natural" female body. Like the apparatus theories, the anti-essentialist arguments (and here she is referring specifically to the work of *m/f*) have paranoically discarded any discussion of the body. In rejecting the idea of a natural female body, they have eliminated questions of the body altogether. Doane fears that the very force of their arguments will lure feminists into a one-dimensional extremist logic (one shared, for example, by the experimental filmmaker Peter Gidal, who refuses to include in his films any representation of a woman on the grounds that the perception of that image is too culturally rooted in an idea of her essential (biological) difference). But we need some conception of the female body, Doane argues, in "order to formulate the woman's different relation to speech, to language" (33). Copjec, in agreement with Doane, acknowledges that the task of putting the body back onto film theory will "often look like a return to biologism" (43); Doane, however, reasons that, in Stephen Heath's words, "the risk of essence may have to be taken,"[36] in order to formulate theories which provide the woman with "an autonomous symbolic representation" (33). In the attempt to find an approach that does not irremediably separate psyche from body, or which does not exclude the *woman's* body, Doane and Copjec, then, take up the theoretical cause of anaclisis as a way of challenging the apparatus theorists and the anti-essentialists. They find support for their challenge in the recently renovated version of anaclisis found in Jean Laplanche's *Life and Death in Psychoanalysis*.[37] Here is Mary Ann Doane's summary of Laplanche on anaclisis:

Jean Laplanche explains the emergence of sexuality by means of the concept of propping or *anaclisis*. The drive, which is always sexual, leans or props itself upon the nonsexual or presexual instinct of self-preservation. His major example is the relation of the oral drive to the instinct of hunger whose object is the milk obtained from the mother's breast. The object of the oral drive (prompted by the sucking which activates the lips as an erotogenic zone) is necessarily displaced in relation to the first object of the instinct. The fantasmatic breast (henceforth the object of the oral drive) is a metonymic derivation, a symbol of the milk: "The object to be rediscovered is not the lost object, but its substitute by displacement; the lost object is the object of self-preservation, of hunger, and the object one seeks to refind is an object displaced in relation to that first object." Sexuality can only take form in a dissociation of subjectivity from the bodily function, but the

> concept of a bodily function is necessary in the explanation as, precisely, a support. (26–27)

If sexuality can be explained only in relation to the body which serves as its "prop," then any discussion of sexuality (in filmic representation or otherwise) will be obliged to account for the role of the body. This raises at least two questions. First, what is *lost* by dropping narcissism from the account of the emergence of the drives and object-relations? And second, is the "anaclitic" body necessarily a feminine body, and is this the body we need to ensure the reconceptualization of the feminine body in film theory?

Doane and Copjec's use of anaclisis to describe the emergence of the drives and the formation of subjectivity should be viewed in the context of recent feminist attempts to align the drives with the body and the body with woman: Julia Kristeva's celebration of the woman's special relation to the pre-Oedipal mother's body, Michèle Montrelay's emphasis on the "real" of the woman's own body which imposes itself prior to any act of construction, Luce Irigaray's mapping of the feminine psyche onto that body's supposedly multiple sexualities.[38] In each case the aim is to give an account of *feminine* sexuality, one which these writers believe that Freud neglected and Lacan either willfully doctored or outrageously construed in the form of a new mysticism of the feminine. "The risk of essence" unabashedly taken by these alternative theories of the feminine typically involves, however, ignoring the important psychoanalytic emphasis on the way that sexual identity is imposed from the "outside." By deriving gendered sexuality from the body, no matter how indirectly, what is in danger of disappearing is the sense of sexuality as an arbitrary identity that is imposed on the subject, as a law. And the phallus, as a sign that belongs to culture rather than to nature, is itself the sign of the law of sexual division. According to this law, each subject, male and female, must take up a position in relation to the phallus — which is *not* of a natural bodily order. In this respect, the most significant insight of psychoanalysis is the theoretical evidence it brings to bear against any notion of a "natural" sexual identity. Because sexual identity is "legislated"[39] rather than autonomously assumed, there is an ill-fit between subject and sexual identity, precisely because it is the result of an *imposition*. This insight agrees with the anti-essentialist claim that femininity is only an awkwardly donned and sometimes inappropriate garb for the woman. The anaclitic account of the emergence of the drives, put forward as an explanation of feminine subjectivity, thus risks (along with the alternative theories of femininity mentioned above) understanding femininity as naturally assumed or a simple product of the body's development. Such an understanding effaces the *difficulty* of femininity as a sexual position or category in relation to the symbolic as well as social order.

It is clear moreover that Laplanche's version of anaclisis does not seek to *substitute* anaclisis for narcissism. As we have seen he is concerned to give an account of the early emergence of the drives and the subsequent paths of object-choice. (In particular, he emphasizes that this description should not be misread as a propping on a "body," but as a propping of the drives on the instincts—16.) In effect, Laplanche provides a description of the metaphorical and metonymical processes or paths leading to the choice of the object. The drives emerge metonymically from the self-preservative instincts (for example, hunger for milk/desire for the breast/desire for the mother) *and* metaphorically in the way sexuality cathects the "outside" (love of one's own double and the doubles of that original double). Laplanche stresses the *meshing* of the metaphorical-metonymical processes; anaclisis is thus a term for him only inasmuch as it is bound up with narcissism.

A further argument against Doane and Copjec's plan for substituting anaclisis for narcissism is that the "body" in question here, if there is one at all (and for Laplanche, as we have seen, there is not), would not be a *woman's* body but a *mother's* body: the moment of the early emergence of the drives and related object choices is *before* the moment when the child can say "My mother is a woman." Once again, in the theoretical search for the "woman," we end up with the "mother," which is not at all the same thing—and feminists[40] have long recognized the crucial need to maintain that distinction, especially since the two terms have a habit of slipping into each other.

We have seen that the argument for anaclisis rests upon the notion that the drives emerge solely by differentiating themselves from the bodily functions. A final problem with this formulation is that it makes it difficult to pose the question of the status of the image or representation itself. Doane and Copjec, for example, follow up Laplanche's claim that the perception of the breast is a fantasmatic one. But what is missing from this account is precisely the whole problematic of splitting and distance that makes representation possible (the object can be represented only if it is absent), and which is provided theoretically by the structural function of narcissism. Repeatedly, then, I have demon-

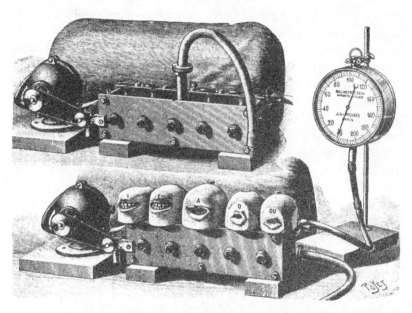

Poyet, wood engraving, 1908 (in La Nature*). Reproduced in* Les Machines Célibataires.

strated the problems involved in turning to anaclisis for a more accurate account of the emergence of the drives of the feminine body, an account "uncontaminated" by the "male" preserves of narcissism and the phallic relation: if anaclisis has any claim to a theoretical existence, then it is in no way autonomous from the question of narcissism.

No matter how carefully these writers attempt to present this concept of anaclisis (or the propping of the drives on the bodily functions) as an alternative logic to that of narcissism and the phallic relation, their effort seems inevitably to reproduce the difficulties endemic to the essentialist position that they are so concerned to avoid, a position which assumes an identity rather than examining it and seeks to answer questions about sexual difference before they are asked. Clearly what we need as a counter to the "maleness" of the cinematic apparatus and its theories is not to reintroduce the *feminine body* into those theories but to insist on a way of theorizing cinema that does not eliminate the question of *sexual difference*. I would argue that the theoretical components for such a project have been presented in the recent feminist work on fantasy in relation to film.[41] An investigation of the construction of fantasy seems to provide a way of accounting for sexual difference that acknowledges difference but which in no way seeks to dictate or predetermine the subsequent distribution of that difference (in terms of sexual identity) in any given film or for any given spectator, male or female. In the psychoanalytic account of fantasy, the drives are sexualized only by way of their articulation in fantasy. The emphasis here is not on the relation to the object but on the subject's desire in relation to a scenario in which he takes part. Although the structure of these scenarios is pre-determined, their contents are not. Laplanche and Pontalis, in an essay indispensable to the discussion of fantasy, "Fantasy and the Origins of Sexuality,"[42] have shown very clearly that the structure of "primal fantasies" serves to answer the subject's questions about *origins*: "The primal scene replays the origin of the individual, the fantasy of seduction pictures the emergence of sexuality; and fantasies of castration represent the origin of sexual difference."[43] The most striking feature of these fantasies though, and the one most relevant here, is that all the possible roles in the narrative are available to the subject, who can be either subject or object and can even occupy a position "outside" the scene, looking on from the spectator's point of view. Again, it is only the formal positions themselves that are fixed (there are "masculine" and "feminine" positions of desire); the subject can and does adopt these positions in relation to a variety of complex scenarios, and in accordance with the mobile patterns of his or her own desire.

The formulation of fantasy, which provides a complex and exhaustive account of *the staging and imaging of the subject and its desire*, is a model that very closely approximates the primary aims of the apparatus theory: to describe not only the subject's desire for the filmic image and its reproduction, but also the structure of the fantasmatic relation to that image, including the subject's belief in its reality. Film analysis, moreover, from the perspective of the structure of fantasy, presents a more accurate description of the spectator's shifting and multiple identifications and a more comprehensive account of these same movements within the film: the perpetually changing configurations of the characters, for example, are a formal response to the unfolding of a fantasy that is the filmic fiction itself. Finally, the model of fantasy would allow us to retain the apparatus theory's important stress on the cinema as an *institution*: in this light, all films, and not just the products of Hollywood, would be seen and studied in their fully historical and social variety as *dream-factories*. The feminist use of the psychoanalytic notion of fantasy for the study of film and its institutions can now be seen as a way of constructively dismantling the bachelor machines of film theory (no need for Luddism) or at least modifying them in accordance with the practical and theoretical demands of sexual modernity.

FEMINISM AND FEMININITY IN GODARD

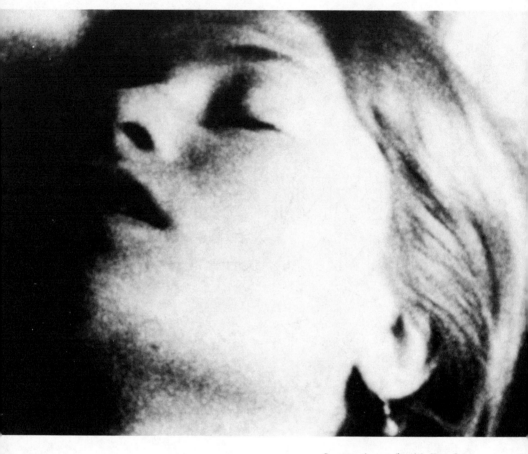

Sauve qui peut (la vie) *(Jean-Luc
Godard, 1980). American title is*
Every Man for Himself.

FIVE

Pornography, Eroticism (on Every Man for Himself)

N EAR THE BEGINNING OF *Sauve qui peut (la vie)*, in a
scene that has been singled out for accusations of
pornography, specifically, pedophilia, "Paul Godard" drops by a
sports field to pick up his eleven-year-old daughter, Cécile. He asks
the coach, who has just remarked that he has a daughter the same age
as Cécile, whether he ever "feels like caressing her tits or fucking her
up the ass?" This scene and others like it that mention or depict bestiality, prostitution, masturbation, sadism, masochism, sodomy, and
voyeurism, do indeed provide the spectator a wide-ranging iconogra-
phy of the pornographic. But is the film pornographic?

In pornography, a fantasy of control and mastery realizes itself
through the spectator's visual negotiation of the scene (sadomas-
ochism, of course, implying a very complex notion of mastery). But
in this film, in several ways, our vision of any given scene is incom-
plete, ambiguous; the fantasy of the full subject necessary to the pornographic scene cannot take hold here. For example, we do not actually see the verbal exchange between Paul Godard and the coach,
because it occurs over Cécile's saccadic step-printed image (a close-up
of her catching and throwing a ball), only cutting to Paul Godard's
face before and after he speaks. Without the typical shot/reverse-shot
dynamic, welding character and dialogue, Paul's speech tends to
"float," and we can even ask if it is *his* speech, delivered by him as a
character in the diegesis, or an incestuous wish "spoken" by the film,
at the level of enunciation. At the very least, "Do you ever feel like
caressing her tits . . . ?" is not unambiguously assignable to Paul Godard, but is possibly a question asked by and in the general fiction of the
film, thus implicating the viewer in its wider address.

In the sports field scene (preceded by the title "Fear"), the spectator is referred several times to an "outside" of the film, and this too works against the narrow fiction, the closed world of the typical pornographic scene. Paul Godard is a fictional character, but he is also meant to be *Godard*. The joke about Castro that he tells the coach ("Have you heard the latest about Castro? . . . He complains that Cubans don't work as hard as Americans") cites something exterior to this scene that is both social (Castro now) and reflexively filmic (Godard's Maoist-era films in which Castro's image often appeared). A further social reference in this supposed pedophilic scene gives the lie to any reading of the scene as simply perverse: following the coach's reply ("No"), Paul complains that it's not fair that mothers can touch their children more easily than fathers. By thus framing Paul's question, the film suggests not that men want to touch their daughters because they have perverse desires, but that they have perverse desires because there are taboos against touching them.

As for Cécile's image, it does not make itself available to any simple voyeuristic pleasure or easy visual mastery, both because of its "startling physics and strange mechanics" (as Jean Epstein described the effects of slow and accelerated motion), and what it shares with other, similar moments in the film where a woman's image is the site of an ambivalence expressed as an idealization/aggression in relation to that image.[1] These various images of women are, in fact, more or less resistant to any subjecting male gaze: the woman at the train station gets slapped but still refuses to choose between two men; the prostitute, Marilyn-Nicole, services her clients while reciting to them a litany of pejorative names for medieval women. And Isabelle, at the moment when she is presented exactly as the inevitable icon of the pornographic lovemaking scene, the close-up of the moaning woman's face serving as the guarantee of pleasure, is thinking about the errands she has to run. For all of its pornographic "images," *Sauve qui peut (la vie)* is, rather, about the refusal or failure of a controlling male gaze, a gaze designated *by this film* as a pornographic one.

"Startling physics and strange mechanics" crop up in the bodily comportment and sexual gestures of the characters throughout the film, and the *ridiculousness* of their movements tends to deflect any pornographic interest. Disobedient prostitutes are usually beaten up by their pimps; here they are spanked. Bestiality is rendered by an extremely rapid shot of a woman presenting her rear to a cow for a lick. People move into an embrace and, irresistibly, begin hitting each other. Orgasm is blatantly faked. The four-way sex scene with Isa-

belle, the prostitute Marilyn-Nicole, and the two businessmen turns into a Rube Goldberg machine. The rhetoric of pornography does not allow such absurd and incongruous gestures.

Important to an understanding of the sports field scene, as well as others marked with the tropes of the pornographic, is its larger narrative frame. *Sauve qui peut (la vie)*'s fictional origin of enunciation is quite possibly Denise, from whose novel-essay-diary we hear extracts throughout the film. (*Isabelle*: "Is your project a book?" *Denise*: "No, but it may be part of one.") The problem that the film sets itself, then, is the relation of these pornographic "images" to a possible origin of enunciation that is a woman's narrative. The reference to Duras, who is diegetically present (she is spoken to, we hear her voice) although we never see her, and the instructions given the students watching her film by Paul Godard to think about "woman's speech" (*parole de femme*) whenever they see a truck passing (as we do several times in the film—a reference to Duras's *Le Camion*) also suggests that the question here is not simply one of "images"—pornographic or not—but of the very possibility of women speaking or writing, and of what they might have to say.

In another way too it is not a question of "images" but of the metaphorical propositions to which they contribute. Godard has adopted a long series of metaphors to designate both the position of the filmmaker in relation to culture and the film industry, and the common workings of sexuality and money: consumerism (*Une femme mariée*), tourism (*Pierrot le fou*), prostitution (*Vivre sa vie, Deux ou trois choses que je sais d'elle*), and, now, pornography. Pornography, however, is one of his most successful metaphors: the filmmaker as pornographer, sex and cinema (in our society) as pornographic. Like prostitution, pornography presents a configuration in which sexuality cannot be seen apart from the selling of it. But pornography as a metaphor has an important advantage over prostitution insofar as it cannot be romanticized. "Filmmaker as prostitute" has an air of proud martyrdom about it that "filmmaker as pornographer" does not. Prostitutes as individuals can be romanticized, as Godard has done repeatedly in his films, but, in pornography, as a business and as a fictional form, there are no martyrs or heroines.

Frequently works that are accused of being pornographic are redeemed by assigning them to the category of the erotic. *Sauve qui peut (la vie)*, if it were pornographic, could never find such redemption because it is deeply anti-erotic. In the erotic formula, masculine and fem-

inine, male and female, are absolute opposites. The fantasy of eroticism is that these two opposites are complementary (to reverse
Lacan—"There *is* a sexual relation"). It is because of this wish that
death is so important to eroticism: if the sexes can be complementary
and can, together, achieve a sort of unity, then there is nothing left to
be desired, and the end of desire is death. The sexes never come together in *Sauve qui peut (la vie)*, and thus the death at the end does not
have to be experienced as a genuine death. Everyone is moving at different speeds. They can't kiss, really. They can't touch, really. The
film is the antithesis of eroticism.

If a criticism is to be made of this film, it cannot be along the lines of
an alleged pornographic debasement of women. The point of disturbance, the site of possible objection, lies, rather, in the film's specific
privileging of women. The men in this film cannot move, Godard has
said, only the women. The women are, for the most part, complex
and powerful, although uncertain where or how to move; but Paul
Godard is truly morbid and only comes to life (here, to self-consciousness) in his "death scene." In the masochistic fantasy of this film Paul
Godard is destroyed by the women, or at least by his passivity in relation to their greater readiness to seek change. In the final scene he lies
dying in the street while the women in his life walk away indifferently.
We do see scenes in this film of women being debased and humiliated;
the women are, however, shown to have a canny awareness of their
situation. Isabelle explains to her sister that the client is primarily interested in humiliating the prostitute; the prostitute Marilyn-Nicole
recites all the pejorative names given to women in the Middle Ages
while she is servicing the businessmen. The film leaves you with the
impression that women are more interesting and forceful than men,
fascinating, but, ultimately, destructive.

When discussing the work that he has done in *France/tour/détour/
deux/enfants* and *Sauve qui peut (la vie)* on changing the rhythms and
temporalities of film through the use of a kind of half-accelerated,
half-slow-motion image, Godard remarked on the far greater degree
of fascination to be found in looking at the image of a woman or a
little girl treated to this variation of rhythms than that of a little boy:

> I concluded that when one changes the rhythms, when one analyzes a
> woman's movements, even ones as simple as buying a loaf of bread for
> example, one notices that there are so many different worlds inside the
> woman's movement. Whereas slowing down the little boy's movements
> was a lot less interesting; every time the image was stopped the same

thing was always going on. But with the little girl, even when she was doing something completely banal, one could suddenly see a look of extreme sadness and then a third of a second later a look of joy: *c'était des monstres* . . . As I am scientific and know certain theories, I had the impression that I was watching different bodies and worlds, galaxies transforming one into another with a series of explosions, whereas the little boy was much less graceful and interesting plastically.

("Propos rompus," *Cahiers du Cinéma* no. 316, Oct. 1980.)

Here, it is clear that women are seen as more engrossing than men: they are *naturally* enigmatic. Further, Godard suggests, this interest is something to be investigated—"As I am scientific and know certain theories."

Seizing on the pornographic as the problem of *Sauve qui peut (la vie)* makes it hard to discern a deeper and more problematic logic located not in individual images (women being slapped, spanked, wrestled to the floor, variously humiliated) or bits of dialogue ("Did you ever feel like caressing her tits?") but in an idea about sexual difference that this film ceaselessly proposes. Although the fictional work of the film takes up sexual difference as a theoretical problem (the possibility in narrative of a feminine origin of enunciation) and as a problem or difficulty in people's lives (Paul's inability, for example, to feel himself as anything but *excluded* from the world of women, from femininity), it constructs this difference as essential, absolute, and irreconcilable to the point of violence. In contrast to classical film, the women here are linked to activity and the man to passivity; in this reversal, femininity becomes the primary term of sexual difference and masculinity its other. Women, then, in this scheme, acquire a certain superiority, but it is at the price of a difference defined as essential (in their nature) and as necessarily bound to extinguish its opposite. The film offers a strikingly different narrative repartition of the terms of masculinity and femininity, but because it leaves unquestioned what it sees as the natural fascination of women, these terms sort themselves out, finally, according to a logic of male masochism as the response to a failed aggression against these idealized women.

Near the beginning of *Sauve qui peut (la vie)* we see a celebration of femininity in its essential difference—Denise in step-printed motion riding her bicycle along a winding country road, her body, face, and movements "like galaxies transforming one into another with a series of explosions." The film ends, however, with the imagined consequences of this difference for men—Paul dying in the street. Although such a death for the man may be a typically Godardian solution, it closes off any consideration of the real questions the film has raised, questions about desire, fantasy, representation, and newer constellations of sexual difference.

LE

TOUR DE LA FRANCE

PAR DEUX ENFANTS

DEVOIR ET PATRIE

LIVRE DE LECTURE COURANTE

AVEC 200 GRAVURES INSTRUCTIVES POUR LEÇONS DE CHOSES

PAR

G. BRUNO

Lauréat de l'Académie française, auteur de *Francinet*.

TREIZIÈME ÉDITION

PARIS

LIBRAIRIE CLASSIQUE D'EUGÈNE BELIN

RUE DE VAUGIRARD, N° 52.

1878

SIX

Les Enfants de la Patrie (on France/Tour/Detour/ Two Children)

But children . . . what do they want?
Jean-Luc Godard[1]

G. BRUNO'S *Le Tour de la France par Deux Enfants* was the most widely read and loved of the nineteenth-century "reading books" or primers used in French schools. Madame Alfred Jules Emile Fouilée, writing under the pseudonym "G. Bruno," tells the story of two orphaned boys who travel through every province and major city of France in search of their uncle and citizenship (born in Alsace-Lorraine, they must decide to be either French or German). Having been taught duty and love of country at an early age (their father's dying words were "La France!"), the journey further strengthens their patriotic devotion. As they go from province to province, they learn about farming, printing, making wallpaper, embroidery, cheesemaking, winemaking, crystal and glass, photography, barrelmaking, basketweaving, and fishing. Helpful citizens along the way teach them about the famous men who made France great. Little homilies sprinkled throughout the book inculcate the values of "Devoir et Patrie": cleanliness, work, godliness, education, devotion to parents and country. The pupil ingests these worthwhile ideas while learning to read, the primer form providing the perfect mesh of ideology and learning—"devoir" suggesting both duty (*devoir*) and homework (*devoirs*).

This famous primer was the loose inspiration for Jean-Luc Godard and Anne-Marie Miéville's twelve-part television series, organized around interviews with two French schoolchildren, *France/tour/détour/deux/enfants* (*France/Tour/Detour/Two Children*, 1978). *Ici et ailleurs* (1978), the first film produced by Godard and Miéville under the com-

pany name Sonimage, raised the problem of how to bring images from "elsewhere" (*ailleurs*) "here" (*ici*) — how to understand images of Palestine brought to France — and their concern has been increasingly with "here" rather than "elsewhere": the French family sitting in front of its television.[2] In "Avant et après" ("Before and After"), the next-to-last program in their other television series, *Sur et sous la communication (Six fois deux) (On and Under Communication [Six Times Two],* 1976), Godard refers to television as a "family affair."[3] Insistently the point is made that the viewing "subject" of television is the family — unlike the cinema spectator who is addressed as an isolated individual. Our tour through the family and through France is taken through the detour — by means of television — of two children, Camille Virolleaud and Arnaud Martin. Godard likes this idea of the *detour,* of the circuitous, roundabout means. In *Letter to Jane* (1972) he and Jean-Pierre Gorin said that it was only by making a "detour through Vietnam" that the photograph of Jane Fonda could be understood. Here our detour remains closer to home.

In *France/tour/détour/deux enfants* "mass communications," and especially television, has taken the place of the primer. As with G. Bruno's primer, televisual literacy implies an intricately structured relation to the state. Like television, Sonimage says, children are "programmed." The interrogation of the children's lives in the interviews ceaselessly points to the serialization, the regulated flow and repetition of their domestic, school, and leisure schedules. As we see the children at home, in school, at play, what seems at first like an obsessive phenomenology ("But what about the night? — Do you think it's space or

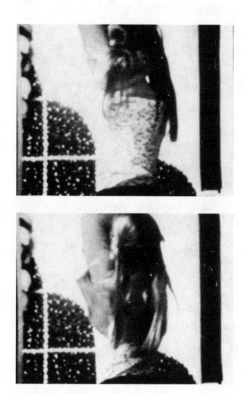

time?" "Instead of your going to school, couldn't we say that it's sometimes the school that goes to you?" "When you're growing, do you think you're moving in time or in space?") is gradually revealed to be an interest in the institutional organization of space and time and in the power of those spatial and temporal grids. This interest is very close to that of Phillipe Ariès, who argues, in *Centuries of Childhood*,[4] that our modern notion of childhood is a product of the increasingly systematic schematization of the school day and the successive years of schooling. "Infancy" and "adolescence" came to be differentiated from adulthood because of the pedagogical need to separate the ages and assign to them tasks of increasing levels of difficulty. Michel Foucault's emphasis on this meticulous control of space and time as a perfected modern means of discipline and domination (*Discipline and Punish*)[5] is reflected in *France/tour/détour/deux enfant*'s unremitting comparison of the school to the prison, the army, and the zoo. Sonimage also take up Foucault's motif of the body as a recording surface, like paper (the many puns on copying and reproduction), and as the machine for making that paper. "Docile Bodies," one of the subheads in Foucault's chapter on the distribution and control of activity to ensure discipline, serves as an apt description of Camille and Arnaud as we see them in the various institutional settings that constitute them as "children." The three most important methods of *scheduling* are the establishment of rhythms, the imposition of particular occupations, and the regulation of the cycles of repetition: capitalizing space and time.[6] Sonimage aims to intervene into the rhythms, regulations, and repetitions of television narrative as well as these same monitorings in the fiction of daily life.

Each "movement," as each of the twelve parts of *France/tour/détour/deux enfants* is called, is structured in the same way. The core is an interview with either nine-year-old Arnaud or eleven-year-old Camille, each child held in a static shot and questioned by an off-screen presence whose voice is unmistakably Godard's. Each program opens in a television studio with Camille and Arnaud alternately holding a boom mike or looking through a television camera. After the title "FIRST MOVEMENT," "SECOND MOVEMENT," etc., we see a short scene— Camille getting ready for bed, a teacher talking to a child in school, Arnaud walking along the street and stealing a newspaper and a pair of jeans, children boisterously playing during school recess. Using the same technique as in *Sauve qui peut (la vie)* (1980), certain movements and gestures are slowed down and then rapidly, yet haltingly, speeded

up ("Slowing down, decomposing," the narrator says) so that we can see and understand the economy of these actions. (Dziga Vertov did nearly the same in *Man with a Movie Camera*, where he took the social gestures of different kinds of labor out of their usual temporalities, breaking them down ("decomposing") and relating them to similar kinds of gestures in other kinds of work.)

The interviews with the children are prefaced by titles that are also seen interspersed throughout, commenting with various degrees of directness on the image: DARK CHEMISTRY, TRUTH, TELEVISION, STORY, YOU, LIGHT, PHYSICS (the most frequently recurring titles are TRUTH and TELE-VISION). Images occur that also relate more or less directly to the statements of the narrating voices: an owl, a freeway at night, people emerging from the Metro, a union demonstration, various magazine advertising photographs. Then, in every program, an off-screen voice, sometimes male, sometimes female, gives a speech on "the monsters": "The monsters go home, with as little delay as possible, like atoms. . . . The monsters have invented machines that dictate a series of orders which they obey. . . . Other monsters fight against this system. . . . For eight hours [the monsters] place themselves at the disposition of the great military–industrial complexes." Evidently, we are all monsters.

The interview begins, punctuated with titles and occasional voice-over comments like, "Despite evidence to the contrary, the reporter is not asking real questions, nor does the child give real answers." At one point the voice wonders what kind of effects the interviews are having on Camille and, at others, why she is so resistant to their questions. "There's something inflexible about her. We'll never see any flights of fancy"; "There's something old about her. She says no more than necessary. Just enough to avoid trouble." The majority of the interviews are noticeably without movement, the frame holding the child in place. In a few of the interviews, however, we see the children engaged in typical and symbolic activities: Camille copying out 50 times, "I must not talk in class" (referred to by the narrator as "forced labor"), and Arnaud working a duplicating machine (his action mimicking a recurring theme: reproduction, copying, imprinting). The questions are idiosyncratic and the tone an odd one for an adult talking to a child; he often uses the formal *vous* to address them. The interviewer does not appear to share the theories of developmental psychologists who would judge his questions to be inappropriate to the age level of the children. The children are often amused by the questions but never volunteer anything. As the series goes along, the little girl, especially, grows more recalcitrant, smiles less, won't look at the interviewer, and seems annoyed or bored. Her slight nervous tic becomes disturbingly more pronounced. The questions, although brilliant in their calculated whimsy and free association, sometimes seem ruthless. They are far more interesting than the children's answers.

What is taking place here is not really an "interview" or a "conversation"; it is more like an Augustinian dialogue, full of puns, tricks and seemingly nonsensical questions that turn into logical traps. In *De Magistro*,[7] St. Augustine intently questions his fifteen-year-old son about the nature of words and signs. Often his son refuses to answer because he knows he is being set up, and, after many twists and turns, is forced to come to certain conclusions about the nature of signification and representation. This wrangling over words and things characterizes exactly Godard's interviews with the children.[8]

There are a lot of things Camille and Arnaud cannot think or say. For example, when Godard asks Camille why her mother doesn't get paid for her work around the house, Camille, nonplused, answers, finally, that no one pays her because there is no one who *could* pay her. Although Arnaud is a precocious "little man" and Camille fascinating in her premature stolidness, they are not "exceptional" children. Within the terms of the program, the implication is that they are *little* monsters.

Toward the end or just after each interview we see the title TELEVI-SION or TRUTH and are told something about television or about the way the narrators are trying to do television differently: "There's never silence on television. It's never live anymore. Management and the unions have banned live TV. . . . " "I dream sometimes of the kind of society in which people, meeting a television reporter, would question him." After each interview we find ourselves in a television studio with a man and a woman (Albert Dray and Betty Berr) who closely resemble television's ubiquitous announcers — smiling, plastic, more actor than journalist. Then we get a "story," always beginning with the same introduction (with "him" or "her," depending on whether it follows an interview with Arnaud or Camille):

Thank you, Robert Linard [presumably the interviewer]. And I think . . . I think it's time for a story. Not *her* story, not a story coming from her. But her coming from a story. And both. But both before. Her before and the story after. The story before and her after. Or superimposed. The story of . . .

The "stories" are often not what we usually think of as stories: "In the beginning, there was paper or a pencil. In the beginning there were squares or circles." The stories are often so tentative and disjointed that it is as if the narrators are not even certain what a story on television would be. Their stories are punctuated with images that may or may not be directly related to what is being said. The themes will sometimes echo ones that have arisen in the preceding interview, but never serve to encapsulate or explain them. Finally, one of the announcers will break it off, saying, "We must stop now" or "Now it's time for a commercial." The other announcer will ask, "Why?" The reply, the same each time, becomes the last words of each "movement": "That's another story."

Sonimage's two television series are the closest thing we have to fulfilling Raymond Williams's "first conditions" for thinking about television: "information, analysis, education, discussion" (*Television: Technology and Cultural Form*)."[9] The two series are important in any debate about television even though we cannot disregard the fact that they were never programmed as intended. Rather than being shown as a prime time series, *France/tour/détour/deux enfants* was slotted into the late Friday night art cinema spot on France's second channel in March and April 1980 (three of the twelve parts were programmed each Friday night). It is interesting to remember that Godard fared even worse with an earlier television program also based on an educational treatise: *Le Gai Savoir* (1968), commissioned by French television as a version of Jean-Jacques Rousseau's didactic fiction, *Emile*, was never allowed to be broadcast.

In *Television: Technology and Cultural Form* Raymond Williams reminds us that it is not always in the state's interest to teach its citizens both to read and write. At the beginning of the industrial revolution in Britain

> when education had to be reorganized, the ruling class decided to teach working people to read but not to write. If they could read they could understand new kinds of instructions and, moreover, they could read the Bible for their moral improvement. They did not need writing, however, since they would have no orders or instructions or lessons to communicate.[10]

"Writing" rather than merely "reading" television comes through as a constant theme in the Sonimage project. Producing local television—

Six fois deux.

making something on video to show your neighbor "without having to go through Paris," "without a SECAM passport"—is part of the solution. But writing television also involves writing, literally. Godard has always written on and with the image, and his "print-out" one-at-a-time letters were one of the most important rhetorical elements of *Numéro Deux*. In *Six fois deux* a video device that allows instant script writing on the image is used lavishly. This anthropomorphization of title lettering gives the feeling of a personal and spontaneous response to the image, and takes many modes: doodling, punning, musing, drawing. Both the writing on the image and the different voices over it question that image rather than merely anchoring its meaning, as is usual in television.

Writing television also means devising new fictions, new ways of presenting information, and new means of addressing the viewer. The tentativeness and obscurity of some of the "stories" told by the narrators in *France/tour/détour/deux enfants*, the interviewer's fear and hesitancy about beginning to question the children, the failure to get the children to speak differently, all seem to say that this is not an easy project, that writing television cannot be accomplished by simply, for example, instituting "community access." Unless television is thought about in terms of its possible fictions, fantasies and forms of address, then what we will see, with the proliferation of channels through cable and satellite, will only be more of the same, the local productions being disappointing amateur versions of "real" network television.

It is impossible not to think about Godard's films when watching these videotapes — details, colors, framing, themes, recall them incessantly. Although it would be historically disingenuous not to recognize all of his films "behind" these television images and sounds, it is important to see this series as *television* and not as cinema or video. It is about television's economics, distribution, themes, temporalities, forms of address, and viewers. However, Godard has often said that working in television is another way for him to think about film.[11]

Fragmentation has been one of the reigning strategies of Godard's filmmaking and he says that television is even more open to this than film:

> I expanded the idea of the fragment up to the point of making a whole film a fragment. . . . I prefer working in television where fragmentationis accepted. In a series, one can program a fragment every day. . . . In the past we had novels like that.[12]

Fragmentation permits a certain kind of intermittent narrative continuity; it can also, as Roland Barthes has shown in *The Pleasure of the Text* and *A Lover's Discourse*, allow another kind of argument, less deductive, non-conclusive, somewhere between fiction and essay. Fragmentation emphasizes the starts and stops of an utterance, its uncertainty rather than its authority. This is just one of the strategies used in the series to ask about the *authorization* of the images and sounds: who speaks on television, to whom, and for what?

A question often raised about Sonimage's television work concerns its particular use of television technology. Although committed to expanding the possibilities of video, Godard, when questioned by technologically oriented video artists like Ed Emshwiller as to why he does not more fully exploit the specificity of video as a medium, replied, characteristically, "Video, film, writing — it's all the same to me."[13] The simplicity of these tapes surprises those who were expecting a video spectacle from the vast technical resources of the Sonimage studios. As in his films, the specificity of the medium is explicitly used as a material in its own right, but it represents the beginning of his interests, not the end.

The first and most apparent difference from "normal" television of *France/tour/détour/deux enfants* can be seen in the way it approaches children and childhood. "It is easier to get an interview with heads of state than spend an hour talking to a child," Godard claims.[14] Most of the places Sonimage chose to film the children were "in-between" places where no one is usually looking at them — on the way to school, getting ready for bed — or places where adults do not usually see children — at school, on the playground. In the Sixth Movement the interviewer gets Camille to admit that, while animals in zoos, inmates in prisons, and patients in hospitals are allowed visitors, children in schools are not. Several times, one of the narrators comments on the fact that they are the first to be going to these places, the first to see what goes on there:

> Parents never come to the classes. And they accept that. Perhaps they even prefer it that way. Nobody ever comes except the children. Today we are quite simply the first to have come.

Of course we see children on television all the time and frequently they are asked for their "opinions." Their replies are typically used to illustrate one of the traits of childhood (or our fantasy of childhood) such as spontaneity, greater happiness, precociousness, "cuteness." Or their answers are seen to offer a special kind of truth unavailable to adults (*The Art Linkletter Show*: "Kids say the darndest things!"). In *France/tour/détour/deux enfants* the children are talked to like beings from another world to whom no one has ever spoken.[15] The "inappropriateness" of the interviewer's questions makes us aware of our preconceived ideas about childhood: Godard's first question to the little girl, after asking her if it is her room they are in, is, "And you pay a lot to live here?"; later, at school, he asks her how much the children are paid for the work they do there. The "truth" that the children are expected to illuminate is not a child-truth: "I was interested [in understanding] what's wrong with the relation between work and love by looking at what children want."[16] But it is equally important here, and no less so than with *The Art Linkletter Show*, to ask what Godard wants.

Another important difference of *France/tour/détour/deux enfants* from "normal" television is its notion of time. To mark that it has another time than television time, each part of the series is called a "movement," rather than a "program," taking its temporal term from music instead of television, and placing the emphasis on *composition*. Television time is the immediate, urgent present — Alexander Haig *now*, Poland *now*, television expansively celebrating its own instantaneous global responsiveness to every "event." From the perspective of television time, these twelve "movements" depict dead time: kids on

the way to school, in school, on the way home, the family dinner, getting ready for bed—these activities are neither newsworthy nor
"now." ("And *now* . . . " is the most repeated phrase of television's
regulated flow.) On Sonimage time, long silences occur—the radical
opposite of the fullness of television. They are not silences meant to
represent, for example, poignance or solemn importance; rather, they
occur when the interviewer has no questions, or the child is bored, or
because there is, at the moment, simply nothing to say.

In "Television: A World in Action,"[17] Stephen Heath and Gillian Skirrow show how the speech and images of the people in the television
documentary on truancy that they examine exist only to make a scene
for television: "The supposed image of the actual is simply the actu-
ality of the image *for television.*"[18] The structural role of any television
scene will be determined by the time and unity of the program:
"People [on television] never have their own time, they have television time."[19] This time and unity, like that of the classical novel and
film, is a fictional construction which simultaneously structures a
point of view for the spectator. The placing of the spectator in relation
to this dramatization of the real, and in its fiction as a "viewer" (the
"citizen [in] a world of communication") is what Heath and Skirrow
refer to as television's role in a "new production of the novelistic."[20]
    To say it another way, the citizen/viewer takes his place in a fiction
of the "family of man," the world's exotic differences (Northern Ire-
land, El Salvador, Pakistan, South Korea, etc.) brought together elec-
tronically not to demonstrate real, historical differences, but to exhibit
the endless varieties of the human essence, its diversity serving only to
comment on its richness.[21] (750 million people watched the Royal
Wedding. What could have been its cultural significance to many
viewers, except the sense of belonging to a global community?) As
Godard puts it, "In a cinema, people are many (together) to be alone in
front of the screen. In an apartment linked to a TV aerial, people are
alone to be many (together)."[22]
    The counterpart of the global "family of man" is the family in front
of its television. Sonimage shows television to be a "family affair"
most pointedly in the anomalous Eleventh Movement which, unlike
the others, does not contain an interview. Instead, we see a silent Camille at the dinner table and hear her family talking animatedly off-
screen. For once, the viewer is not implicated in the off-screen space of
Godard-the-interviewer, but shares the implied off-screen space of the

family. We are no longer watching Camille to observe how she will respond to questions, we are seeing her as her family sees her, or, rather, does not see her, as they seem oblivious to her silence and withdrawal. The narrators are dissatisfied, though, and do not think they got very much out of focusing on this family scene, of making concrete the idea of television as a family affair." "Something . . . doesn't come across," they say, voicing the pessimism about the possibilities of television heard increasingly throughout the programs.

Interviewing is an extreme form of demand. The television interview is conducted under the pressure of television time. It must look as much like a conversation as possible even though spontaneity and silences are not permitted inside that structure. Unlike what occurs in a conversation, the person interviewed is typically required to verify or refute a point introduced by the interviewer. From the way Godard sets up the positions of interviewer and interviewed, and from the manner in which he poses his questions, it is clear that he is not trying to get across the optimistic fiction of the television interview, that an exchange of information, a communication, a dialogue, has taken place between two persons. In the First Movement, the male narrator says of the interviewer and Camille:

> I don't believe he wants to get an image of her—whatever one might think—or a sound. He's simply sending out a signal and waiting to see what happens when the signal reaches her. Often it reaches her and conveys nothing.

And, at another point:

> Despite evidence to the contrary, the reporter is not asking real
> questions. Nor does the child give real answers.

If one does not start with pre-given questions and answers, and if a
situation is not set up in which "communication" is sure to take place
between two carefully designated positions, then something different
is going to happen. Silences, yes, but also perhaps another kind of
knowledge than that available to us through the usual forms of television rhetoric.

Interviews never stand by themselves on television. They are introduced, provided with a context, summarized afterward, and often
given an editorializing finish. The person interviewed furnishes the
"raw information," which is guided and shaped by the questions of
the interviewer. The narrator, if there is one, supplies the final, ratio-
nalizing commentary. In *France/tour/détour/deux enfants*, however, this
smooth narrative embedding does not occur; difficulties arise among
all of the designated positions of "person interviewed," "interviewer," and "narrator." The children being interviewed do not always understand the questions and do not have much to say. The interviewer's questions are often obscure and seemingly inappropriate.
The narrators are frequently at a loss to "make sense" of the interviews (or at least the spectator has difficulty understanding the perti-
nence of their comments to the interview preceding it), and are concerned that the interviews are not being conducted properly. In the
Eighth Movement the female narrator says to "Robert" (the interviewer), who has just played a trick on Arnaud:

> No, No, Robert, you mustn't say that to him. It's obvious he no longer
> believes you when you say the money is from you. It isn't true anyway.
> It's the company's money.

Immediately following this interjection, there is a complete break-
down:

> He doesn't hear me. What's wrong with the mike? Robert! Robert! He
> doesn't hear me!

The usual narrative embedding of the interview, which functions to
give credence to the speech of each party (and the final truth to television itself), simply disintegrates here. "Communication" is not taking place in any of the ways we usually imagine it occurring on television.

Where are *we* as viewers in these interviews? Traditionally in television interviews we are looking on at an oblique angle, sometimes seeing the interviewer partly in frame, or even cutting back and forth between the interviewer and the person interviewed. This is especially so when both are known "personalities"; in an interview situation, however, everyone is a "personality" even if only for the time of the interview. (When Dick Cavett interviews, for example, Jean-Luc Godard, it is supposed to be as interesting to us that the interviewer is Cavett as that the person interviewed is Godard. The spectacle of the interview is just as much our interest in watching Cavett's interviewing skills being challenged by a "difficult" personality as it is in listening to Godard.) In a typical interview we overhear and overlook an exchange.[23] But in *France/tour/détour/deux enfants* we are not given the usual choreography of shot/reverse-shot and the "reaction shot," as we never see the interviewer. This arrangement effectively implicates the viewer in the scene far more than having us look on and overhear the interviewer from a position outside it. We share the imaginary off-screen space of the interviewer and this is a distinctly uncomfortable place in which to be.

Sometimes the interviewer's questions simply appear to be mean; the children, although amused at first with some of the tricky questions, grow bored or annoyed as the series goes on. In the Twelfth and last Movement, Arnaud is sitting up and answering the questions as best he can, but is obviously getting sleepy. He lies down in bed, his eyelids droop, but the interviewer persists, even when it is plain that Arnaud can no longer fight off sleep. In an earlier Movement, the interviewer embarrasses Arnaud by getting him to admit on television that he received a bicycle as payment for being in the series. Sometimes the interviewer is merely distracted; once he says something Arnaud cannot understand; Arnaud asks, "What?" and the interviewer replies, "I was talking to myself."

Although the "inappropriateness" of the interviewer's questions to the children serves to bring into relief our received ideas about childhood, it is also disconcerting in another, deeper sense. We have clear linguistic and social conventions governing the way adults speak to children; we simply do not speak to them in the same manner that we speak to other adults. Disrupting these linguistic conventions makes ambiguous the conventions regulating other forms of behavior, such as sexual, between adult and child. Refusing to speak to the children as children suggests that there is at work here an unconscious fantasy of sexual equality and the possibility of a reciprocated desire. It is for this reason that we feel particularly discomfited in the First Movement when the interviewer, in his very untypical adult-to-child tone, addresses Camille in her nightgown, on her bed. Before the interview we saw Camille undressing for bed. The male narrator's voice-over, during the interview, comments on the vision and desire of the interviewer:

> He's still there, facing her, and the night is breaking. As she neglected to tell him earlier, at the beginning of the program, she didn't want to show her bottom, he didn't make a point of it, so that now he can only see part of her shoulders and a mass of thick blond hair.

Our uneasiness about the interviewer's behavior is particularly strong because we are not outside looking on, or merely overhearing. Normally exterior to the scene of the interview (watching the play of shot/reverse-shot, looking at a two-shot or over the interviewer's shoulder), we are here implicated in the off-screen space of the interviewer. This sometimes forces us to share his idiosyncratic point of view, making that space palpable in a way that it usually is not. The viewer has to ask, "What is the demand being voiced here? What is he trying to say or trying to get the child—who is not exactly being treated as a child—to say? What does Godard want?"

But although we are sometimes uneasy (linguistically, sexually) about the manner in which the interviewer addresses the children, it is too simple to say that the interviewer's speech requires the children to respond as *adults*. Godard said that in speaking to the children he did not address them by saying, "Oh you sweet little things," but neither did he speak to them as adults: "I saw them as beings from another world to whom no one had ever spoken, until the moment I talked to them."[24] Here we are very close to seeing what Godard wants, at least consciously, from these children. He says that he posed to the children a mélange of eminently practical and deeply metaphysical questions in order to get them to speak differently, so that, "Perhaps afterwards, when we are making fiction films again, we can get men and women to speak a little differently, something which today no one yet knows how to do very well."[25]

Many people are surprised when they first hear that Godard-Miéville's two television series center around interviews with "marginal" types: children, women, the unemployed, an amateur filmmaker, a peasant, two "mad" people (the other, smaller category of people interviewed consists of those who professionally manage words or images: a writer and a news photographer). Godard has never adopted the common political film strategy of letting the oppressed speak directly, "in their own words." In his films, prostitutes, children, revolutionaries, housewives, are clearly always giving speeches not originating from themselves. Indeed this Brechtian separation of speech and person has been an important strategy throughout his films. Even when Godard himself "speaks" in his two television series, it is never direct and unmediated. In the "Jean-Luc" section of *Six fois deux* he can barely be seen in the dim light, and a view of his face is more often than not blocked by the back of the *Libération* journalist's head. And in "Avant et après," which includes the most directly didactic statements about the Sonimage project, Godard's words are transmitted to us by someone listening to his coaching whisper over a set of earphones. Thus, even when amassing interviews with "ordinary" people, the political project here is not simply one of allowing them to express directly their life experiences. Television does this all the time and gives us nothing but the spectacle of people telling their "stories," which are in fact never theirs but only another installment in television's ongoing novelization of experience. In "No One's There" (from *Six fois deux*), Godard does not interview the unemployed to get them to tell their life stories and feelings about being out of work, he asks them about the details of their work and how they would go about *representing* their labor with sounds and images for people in other countries to see. Throughout Godard's work, the act of speech is integrated into an analysis of that act in relation to film or television representation.

But something goes awry with this strategy in *France/tour/détour/deux enfants*. Even though the interviews with the children are not "normal" television interviews, we are still supposed to believe that these are real children talking about their lives, not child–actors giving prepared speeches. Thus there is a conflict here between two aesthetic/political strategies, one wishing to give speech and the "means of representation" to the children (the interviews; Camille and Arnaud with the microphone and television camera at the beginning of each program), and another—more in line with Godard's previous approach—which offers an analysis of the limitations, or even the *impossibility* of that speech (the prevailing theme of the series: we are all thoroughly regulated by capitalism, no one escapes—the "monster" thesis). Godard and Miéville want to know what children want, but they also want the children to be a certain way for them, for the "dramatic" structure of the program, for their project of doing television differently. Such a double and contradictory demand often takes the following form in the interviews: reveal to us, through your precociousness, what only children can reveal (what children today think and want); represent for us, by your opaqueness, what we (Sonimage) see as widespread political and social ignorance (the monstrosity of capitalism's limitations of thinking and being).

It is as if Godard and Miéville, when taking up questions of direct interest to feminism—"childhood" and "family" as complex representations, as particular orderings of subjectivity and power—can only do so in *France/tour/détour/deux enfants* by incorporating, without sufficient scrutiny, feminism's most commonly used aesthetic strategy: a politics of representation based on personal experience as the site of truth. This results in an uneasy and contradictory relation between Godard's usual analytic technique—in which the speaking subject is made to be the field of an interplay of discourses—and an essentialist approach which would want the children to speak "for themselves."

This conflict can also be shown from another angle. The programs use the children to make three different arguments that are sometimes contradictory. First, the "inappropriate" questions put to the children are used to undermine our received notions about childhood. Second, the children's taciturnity and lack of spontaneity are used to demonstrate the completeness of their submission to capitalism's "programming." Third, and in contradiction to the second representational use of the children, the repeated comparison of them to prisoners and workers, and the reference to the children as "marginals," argues that they are to be seen as inherently or potentially radical. In addition, the demonstration of their radicalness in relation to the social goes no further than these glib comparisons;[26] we are given no indication of the possible origins or causes of the inherent radicalness of children as a class, thus opening the way to an easy (and, again, contradictory) romanticization of children.

In addition to the casual, though incongruous, adoption of the feminist strategy of a politics of representation based on personal experience as the site of truth, Sonimage also accepts too readily the facile mirroring of Marxism and feminism found in the pun on social/economic "reproduction" and human biological "reproduction." The programs are structured around a lengthy series of puns on "copying," "duplicating," and "programming." Finally (in the Fifth Movement), we see a pregnant, naked secretary being given orders by her boss. The female narrator's voice tells us, "One realizes that men, by nature incapable of imagination, that most men condemn the majority of women to dictation, to copy-typing, to reproduction." Leaving aside the essentialist assertion that inequality between the sexes results from something in the *nature* of men (incapable of imagination), there still remains the fundamental problem of conflating two critically different though interconnected realms: the economic and the economy of sexuality.

The seduction of metaphor strikes again, in the Fourth Movement, when the narrator, over an image of waitresses at a lunch counter in slow/fast motion, says:

> And someone you don't know is a "what's-his-name." In French we say: *machin*. And for a woman: *machine*. With her body machine. Slowing down the machine. The machinery of state.

In Godard's work the woman's body has had to carry a heavy representational load: in *Two or Three Things I Know about Her*, as a prostitute, she is Paris and consumer culture, in *Numéro Deux*, she is a factory, in *France/tour/détour/deux enfants*, she is the embodiment of "reproduction," the machinery of the state. It is not very effective to oppose this metaphorical use of the woman's body with a demand for Sonimage to give us "real" women, women engaged in productive labor, in activities not metaphorically linked to their gender or sexuality (for example, women as factory workers rather than prostitutes).[27] This is because a non-metaphorical representation of the body would be impossible for both women and men if one accepts that sexual difference is a result not of biology but of the subject's positioning in language and culture. Thus, conceptions of bodies and sexes are necessarily metaphorical, that is, always seen in terms of something else. Historically, of course, women's bodies and men's bodies have accrued different representational values. Surprisingly, Sonimage's acute reflexiveness about language and representation (in relation to television, the family, the state) does not extend to questioning certain received metaphorizations of the woman's body: woman as state, as machine of reproduction, as sexuality itself. The repeated use of these metaphors of the woman's body has always posed problems for feminists discussing Godard's work. Now, however, with Sonimage's increasingly direct engagement with feminist concerns, these question-able metaphors are thrown into even sharper relief.

Also problematic is another aspect of the way Sonimage attempts to incorporate feminist questions. Godard-the-interviewer's voyeurism and manipulation is severely reprimanded in the "Nanas" ("Chicks") section of *Six fois deux*. He is interviewing an elderly woman and, just as he is asking her if she would mind talking about sex, a woman's voice explodes on the sound-track, bitterly criticizing him for the way he sets up the women in the interviews, more or less tells them how to reply, and then is always surprised when they aren't as interesting as he'd hoped they'd be. The woman's-voice-as-super-ego is similar in function to the woman's voice that comes on over the image of the Palestinian woman in *Ici et ailleurs*, accusing Godard of having chosen a young, beautiful woman for the scene and having said nothing about it: "It's a small step from this kind of omission to fascism." To assign a censoring and denunciatory role to a woman's voice that is narra-tively one step removed from the diegesis is to make of feminism a superior, authoritative truth that stands as a corrective to the sexism of men. It is to make feminism into a moral truth rather than a political theory and set of strategies. Endowing feminism with such inordinate power implies a masochistic relation for men to that excessive po-tency. That a masochistic fantasy is at work here can be seen most con-spicuously at the end of *Every Man for Himself* when the mise-en-scène requires the "Paul Godard" character to die under (as a result of?) the disaffected gazes of the women in his life. [28]

Decentralization, local autonomy, personal and community produc-tion rather than broadcasting for mass consumption: these are the terms of a new television politics proposed by Sonimage. But, to put it bluntly, what about politics *in* the programs? Explicit statements made by the narrators reveal an anti-authoritarian, anti-hierarchical, anarcho-syndicalist stance. Here, the "political" includes a politics of sexuality, family relations, and daily life. Thus the narrators of these programs can punningly yet seriously refer to children's activities in elementary school as "class struggle," or to the children themselves as "political prisoners." The political problem identified in this series is focused around the theme of "the monsters." The monsters are all of us subjected to capitalism's "disciplines," which impose the condi-tions to ensure our docility and utility. This is one of those "global critiques" that brings with it the seductiveness of the sweeping statement and the easy nihilism of its totalness. If we are all monsters, then who will be able to change or bring about change? Leftists too are considered to be monsters: "Politicals, go to hell!" the female narrator tells us in the Fifth Movement. In speaking about a politics of "autonomy," she says, "In France there are struggles which reject the right, the left and the leftists; there are people fighting with their own resources. We want to join them." One of the few political actions proposed here is organized theft—stealing from the Metro, from the supermarket, "*everything* can be taken." "Stealing alone, one may get caught. A hundred or two hundred makes it more difficult. . . . We must steal together and assume responsibility together" (Fifth Movement). This same political solution was put forward near the end of *Tout va bien* (1972), when Jane Fonda is seen walking through a supermarket being looted by leftists. At another point the narrators suggest a new kind of terrorism: taking ordinary people hostage—whether they are guilty of something or not:

> Guilty of no more than having slapped their child. Having refused to drink with their friends. Having failed to gripe about the quality of pullovers today or the cost of medicine (Fourth Movement).

The politics of the personal and of daily life which provide such a rich starting point for *Numéro deux* and *France/tour/détour/deux enfants* are cynically turned into an attack on the possibility of any form of organized political action. Although this attitude must be seen in the context of widespread French leftist disenchantment with party authoritarianism and bureaucratization, it is still a peculiarly derisive stance. If, as the series claims, we are all monsters, then what is the position from which these narrators are speaking to us? Who makes up this vanguard which has managed to escape the total submission to capitalism and which can tell us to reject both right and left? Sonimage's tactics aim to subvert the *truth* of television; but, in the sections on the monsters, we are being given a substitute truth, a voice of authority that paradoxically urges us to refuse authority.

What is at stake in *France/tour/détour/deux enfants*, through the problem of the family, is France in general and television in particular. Sonimage wants to change the programing, it wants to reschedule. Most of all, Sonimage would like to make "local" television (television's version of home movies), programs that we would make to show others, telling them about our lives and work. For the "No One's There" segment of *Six fois deux*, Sonimage placed a job announcement, advertising for people willing to talk on television about what they do for a living. They found very few people—only a cleaning woman and a welder—who could be persuaded to speak about their work. Godard asks the cleaning woman if she would be willing to make a film that would be called *Madame Jeanne Becq Looks for a Job France 1976* (he would help her technically, he says), and then get on an airplane and take the film to show to women who do manual work in other countries.

Similarly, Sonimage wants television to be going out of the home as well as into the home: people should be producing television as well as receiving it; a "channel" has two directions. In the Fourth Movement the narrators say that they want television transmitted from the classrooms, not for surveillance, but to broadcast classroom activities just like sports or light entertainment. However, in the Eleventh Movement, they finally get a scene that is "the sort of television we said we should have. Which transmits just what is happening"—a family dinner scene. They admit, however, that "there's something that doesn't come across. . . . It's cinema."

As a critical and oppositional primer on the subject of television, how successful pedagogically is *France/tour/détour/deux enfants?* It offers a comprehensive survey of television-as-institution (the criticism of the idea of "broadcasting"), the subject-spectator of television (the family as viewer), and the characteristic fiction-effect of television (its "novelization of experience"). And we do get, as Raymond Williams suggested, "information, analysis, education, discussion." Yet the narrators themselves voice two doubts about their own strategies. The first concerns their failure to get things across: "In our questioning it looks as though we always want to have the last word, whereas it's the first that we want." Their second misgiving focuses on the lack that they see in television, even in their different version of television: what doesn't come across, they say enigmatically, is "cinema." These two apprehensions are, in fact, linked, because both speak to Sonimage's limitations in dealing with the overweening *authority* of the television image and voice.

Television as the voice of truth haunts *France/tour/détour/deux enfants* even though its stated aim is to subvert that truth. Wanting to have the first word, but always appearing to have the last word, is an apt way to describe the contradictory representational strategies at work in the series: trying to get the children to speak ("the first word") versus im-

Le Gai Savoir *(Jean-Luc Godard, 1968).*

posing an a priori analysis on the children's speech ("the last word"). Television, as it now exists, always has the last word. Similarly, in its moralistic and global denunciation of "the monsters," Sonimage cannot resist the temptation to use television to broadcast another version of the truth. This inability to forgo the truth of television is perhaps the reason for Sonimage's ultimate pessimism about the possibility of doing television differently. "Make movies," Godard advises.[29]

Where could we find that missing element, "cinema"? One place to look might be *Le Gai Savoir*, made ten years earlier, a film that also began as a treatise on education and ended up as a discussion of language and television. In *Le Gai Savoir*, the problem of language and television, the investigation of sounds and images, is taken up by means of two fictional characters, Patricia Lumumba and Emile Rousseau, in the fictional space of a darkened set that we are told is a television studio. Perhaps what is felt to be lacking in *France/tour/détour/deux enfants* is that distance from the authority of person, image, and sound that filmic fiction can offer. It is not that it is the essence of film to be fictional and the essence of television to be something else, like documentary or reportage. But the historical uses of film and television have been very different, and with the minor exception of art video, television is most often *the* medium for disseminating a seemingly authoritative and univocal truth about the world. Film, historically, and certainly with the example of Godard, has had room (aesthetically, institutionally) to be more reflexive and more playfully subversive than television with the "truth" of images and sounds. At this point, the range of what can be thought and said on film — its *intelligibility*[30] — is greater than that of television.

For twenty years Godard has been insisting that he wanted to do television, and he has had very distinct ideas about what could and should be done with the medium (1962: "[Television] should not be regarded as a means of expression but of transmission, and it should be used as such").[31] His detour through television, though, appears to have made him much less optimistic about its aesthetic and political possibilities (1980: "TV is too big").[32] He now prefers to speak of his television work as "research,"[33] just as he often calls his films "essays." It is perhaps through this idea of research (with its paradoxical connotations of pretentious scientism and intellectual open-endedness) that we can best appreciate the pedagogical successes and failures of Sonimage's primer on television, the family, and France.

SEXUAL DIFFERENCE
IN POPULAR CULTURE

The Terminator *(James Cameron, 1984)*.

SEVEN

Time Travel, Primal Scene, and the Critical Dystopia (on The Terminator and La Jetée)

*I*F THE SURE SIGN of postmodern success is the ability to inspire spin-offs, *The Terminator* was a prodigy. The film was quickly replicated by *Exterminator*, *Re-animator*, *Eliminators*, *The Annihilators*, and the hard-core *The Sperminator*, all sound-alikes if not look-alikes. It then went on to garner one of popular culture's highest accolades when a West Coast band named itself *Terminators of Endearment*. And just to show that modernity knows no boundaries, national or otherwise, an oppressively large (2 ft. x 3 ft.) and trendy new Canadian journal has appeared, calling itself *The Manipulator*.

For some science-fiction critics, Fredric Jameson among them, *The Terminator*'s popular appeal would represent no more than American science fiction's continuing affinity for the dystopian rather than the utopian, with fantasies of cyclical regression or totalitarian empires of the future. Our love affair with apocalypse and Armageddon, according to Jameson, results from the atrophy of utopian imagination, in other words, our cultural incapacity to imagine the future.[1] Or, as Stanislaw Lem puts it, in describing the banality and constriction of most American science fiction, "The task of the SF author today is as easy as that of the pornographer, and in the same way."[2] But surely there are dystopias and dystopias, and not all such films (from *Rollerball* to *The Terminator*) deserve to be dismissed as trashy infatuations with an equally trashy future. While it is true that most recent dystopian films are content to revel in the sheer awfulness of The Day After (the Mad Max trilogy and *A Boy and His Dog* come readily to mind), there are others which try to point to present tendencies that seem likely to result in corporate totalitarianism, apocalypse, or both. Although *The Terminator* gives us one of the most horrifying post-apocalyptic visions of any recent film, it falls into the latter group because it locates

the origins of future catastrophe in decisions about technology, war-
fare, and social behavior that are being made today. For example, the
new, powerful defense computer that in *The Terminator* is hooked into
everything—missiles, defense industry, weapons design—and trusted
to make all the decisions, is clearly a fictionalized version of the bur-
geoning Star Wars industry. This computer of the near future, forty
years hence, gets smart—a new order of intelligence. It "began to see
all people as a threat," Reese tells Sarah as he tries to fill her in on the
future, "not just the ones on the other side. It decided our fate in a
microsecond. Extermination."

A film like *The Terminator* could be called a "critical dystopia" inasmuch as it tends to suggest causes rather than merely reveal symptoms. But before saying more about how this film works as a critical
dystopia, two qualifications need to be made. First, like most recent
science fiction from *V* to *Star Wars*, *The Terminator* limits itself to solutions that are either individualist or bound to a romanticized notion
of guerrilla-like small-group resistance. The true atrophy of the utopian imagination is this: we *can* imagine the future but we *cannot* con-
ceive the kind of collective political strategies necessary to change or
ensure that future. Second, the film's politics, so to speak, cannot be
simply equated with those of the "author," James Cameron, the director of *The Terminator*, whose next job, after all, was writing *Rambo*.
(His disclaimers about Stallone's interference aside, he agreed to the
project in the first place.) Instead *The Terminator* can best be seen in
relation to a set of cultural and psychical conflicts, anxieties, and fantasies that are all at work in this film in a particularly insistent way.

Tech Noir

What are the elements, then, of *The Terminator*'s critical dystopian
vision? Although the film is thought of as an exceptionally forward-
thrusting action picture, it shares with other recent science-fiction
films, like *Blade Runner*, an emphasis on atmosphere or "milieu," but
not at the price of any flattening of narrative space (in this respect it is
closest to *Alien*). *The Terminator* is studded with everyday-life detail,
all organized by an idea of "tech noir." Machines provide the texture
and substance of this film: cars, trucks, motorcycles, radios, TVs,
time clocks, phones, answering machines, beepers, hairdryers, Sony

Walkmen, automated factory equipment. The defense network computer of the future that decided our fate in a microsecond had its humble origins here, in the rather more innocuous technology of the film's present. Today's machines are not, however, shown to be agents of destruction because they are themselves evil, but because they can break down, or because they can be used (often innocently) in ways they were not intended to be used. Stalked by a killer, Sarah Conner cannot get through to the police because the nearest phone is out of order. When she finally reaches the LAPD emergency line, on a phone in the Tech Noir nightclub, it is predictably to hear, "All our lines are busy . . . please hold . . . ." Neither can she get through to her roommate, Ginger, to warn her because Ginger and her boyfriend have put on the answering machine while they make love. But Ginger wouldn't have been able to hear the phone, in any case, because she'd worn her Walkman to bed. Tech turns noir again when the Terminator, not Ginger, takes the answering-machine message that gives away Sarah's location. Later Sarah will again reveal her whereabouts when the Terminator perfectly mimics her mother's voice over the phone. And in one of the film's most pointed gestures toward the unintentionally harmful effects of technology, the police psychiatrist fails to see the Terminator entering the station when his beeper goes off and distracts him just as their paths cross. Lacking any warning, scores of policemen are killed and the station destroyed. The film seems to suggest that if technology can go wrong or be abused, it will be. To illustrate this maxim further, Kyle Reese is shown having a nightmare of his future world where laser-armed hunter-killer machines track down the few remaining humans; he wakes to hear a radio ad promoting laser-disk stereos. It comes as no surprise, finally, to see that his futuristic concentration-camp number is the ubiquitous bar code stamped on today's consumer items.

That tech turns noir because of human decision-making and not something inherent in technology itself is presented even more forcefully in the "novelization" of *The Terminator* by Randall Frakes and Bill Wisher.[3] The novelization adds a twist, perhaps one that originally appeared in the script but was discarded because it would have generated a complicated and digressive subplot. Or perhaps the authors of the book made it up on their own, unable to resist pointing out, once again, that it is humans, not machines, that will bring on the apocalypse. Near the end of the book, after the Terminator has been destroyed, a man named Jack, a Steve Wozniak-like computer prodigy, discovers a microchip in the debris. His entrepreneur friend, Greg, decides that they will go into business for themselves, once they figure out how to exploit what they take to be a new kind of micro-processing unit. Sixteen months later, they incorporate under the name Cyberdyne Systems . . . the company that goes on to make the same defense network computer that will try to destroy humanity in Reese's day.[4] Here the case is being made not so much against the tunnel vision of corporate greed, but against the supposedly more benign coupling of golly-gosh tech-nerd enthusiasm with all-American entrepreneurship.

The film, moreover, does not advance an "us against them" argument, man versus machine, a Romantic opposition between the organic and the mechanical, for there is much that is hybrid about its constructed elements. The Terminator, after all, is part machine, part human—a cyborg. (Its chrome skeleton with its hydraulic muscles and tendons of flexible cable looks like the Nautilus machines Schwarzenegger uses to build his body.) And Kyle's skills as a guerilla fighter are dependent upon his tech abilities—hot-wiring cars, renovating weapons, making bombs. If Kyle has himself become a fighting machine in order to attack the oppressor machines, Sarah too becomes increasingly machine-like as she acquires the skills she needs to survive both the Terminator and the apocalypse to come. The concluding irony is that Kyle and Sarah use machines to distract and then destroy the Terminator when he corners them in a robot-automated factory. At the end of one of the most harrowing, and gruelingly paced, chase scenes on film, Sarah terminates the Terminator between two plates of a hydraulic press. This interpenetration of human and machine is seen most vividly, however, when Sarah is wounded in the thigh by a piece of exploding Terminator shrapnel. Leaving aside the rich history of sexual connotations of wounding in the thigh,[5] part of a machine is here literally incorporated into Sarah's body ("a kind of cold rape," the novelization calls it). While the film addresses an ultimate battle between humans and machines, it nonetheless accepts the impossibility of clearly distinguishing between them. It focuses on the partial and ambiguous merging of the two, a more complex response, and one typical of the critical dystopia, than the Romantic triumph of the organic over the mechanical, or the nihilistic recognition that we have all become automata (even if those automata are better than we are, more human than human, as in *Blade Runner*).[6]

Time Travel

The Terminator, however, is as much about time as it is about machines. Because cinema itself has the properties of a time machine, it lends itself easily to time-travel stories, one of the staples of science-fiction literature. Surprisingly, however, there have been relatively few attempts in film to create stories around the idea of time travel. Hollywood, to be sure, has always been more drawn to conquering space and fighting off alien invaders than thinking through the heady paradoxes of voyaging through time. The exceptions have been very successful, however, and so it is curious that the industry has not made more effort to produce such stories. George Pal's *The Time Machine* (1960) was so exquisite (it brought the MGM look to science-fiction film) that one even forgave the film's suppression of H. G. Wells's kooky class analysis of the Eloi and the Morlocks, which was, after all, the conceptual center of the original tale. And the runaway success of the banal and clumsily made *Back to the Future* should have convinced Hollywood that there is something commercially expedient about the idea of time travel. Indeed, *The Terminator*'s appeal is due in large part to the way it is able to put to work this classical science-fiction theme.

Compared to the complexity of many literary science-fiction time-travel plots, *The Terminator*'s story is simple: in 2010 a killer cyborg is sent back to the present day with the mission of exterminating Sarah Conner, a part-time waitress and student, the future mother of John Conner, the man who will lead the last remnants of humanity to victory over the machines that are trying to rid the world of humans. John Conner chooses Kyle Reese, a young and hardened fighter, to travel back in time to save Sarah from the Terminator. If the Terminator succeeds in his mission, John Conner, of course, will never be born, and the humans will never be able to fight back successfully against the machines. Kyle has fallen in love with Sarah through her photograph, given to him by John Conner. He says he always wondered what she was thinking about when the photo was taken for she has a faraway look on her face and a sad smile. "I came across time for you," he professes. "I love you. I always have." They make love, he is killed soon after, Sarah destroys the Terminator and leaves for the mountains to give birth to her son and wait out the holocaust to come. The film ends South of the Border with a Mexican boy taking a Po-

laroid of Sarah as she is thinking of Kyle. It is the photograph that John
Conner will give to Kyle, forty years later, knowing that he is sending
his own father to his death.

This sort of story is called a time-loop paradox because cause and
effect are not only reversed but put into a circle: the later events are
caused by the earlier events, and the earlier by the later.[7] If John Conner had not sent Kyle Reese back in time to be his father, he would
never have been born. But he was born, so Kyle Reese must *already*
have traveled back to the past to impregnate Sarah Conner. As another
instance of paradox, John Conner's fighting skills were taught him by
his mother. Sarah Conner, however, learned those skills from Kyle
Reese, who had himself learned them while fighting at John Conner's
side. (The novelization adds another time-loop paradox in locating the
origin of the defense network computer in the microchip found in the
Terminator debris.) Small wonder then that Sarah looks slightly be-
wildered when Kyle says he has "always loved" her. How could this
be true when, from the perspective of her point in time, he hasn't been
born yet?

What is the appeal of time-loop paradox stories? They are so fascinating that many people who used to read science fiction but have
long since given it up will usually remember one story in particular,
Ray Bradbury's "A Sound of Thunder," even if they can no longer
recall the author or the title (others have also noted this phenomenon).
In this famous story, big-game hunters from the future travel back to
the age of the dinosaurs. They don't have to fear that their shooting
will affect the future, however, because dinosaurs will soon be extinct
anyway. They are strictly warned, though, not to step off the walk-
way that has been prepared for them over the primeval jungle. One
hunter disobeys and in doing so crushes a tiny butterfly under his
boot. When the hunting party returns to the future, everything is ever
so slightly different, the result of killing one small insect millions of
years earlier.

Primal Scene

The essential elements of time travel and its consequences are witnessed in a very succinct way in "A Sound of Thunder." That is why
the story is remembered. But when plots of this kind become more

complex, one theme tends to predominate: what would it be like to go back in time and give birth to oneself? Or, what would it be like to be one's own mother and father? Robert Heinlein has given us the seminal treatment of this paradoxical situation in "All You Zombies." A time traveler who has undergone a sex-change operation not only encounters both earlier and later versions of himself but turns out to be his own mother and father. Similarly, in David Gerrold's *The Man Who Folded Himself*, each time the protagonist travels in time, he reduplicates himself. Eventually this results in a large group of identical men who find each other to be ideal lovers. One of them goes very far back in time and meets a lesbian version of himself. They fall in love, have children, and then break up, to return to their copy-lovers. (As the narrator says in "All You Zombies," "It's a shock to have it proved to you that you can't resist seducing yourself.") The appeal of *Back to the Future* should now be apparent—it is only a more vulgar version of the desire manifested in these stories. There is of course a name for this desire; it is called a primal-scene fantasy, the name Freud gave to the fantasy of overhearing or observing parental intercourse, of being on the scene, so to speak, of one's own conception. The desire represented in the time-travel story, of both witnessing one's own conception and being one's own mother and father, is similar to the primal-scene fantasy, in which one can be both observer or one of the participants. (The possibility of getting pregnant and giving birth to oneself is echoed in *Back to the Future*'s TV ad: "The first kid to get into trouble before he was ever born.") The reconstruction of a patient's primal scene assumes, in fact, a great deal of time travel. (Freud said the most extreme primal-scene fantasy was that of observing parental intercourse while one is still an unborn baby in the womb.[8]) The Wolf-Man, supine on the analytic couch, is sent further and further back in time to "remember" the moment when, as a child, he saw his parents having sex. Although Freud's interpretation depends upon the Wolf-Man's having witnessed such a scene, he decides, finally, that it was not necessary for the event to have *actually occurred* for it to have had profound effects on the patient's psychical life. A patient can consciously fabricate such a scene only because it has been operative in his or her unconscious, and this construction has nothing to do with its actual occurrence or nonoccurrence. The idea of returning to the past to generate an event that has already made an impact on one's identity, lies at the core of both the primal-scene fantasy and the time-loop paradox.

What is *The Terminator*'s primal scene? The last words that Kyle Reese flings at the Terminator, along with a pipe bomb, are "Come on, motherfucker!" But in the narrative logic of this film it is Kyle who is the mother fucker. And within the structure of fantasy that shapes the film, John Conner is the child who orchestrates his own primal scene, one inflected by a family romance, moreover, because he is able to choose his own father, singling out Kyle from the other soldiers. That such a fantasy is an attempted end-run around Oedipus is also obvious: John Conner can identify with his father, can even *be* his father in the scene of parental intercourse, and also conveniently dispose of him in order to go off with (in) his mother.

Recent film theory has taken up Freud's description of fantasy to give a more complete account of how identification works in film.[9] An important emphasis has been placed on the subject's ability to assume, successively, all the available positions in the fantasmatic scenario. Extending this idea to film has shown that spectatorial identification is more complex than has hitherto been understood because it shifts constantly in the course of the film's narrative, while crossing the lines of biological sex. In other words, unconscious identification with the characters or the scenario is not necessarily dependent upon gender. Another element of Freud's description of fantasy that also deserves attention, particularly in discussing fantasy in relation to popular film, is the self-serving or wish-fulfilling aspect of fantasy. In "The Paths to the Formation of Symptoms," Freud constructs two analogies between the creation of fantasy and instances drawn from "real life." He begins by saying that a child uses fantasies to disguise the history of his childhood, "just as every nation disguises its forgotten prehistory by constructing legends" (368). A fantasy is thus not "just a fantasy" but a story *for* the subject. The fantasy of seduction, for example, serves to deny the subject's acts of auto-eroticism by projecting them onto another person (such fantasy constructions, Freud says, should be seen separately from those real acts of adult seduction of children that occur more frequently than is acknowledged). Similarly, in the "family romance," the subject creates another parent, an ideal one, to make up for the perceived shortcomings of the real mother or father. Thus a film like *The Terminator* that is so clearly working in relation to a primal fantasy, is also working in the service of pleasure (already a requirement for a mass-audience film), a pleasure that depends upon suppressing conflicts or contradictions. (Because such suppression does not always work, and because desire does not always aim for pleasure—the death drive—much recent film analysis is devoted to examining those aspects of film that go distinctly "beyond the pleasure principle."[10])

Take, for example, the seemingly contradictory figure of Kyle Reese. The film "cheats" with his image in the same way that *The Searchers* "cheats" with Martin Pauley's image, which is, variously, wholly Indian, "half-breed," "quarter-blood" Cherokee, one-eighth Cherokee, or wholly white, depending upon the unconscious and ideological demands of the narrative at any given moment.[11] In *The Terminator* Kyle is the virile, hardened fighter barking orders to the terrified Sarah, but alternately he is presented as boyish, vulnerable, and considerably younger in appearance than she is. His childishness is underscored by Sarah's increasingly maternal affection for him (bandaging his wounds, touching his scars), and in the love scene, he is the young man being initiated by the more experienced, older woman. Kyle is thus both the father of John Conner and, in his youth and inexperience, Sarah's son, John Conner. The work of fantasy allows the fact of incest to be both stated and dissimulated. It is only in fantasy, finally, that we can have our cake and eat it too (or as the French equivalent puts it, even more aptly, that we can be and have been—*peut être et avoir été*).

Freud also compared the mental realm of fantasy to a "reservation" or "nature reserve," a place set aside where "the requirements of agriculture, communication and industry threaten to bring about changes in the original face of the earth which will quickly make it unrecognizable" (almost a description of a post-apocalyptic landscape). "Everything, including what is useless and even what is noxious, can grow and proliferate there as it pleases. The mental realm of fantasy is just such a reservation withdrawn from the reality principle" (372). Can a film like *The Terminator* be similarly dismissed as merely escapist, appealing as it does to a realm of fantasy "withdrawn from the reality principle," where even our incestuous desires can be realized? For one possible answer we can turn to the end of Freud's essay on symptom formation, where he tells us that there is "a path that leads back from fantasy to reality—the path, that is, of art." An artist, he says, has the ability to shape a faithful image of his fantasy, and then to depersonalize and generalize it so that it is made accessible to other people. Even if we do not have as much faith in "art" or the "artist" as Freud has, we can still draw some useful conclusions from what he says. One could argue that *The Terminator* treads the path from fantasy back to reality precisely because it is able to generalize its vision, to offer something more than this fully, though paradoxically, resolved primal fantasy. This *generalizing* of the fantasy is carried out through *The Terminator*'s use of the topical and everyday: as we have seen, the film's texture is woven from the technological litter of modern life. But this use of the topical is not, for example, like *ET*'s more superficial referencing of daily life through brand name kid-speak, that is, topicality for topicality's sake. Rather, it is a dialogue with Americana that bespeaks the inevitable consequences of our current technological addictions. To give another example, the shopping mall in George Romero's *Dawn of the Dead* is more than a kitsch ambience, it is a way of concretely demonstrating the zombification of consumer culture. By exposing every corner of the mall—stores, escalators, public walkways, basement, roof—the location becomes saturated with meaning, in a way that goes far beyond *ET*'s token gesturing toward the commodification of modern life. If *The Terminator*'s primal-scene fantasy draws the spectator into the film's paradoxical circle of cause and effect and its equally paradoxical realization of incestuous desire, its militant everydayness throws the spectator back out again, back to the technological future.

Science Fiction and Sexual Difference

In the realm of the unconscious and fantasy, the question of the subject's origin, "Where did I come from?" is followed by the question of sexual difference, "Who am I (What sex am I)?" It is by now well-known that the narrative logic of classical film is powered by the desire to establish, by the end of the film, the nature of masculinity, the nature of femininity, and the way in which those two can be complementary rather than antagonistic.[12] But in film and television, as elsewhere, it is becoming increasingly difficult to *tell the difference*. As men and women are less and less differentiated by a division of labor, what, in fact, makes them different? And how can classical film still construct the difference so crucial to its formula for narrative closure? Ironically, it is science-fiction film—our hoariest and seemingly most sexless genre—that alone remains capable of supplying the configurations of sexual difference required by the classical cinema.[13] If there is increasingly less practical difference between men and women, there is more than enough difference between a human and an alien (*The Man Who Fell to Earth, Starman*), a human and a cyborg/replicant (*Android, Blade Runner*), or a human from the present and one from the future (*The Terminator*). In these films the question of sexual difference—a question whose answer is no longer "self-evident"—is displaced onto the more remarkable difference between the human and the other. That this questioning of the difference between human and other is sexual in nature can also be seen in the way these films reactivate infantile sexual investigation. One of the big questions for the viewer of *Blade Runner*, for example, is "How do replicants *do it?*" Or, of *The Man Who Fell to Earth*, "What is the sex of this alien who possesses nothing that resembles human genitals (its sex organs are in its hands)?"

But if recent science-fiction film provides the heightened sense of difference necessary to the classical narrative, it also offers the reassurance of difference *itself*. In describing one important aspect of the shift in the psychical economy from the nineteenth century to the twentieth century, Raymond Bellour maintains that in the nineteenth century men looked at women and feared they were different, but in the twentieth century men look at women and fear they are the same.[14] The majority of science-fiction films work to dissipate that fear of the same, to ensure that there is a difference. A very instructive example is the NBC miniseries *V*, broadcast during the 1983–84 season. A rare instance of science fiction on television (*Star Trek* to the contrary, the television industry insists that science fiction does not work on television), *V* tried to be as topical and up-to-date as possible, particularly in the roles it gave to women. The Commander of the alien force that takes over Earth's major cities, the Supreme Commander of the aliens, the leader of the Earthling guerrillas, and the leader of the alien fifth column aiding the Earthlings, are all played by women. They are seen performing the same activities as the men (planning, fighting, counterattacking, infiltrating, etc.), thus removing the most important visible signs of difference. The only difference remaining in *V* is that between the aliens (scaly, green reptiles in human disguise) and the humans. That difference, however, comes to represent sexual difference, as if the alien/human difference were a projection of what can no longer be depicted otherwise.[15] The leader of the guerrillas is captured and brainwashed by the alien commander. Although she is eventually rescued by her comrades, they fear that the brainwashing has turned her into an alien. She even begins using her left hand rather than her right one, a reptile-alien characteristic. Thus when she and her boyfriend, the second in command of the guerrillas, are shown making love, we realize, as they do, that this could be interspecies sex—the blonde, all-American Julie may be a lizard underneath it all, whether in fact or in mind. It gives the otherwise banal proceedings a powerful source of dramatic tension, while it reassures TV-viewing audiences everywhere that there is a difference. (Such a radical disposition of difference always risks, of course, tipping over into the horror of *too much* difference.)

Similarly, it is instructive to see how *Aliens*, directed by James Cameron following his success with *The Terminator*, cracks under the strain of trying to keep to the very original *lack* of sexual differentiation in its precursor, Ridley Scott's *Alien* (not counting, of course, the penultimate scene of Ripley in her bikini underwear). Dan O'Bannon's treatment for the first film was unique in writing each role to be played by either a man or a woman.[16] Ridley Scott's direction followed through on this idea, producing a film that is (for the most part) stunningly egalitarian. In attempting to repeat the equal-opportunity comraderie of the first film, Cameron's sequel includes a mixed squad of marines, in which the women are shown to be as tough as the men, maybe tougher. And Ripley is, again, the bravest and smartest member of the team. But this time there is a difference, one that is both improbable and symptomatic. Ripley develops a maternal instinct, risking her life to save the little girl who is the only survivor of a group of space colonists decimated by the aliens. Tenaciously protective, she takes on the mother alien, whose sublime capacity for destruction is shown nonetheless to result from the same kind of maternal love that Ripley exhibits. Ripley is thus marked by a difference that is automatically taken to be a sign of femininity (we do not see Hicks, for example—played by Michael Biehn, who was Kyle Reese in *The Terminator*—acting irrationally in order to rescue a child who is probably already dead). *Aliens* reintroduces the issue of sexual difference, but not to offer a newer, more modern configuration of that difference. Rather, by focusing on Ripley alone (Hicks is awkwardly "disappeared" from the film in the closing moments), the question of the couple is supplanted by the problem of the woman as mother. What we get finally is a conservative moral lesson about maternity, futuristic or otherwise: mothers will be mothers, and they will *always* be women. We can conclude that even when there is not much sex in science fiction, there is nonetheless a great deal about sexuality, here reduced to phallic motherhood: Ripley in the robot-expediter is simply the Terminator turned inside out.

Just as it is ironic that science-fiction film can give us the sharper notion of sexual difference lost from contemporary classical film, so too it is ironic that when this genre does depict sexual activity, it offers some of the most effective instances of eroticism in recent film. The dearth of eroticism in current filmmaking is pointed up by Woody Allen's success in providing the paradigm of the only kind of sexual difference we have left: the incompatibility of the man's neuroses with the woman's neuroses. Understandably, this is not very erotic. But science-fiction film, in giving us an extreme version of sexual difference, coincides with the requirements of the erotic formula, one which describes a fantasy of absolute difference and absolute complementarity (the quality of being complementary, of course, depending upon the establishment of difference). In contrast to classical cinema, the science-fiction couple is often not the product of a long process of narrative differentiation; rather, the man and the woman are different *from the very beginning*. The narrative can then focus on *them together* and the *exterior* obstacles they must overcome to remain a couple. The erotic formula has, in fact, two parts: first, the two members of the couple must be marked as clearly different (in nonscience-fiction film, for example, she is a nun, he is a priest; she is white, he is black, she is a middle-class widow, he is a young working-class man; she is French, he is German/Japanese, etc.). Second, one of the two must die or at least be threatened by death. If the man and the woman, in their absolute difference, are absolutely complementary, then there is nothing left to be desired. Something has to be taken away to regenerate desire and the narrative. Thus, although the lovemaking scene in *The Terminator* is not a very distinguished one in terms of the relatively perfunctory way that it was filmed, it nonetheless packs a strong erotic charge, *in its narrative context*, because it is a kiss across time, a kiss between a man from the future and a woman from the present, an act of love pervaded by death. For Kyle has to die in order to justify the coda, in which Sarah ensures the continuity of the story, now a legend, of their love for each other.

Time Travel as Primal Scene: La Jetée

If time-travel stories are fantasies of origins, they are also fantasies of endings. Mark Rose has pointed out that many of the narratives that deal with time travel tend to be fictions of apocalypse.[17] (As in *The Terminator*, however, these visions of endings may also be visions of new beginnings—in the Genesis version, after God destroys the world by flood, it is Sarah who is anointed "mother of all nations.") Rose cites Frank Kermode's *The Sense of an Ending* to show that we create fictions of endings to give meaning to time, to transform *chronos*— mere passing time—into *kairos*, time invested with the meaning derived from its goal. History is given shape, is made understandable by spatializing time, by seeing it as a line along which one can travel. Such spatialization of time, however, introduces the paradox of time travel. "Much of the fascination of the time loop is related to the fact that it represents the point at which the spatialization of time breaks down" (Rose, 108). If I could travel back into the past, I could (theoretically) murder my own grandmother. But I would cease to exist. How then could I have murdered her?

If this example illustrates the collapse of time as we know it, it also shows that it is impossible to separate ourselves from time (the time traveler who murders her grandmother ceases to exist). Thus time-travel paradox narratives typically explore either the question of the end of time or the reciprocal relation between ourselves and time (Rose, 108). Although *The Terminator* is concerned with both apocalypse and the question of time in relation to personal identity, another film which preceded it by more than 20 years, Chris Marker's *La Jetée*, weaves the two together in a way that still haunts the spectator of this stunning film. *The Terminator*, in fact, bears such an uncanny resemblance to *La Jetée* that Cameron's film could almost be its mass-culture remake. Marker's film too is about a post-apocalyptic man who is chosen to be a time traveler because of his fixation on an image of the past. It too involves a love affair between a woman from the present and a man from the future, and an attempt to keep humanity from being wiped out.

A crucial difference between *The Terminator* and *La Jetée*, however, is that Marker's film explicitly addresses the paradox of time travel. After being sent on numerous journeys through time, *La Jetée*'s time traveler attempts to return to the scene from his childhood that had

La Jetée *(Chris Marker, 1962)*.

marked him so deeply. On that day, a Sunday afternoon before a third
World War that will drive the few remaining survivors underground,
his parents had brought him to Orly to watch the planes take off. He
remembers seeing the sun fixed in the sky, a scene at the end of the
jetty, and a woman's face. Then, a sudden noise, the woman's gesture,
a crumbling body, the cries of the crowd. Later, the voice-over tells
us, he knew that he had seen a man die. When he tries to return to that
Sunday at Orly, he is killed by one of the scientists from the underground camp who had sent him voyaging through time; they no
longer have any use for him. The moment, then, that he had been
privileged to see as a child and that had never stopped haunting him
was the moment of his own death. In the logic of this film he *has* to
die, because such a logic acknowledges the temporal impossibility of
being in the same place as both adult and child. In *La Jetée* one cannot
be and have been.

The film goes even further when it insists on the similar paradox at
work in the primal-scene fantasy by depicting the psychical consequence of attempting to return to a scene from one's childhood: such a
compulsion to repeat, and the regression that it implies, leads to the
annihilation of the subject.[18] But the subject is also extinguished in another way, this time through a symbolic castration depicted as a very
real death. The woman he is searching for is at the end of the jetty, but
so is the man whose job it is to prevent him from possessing her, the
man and the woman on the jetty mirroring the parental (Oedipal) couple that brought the little boy to the airport. This film's version of the
Terminator succeeds in its mission. While *The Terminator* gives us a
time-travel story that depends upon a primal-scene fantasy for its unconscious appeal, its fantasmatic force, *La Jetée* shows that the two are
one and the same: the fantasy of time travel is no more nor less than
the compulsion to repeat that manifests itself in the primal-scene fantasy. Moreover, since *La Jetée*'s circular narrative is wholly organized
as a "beginning toward which [one] is constantly moving,"[19] it suggests that all film viewing is infantile sexual investigation.

The *Terminator*, in many respects, merely abstracts and reifies *La
Jetée*'s major elements. Its narrative, for example, circles around a single photograph, while Marker's film is composed of hundreds of still
images dissolving in and out of one another in a way that constantly
edges toward the illusion of "real" filmic movement. As Thierry
Kuntzel has pointed out,[20] such a technique allows *La Jetée* to be a film
about movement in film, and our desire for movement. Using still

images to make a film is also a perfect way to tell a time-travel story because it offers the possibility of mixing two different temporalities: the "pastness" of the photographic image and the "here-nowness" of the illusionistic (filmic) movement.[21] *La Jetée* thus recreates the primal-scene/time-loop paradox at both a formal and thematic level.

Although I suggested that *The Terminator* could be seen as the industry remake of *La Jetée*, it should now be clear that Marker's film could not be remade because in its very structure it is *unrepeatable*. Inasmuch as it acknowledges the paradox of the time loop and rejects the rosy nostalgia of a wish-fulfilling version of the primal-scene fantasy, it is not likely remake material with respect to popular film's demand for pleasure without (obvious) paradox. Similarly, one could not imagine a *sequel* to *La Jetée* because of the way the film collapses time in its rigorous observance of the fatalistic logic of time travel. But one can be sure that *Terminators* is already more than a gleam in a producer's eye. After all, what is to stop John Conner, in another possible future, from sending Kyle Reese back in time again, but at a later date, perhaps so that he could rendezvous with Sarah in her South of the Border hide-out?

Would it not be too easy, however, to conclude by pitting *La Jetée* against *The Terminator*? To end by falling back on less-than-useful dichotomies like the avant-garde versus Hollywood or even the Symbolic versus the Imaginary? It is true that *La Jetée* is governed by "the laws of recollection and symbolic recognition" (in Lacan's terms) while *The Terminator* is ruled by "the laws of imaginary reminiscence."[22] But it is precisely the way *The Terminator* harnesses the power of "imaginary reminiscence" (the primal-scene fantasy of time travel) that allows it to present one of the most forceful of recent science-fiction tales about the origins of techno-apocalypse. The film is able to do so, as I have argued, by generalizing its core of fantasy through the systematic use of the topical and everyday, reminding us that the future is now. As a critical dystopia, *The Terminator* thus goes beyond the flashy nihilism of apocalypse-for-the-sake-of-apocalypse to expose a more *mundane* logic of technological modernity, even if it is one that is, finally, no less catastrophic.

EIGHT

The Cabinet of Dr. Pee-wee: Consumerism and Sexual Terror

> *E*very evening at lighting up o'clock sharp and until further
> notice in Feenichts Playhouse. . . . By arraignment,
> childream's hours, expercatered. . . . With nightly
> redistribution of parts and players by the puppetry producer.
>
> James Joyce, *Finnegans Wake*

What goes on in *Pee-wee's Playhouse?* What goes on outside *Pee-wee's Playhouse?* On the inside we have the hi-tech, low-taste spectacle of sexually ambiguous adults, not exactly pretending to be kids, yet inhabiting this child's fantasy-land with hyperactive glee. Outside and around the Playhouse we have the world of Saturday morning television and its efforts to deliver the children to the advertisers. What then does the outside of the Playhouse have to do with the inside?

What goes on *in* the Playhouse is that Pee-wee and his guests are "playing house." This is literally so in one episode that takes place on a rainy day when everyone has to stay inside. "Let's play war!" is one suggestion. "Let's play headhunter!" is another. But it is Miss Yvonne who prevails, insisting that they "play house," even over Pee-wee's objection that "that's girl stuff." Pee-wee dutifully, if grudgingly, takes up his assignment to play Daddy to Miss Yvonne's Mommy, but balks at her demand that Daddy give Mommy a kiss. He relents, under pressure, and gives her a kiss whose passion is just this side of Ward Cleaver's. Another episode makes more explicit what playing house involves when Pee-wee, in otherwise innocent circumstances, says, "I'll show you mine if you'll show me yours." (In the second season of the show they finally get around to playing "doctor.") Indeed, the dialogue and visuals of *Pee-wee's Playhouse* abound with weenie jokes, for the most part of the size variety. "Think you got a big   *141* enough pencil there?" Reba the mail-lady asks Pee-wee as he hauls out a giant pencil to write a letter to his seafaring friend Captain Carl. But before Pee-wee can get the letter in the mail, Captain Carl shows up with an equally oversize extendable telescope as a present for *him*. On another day in the Playhouse, Mrs. Steve, the local snoop and mean-lady, is looking for Randy, the eponymous bad-boy puppet who has stolen apples from her orchard. "I have a bone to pick with you," she shrieks at Randy. "Where are you hiding the little thing," she asks Pee-wee accusingly. Tracking Randy down to his hiding place under the bunk beds, she snarls, "Come out here, you little dickens."

But what girls have, or do not have, is also the subject of investigation at the Playhouse when Pee-wee, rendered permanently invisible by a magic trick that backfires, takes the opportunity to look up Miss Yvonne's dress and begins the childhood chant, "I've seen London, I've seen France . . . ," until Miss Yvonne makes her escape. ("Oh, Pee-wee!" is one of Miss Yvonne's most frequently uttered lines, always in a tone of feigned outrage.) The putative difference between little boys and little girls is once again the topic, this time of a Penny cartoon, in which the narrator rapidly and cannily speculates on a whole range of differences, wrapped up in the final observation that "girls grow to maturity faster than boys."

Frequently then in the Playhouse, "playing house" involves a fever-pitch investigation of sexual identity, most succinctly stated in Pee-wee's now notorious line, another recycled childhood taunt, "I know you are, but what am I?" Also posed throughout the show is the kindred question of the relation between the sexes. In one episode Pee-wee throws a party "to celebrate friendship." All the Playhouse regulars show up, dressed to the nines. They play pin-the-tail-on-the-donkey and eat fifties hors d'oeuvres like pigs-in-a-blanket. Then everyone starts dancing. Among the couples is Miss Yvonne and Tito, the muscular lifeguard, usually seen only in skimpy bathing trunks, and a libidinal object for any number of the Playhouse regulars. Pee-wee taps him on the shoulder, asking "May I cut in?" Tito steps back, Pee-wee steps in, but only to turn and begin dancing with Tito, not Miss Yvonne. After a few seconds, Pee-wee gives a wicked laugh and turns back around to Miss Yvonne ("Oh, Pee-wee!). All tension is dissolved in the next scene, however, when everyone begins to dance the Hokey-Pokey, the elementary-school game designed to help children make distinctions not between the sexes, but between their right foot and their left foot.

The question of sexual relations is posed once again when Miss Yvonne asks Cowboy Curtis for a date. Cowboy Curtis exclaims, "Well, if that don't beat all, a *woman* asking a *man* out on a date!" What is implied, of course, is that he has never been out with a woman before and, in fact, considers it a pretty wild idea. Worried that he "won't know how to act," he is rescued from his pre-date jitters by the Cowntess, the aristocratic bovine who claims that her specialty is "dating dilemmas." To demonstrate to Cowboy Curtis what to do on a date, the Cowntess sets up a role-playing game and asks Pee-wee to be Miss Yvonne. He objects at first, but then takes to his role with gusto. The game comes crashing to a halt, however, when Cowboy Curtis, carried away with *his* role, tries to give Miss Yvonne/Pee-wee a goodnight kiss. Things go pretty far before Pee-wee pulls back to exclaim, "No!, none of that stuff! Game's over!"

It is not until the second season, however, that the inevitable question of where babies come from is raised. The King of Cartoons springs a surprise by bringing along, for the first time, the Queen of Cartoons and their new son, the Prince of Cartoons. Pee-wee plays kitchy-koo with the Prince, and then asks, "Where'd you find him, King, did a stork bring him?" "Not *exactly*," the King replies. Cowboy Curtis guesses that the Prince appeared on the castle doorstep in a basket. "No, no," the King says, "don't you know where babies come from?" Chairy offers still another hypothesis: "Silly, you buy babies in the Baby Department at the hospital." Pee-wee nods in agreement. Since Cowboy Curtis and Pee-wee have just been experimenting with sprouting a grapefruit seed, Cowboy Curtis opines that perhaps babies grow "kinda like seeds." The King agrees, "Yes, kinda like that," and then asks the ever-helpful Magic Screen "to show us some information on the subject." Magic Screen complies by showing them and us what looks like an early sixties educational film on reproduction, which is about as helpful as the preceding hypotheses on where babies come from: we are told about the "miracle of reproduction" while watching a baby chick hatch. When it is over, Pee-wee looks at the camera and says, "Gee, you learn something new every day!" But all that has been learned here is that traditional pedagogical ideas about how to give sexual information to children result in stories that are as fantasmatic as the children's own attempts to make sense of reproduction.

It is highly appropriate that it is the figure of the Sphinx that adorns the exterior of the Playhouse, inasmuch as Freud declared the Sphinx's

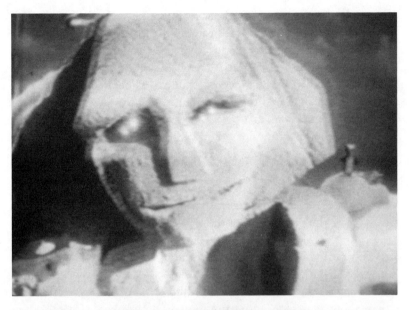

riddle to be the very model of the sexual questions invariably posed by children.[1] The Sphinx therefore becomes the icon or emblem of infantile sexual investigation, a repetitious line of questioning that wants to know "Where did I come from?" "What sex am I?," and "With whom is it possible to have sexual relations?" In its deliberate playing to two audiences, one child and the other adult, *Pee-wee's Playhouse* suggests that these are questions that never cease to insist, even in fully Oedipalized adulthood. How does the Playhouse play to two audiences? Take the following example, in which the question of "With whom is it possible to have sexual relations?," which necessarily includes the question of *how* one has sexual relations, is given, for adult viewers at least, a modern and tragic twist. In this episode, the first of the second season, after the production of the show had moved from New York to Los Angeles, Pee-wee is remodeling the Playhouse. Miss Yvonne arrives, as usual looking as if she is gliding down the Miss Universe runway. Since the Playhouse is such a mess, Pee-wee is worried that Miss Yvonne is going to get dirty. But Miss Yvonne says, "Don't worry about that, you know my motto." "No, what's that?," Pee-wee asks. "Be Prepared!," she exclaims, as she whips out a clear plastic raincoat to cover her pale chiffon dress and billowing crinolines. Pee-wee helps her put it on, along with a transparent plastic cap to protect her large, dome-shaped bouffant hairdo. They walk over to the hipster leader of the Playhouse band, a dog-puppet that speaks in syncopated rhyme. "Dig that crazy plastic dress," he exclaims. "That's in case I make a mess," Miss Yvonne coyly replies. Adults are sure to get the safe sex allusion here, but it is an allusion that is probably not immediately available to the child viewers of this show, ages 2–11. In the same way, the program's references to homosexuality, as in the episodes where Pee-wee rejects Miss Yvonne to dance with Tito or where Cowboy Curtis tries to give Pee-wee a kiss when he's playing Miss Yvonne, are probably taken by children as no more than a perfectly adequate representation of their own dismissal of the opposite sex and all that "icky stuff."

But what does the Playhouse's network, CBS, think of all that "icky stuff," heterosexual or otherwise? CBS no longer has an internal censorship board, but informal self-censorship is still very much at work. Why then did no one object, for example, to Pee-wee's giant underpants skit, in which he places a pair of truly humongous Fruit of the Looms over his head to show how this simple, everyday garment can be turned into a nun's habit or Rapunzel's flowing hair? Once one has noticed the very adult sexual antics mixed in with the childsplay on this show, one inevitably wonders how this is allowed to go on, especially on CBS, traditionally the staidest of the three major networks, indeed the "quality" or "family" network. Could it be that the CBS executives have *scotomized* the show's sexuality, and specifically its homosexuality? That is, they like children who are not yet developmentally or psychically prepared to receive certain sexual information, *see* it but do not *register* it? I shall return to this question of CBS's sexual knowledge, or lack of it, later on.

Infantile sexual investigation is, of course, no more innocent than playing house, and it has its own terrors. Pee-wee's Playhouse is, in fact, a haunted house. There is something uncanny about it, as we shall see. CBS's decision to produce *Pee-wee's Playhouse* for the 1986 season broke a cardinal rule of Saturday morning kidvid programing: the familiarity principle. As ABC's vice-president of children's programing (awkwardly) put it: "Each of our shows has newness about it, yet with familiarity built in."[2] "Familiarity" arises from the product tie-in, the show derived from a toy, *Lady Lovely Locks and Pixie-tails*, for example, or the show spun off from a popular TV series or movie, like *The Flintstone Kids* or *Real Ghostbusters*. *Pee-wee's Playhouse* has none of these advantages; it lacks product recognition or an audience already *familiar* with its images. Is there then something *unfamiliar* about *Pee-wee's Playhouse*, what Freud, in his essay on "The 'Uncanny',"[3] called *unheimlich*, literally, "unhomely"? Let us look at a story that Freud confesses had an uncanny effect on him. He reports that:

> In the middle of the isolation of war-time a number of the English *Strand Magazine* fell into my hands. . . . I read a story about a young married couple who move into a furnished house in which there is a curiously shaped table with carvings of crocodiles on it. Towards evening an intolerable and very specific smell begins to pervade the house; they stumble over something in the dark; they seem to see a vague form gliding over the stairs—in short, we are given to understand that the presence of the table causes ghostly crocodiles to haunt the place, or that the wooden monsters come to life in the dark, or something of the sort. (244–45)

"It was a naive enough story," Freud says, "but the uncanny feeling it produced was quite remarkable." This can only make us wonder what Freud would have thought of the goings-on in Pee-wee's fridge—ice cubes, popsicles, vegetables, and leftovers performing trapeze acts,

staging an opera, dancing the Can-Can — because it is not only croco-
diles that come to life in the Playhouse. Radically anthropomorphized,
everything is animated: Conky the robot, Chairy the chair, Globey the
globe, Magic Screen, Mr. Kite, Mr. Window, and, in the second season, Clocky the clock and Floory the floor, just to name a few. And it
is precisely this animation of the animate that characterizes the uncanny: sentient furniture, dolls coming to life, dismembered limbs, a
severed head, a hand cut off at the wrist, feet that dance by themselves.
Pee-wee's Playhouse teems with such partial objects. Pee-wee himself
seems like a bright-cheeked puppet that has come to life, and it is
doubtless for this reason that he was chosen to play Pinocchio in Shelley Duval's *Fairy Tale Theater*. The mutant toys, Jambi's head in the
genie box, and the hands he receives in the mail in the original *Pee-wee
Herman Show*, Pee-wee's headless torso when Jambi has been only partially successful in bringing him back from invisibility, all of these recall the *jouissance* of dismemberment and other bodily mayhem in the
silly and sadistic cartoons of the thirties and forties which set the tone
for much of what goes on in the Playhouse.

For Freud, however, the uncanny does not arise simply from intellectual uncertainty (Is it alive or not?). "Something has to be added to
the novel and unfamiliar in order to make it uncanny" (221). The first
dictionary definition of *heimlich*, Freud shows, links it to the
"homely," the "familiar," and thus its opposite, *unheimlich*, becomes
that which is frightening, or arouses dread and horror, precisely because it is unfamiliar. But the second definition of *heimlich* is quite different from the first, and means "concealed," "kept from sight." Thus
the second definition of *heimlich* bizarrely turns into its opposite, *unheimlich,* that which is eerie, weird. The dictionary example Freud offers takes us right back to Pee-wee: "These pale youths are *unheimlich*
and are brewing heaven knows what mischief" (224). Freud uses the
ambivalence in the dictionary definition of *heimlich* to demonstrate
that what is unfamiliar is actually the familiar. Repetition, the instinc-
tual compulsion to repeat, is powerful enough, he says "to overrule
the pleasure principle" (238), and is a source of the uncanny. For
Freud, what is repeated is that which has been previously repressed: an
earlier way of psychically negotiating the world. Once again notori-
ously collapsing phylogeny and ontogeny, Freud argues that both
primitive humans and each of us in our own earlier development had
an animistic conception of the universe, manifested in the belief that
the world is peopled by the spirits of human beings. This idea arises

from the subject's narcissistic overvaluation of his own mental processes, the belief in the omnipotence of his own thoughts and wishes. Jambi, you will recall, allows Pee-wee one wish a day, which is (almost) always perfectly fulfilled.

For Freud, of course, this kind of uncanniness depends mainly upon its proximity to the castration complex. This is perhaps why one cannot go through the saw-toothed door of Pee-wee's Playhouse without passing a giant pair of scissors hanging on the wall (although they disappear in the second season). And as for the name Pee-wee itself, beyond its myriad connotations of smallness, lurks the threat of castration. For Freud says in his essay on "The Dissolution of the Oedipus Complex" that castration threats come so often not as warnings about masturbation, but about bedwetting.[4]

But is the Playhouse, in fact, *unheimlich*, unhomely, uncanny? Freud admits that fairy tales, no matter how much they adopt animism and omniscience of thought, do not have an uncanny effect. As long as the events or objects are enclosed in a fictional world, we do not feel them as uncanny. We are not asked to decide on their reality or not; we take them as fiction. However, the situation is altered, he says, as soon as the writer begins to move in the world of common reality. I want to suggest that *Pee-wee's Playhouse* does have an uncanny effect, precisely because it moves in the world of common reality, as Freud calls it, or consumer reality, as we might now call it. *Pee-wee's Playhouse* differs significantly from the fairy tale in that it does not try to pass itself off as a seamless fiction, separate from the "real world." Instead, it fully acknowledges its continuity with what is outside and around the Playhouse, namely the world of children's Saturday morning television.

We do not find a moralistic "No Trespassing" sign posted on the edge of Pee-wee's premises. First of all, there is the Chinese box or mise-en-abîme effect of the ubiquitous Broadcast Arts aesthetic (the "look" provided by the producers of the first season of the *Playhouse*). This is seen throughout the Playhouse, then in the "stay tuned" bumpers that Broadcast Arts designed for CBS to distinguish the Saturday morning programs from the commercials, and, finally, in the commercials themselves, some of them created by Broadcast Arts for the sponsors, the manufacturers of Fruit-Flavored Trix, for example. All of these bear the distinctive Broadcast Arts look, which combines live action filmmaking with a variety of special-effects techniques, including clay animation, stop-motion animation, cel animation, motion graphics, motion control photography, and the use of models, miniatures, mattes, and computer graphics.[5] Frequently, then, there is remarkably little visual difference between the inside and outside of *Pee-wee's Playhouse*. Broadcast Arts and Pee-wee Pictures, in both their production methods and their characteristic looks, exuberantly play up the continuity between art and commercialism.

But, one might ask, what about the figure of the Salesman, the giant puppet somewhat resembling Richard Nixon who comes to the door in each episode, only to have it slammed in his face as Pee-wee once again refuses his high-volume "incredible offer," screaming "Salesmen!" (or "Sandman!," as I heard it the first six or seven times I saw the show)? Is not this refusal to be seen as *this* show's rejection of the blatantly manipulative commercialism that pervades children's television programing? Yes and No. While it is true that the Salesman's attempted hard-sell is exactly repeated and rejected each week during the first season, an exception is made in one episode. Pee-wee is having a party to which all the regulars have been invited. Everyone was to have brought a present for someone else, but somehow Pee-wee has been left out. When we hear the pounding on the door, we know that it is the Salesman. Pee-wee opens the door and, this time, responds to the sales pitch because his feelings are hurt at not having been given a present. Instead of slamming the door, he hesitates and asks, "What's the offer?" The Salesman makes him an offer he can't refuse, free foil for his ever-expanding foil ball. Pee-wee grabs the foil, invites the Salesman in, and even directs him to the refreshment table. Everyone has a price. Repeatedly in the Playhouse, a moral stance is established—here, an objection to the kind of corporate decision-making that turns every kids' show into a half-hour commercial—and then blithely undermined.

When Stephen Oakes, executive producer of the first season of the *Playhouse*, was asked why his company had not tried to market any of the mutant toys seen by millions of kids every week on Pee-wee's toy-shelf, he replied, somewhat tongue-in-cheek, "Bad management."[6] He wryly admitted, however, that it might not be such a commercially successful idea since any child can easily create his or her own mutant toy through even the most half-hearted efforts at dismemberment and recombination. Paul Reubens, who plays Pee-wee Herman both on and off screen (reporters are warned that they will be interviewing *Pee-wee*, not Paul Reubens), constantly threatens to market toys based on the show. But when he begins to discuss the Pee-wee products he would like to merchandise and license, it is clear that his

ideas are only an extension of Pee-wee's typical attitude toward the
Salesman. In *Interview* magazine Pee-wee revealed that "Ralston-
Purina is developing a cereal with me called 'Pee-wee Chow,' and it'll
be in the shape of little dog-food stars. . . . I want the television commercial for it to show a mother pouring it into a bowl and putting it
on the floor, and the kids crawling over and eating it like dog food."
Another of his marketing schemes involves permanent Pee-wee tattoos: "I always thought it would be fun to have permanent tattoos and
not say they were permanent. Kids would put them on their arms and
stuff and their parents would be scrubbing them and scrubbing them
and they wouldn't come off. It would be good advertising for the
show in the future. A whole generation of kids with these big Pee-wee
tattoos."[7] However, a Pee-wee Herman talking doll was successfully
introduced in the 1987 Christmas season and is already a collector's
item.

In another way too *Pee-wee's Playhouse* is both continuous and dis-
continuous with the world of commercialized children's television
programing. When it first appeared in 1986, the *Playhouse* was most
notably different in being the only Saturday morning show to have
live characters on it (even if the look and gestures of the Playhouse
gang seem governed by an animated cartoon aesthetic). But it is significant that Pee-wee *leaves* the Playhouse at the end of each episode,
saying good-bye to his guests and riding/flying his scooter off into an
imaginary geography of America, as well as into the credits sequence,
which segues into an announcement to stay tuned for *Teen Wolf* and
Galaxy High, the CBS programs to follow. If in these numerous ways
the Playhouse is not sealed off from common reality, or here, consumer reality, then, according to Freud, the viewer would be confronted with an intellectual uncertainty about the boundaries between
the real and the unreal, the animate and the inanimate (or, here, the
commercial and the noncommercial) that in part characterizes the uncanny. In all the senses of the uncanny the Playhouse can therefore be
said to fit the bill: its investigation of sexual identity, with the threat of
castration always in the wings; its animation of the animate, so linked
to childhood narcissism and the fantasy of omnipotent thought, and
the conceptual uncertainty it raises about borders, limits, and boundaries.

No television show or program can be understood outside of its en-
vironment, the ads that are embedded in it and the other programs
around it. *Pee-wee's Playhouse*, as we have seen, is clearly not separate

from these considerations of commercialism and scheduling, and the confusion over where the show begins and ends even contributes to its uncanny effect, as we have seen. But there is one way that *Pee-wee's Playhouse is* distinct from its surroundings. All the other Saturday morning shows, as well as most of the commercials, are marked by an extreme sexual differentiation. The network programs aim for what is called "girl appeal," especially in the 1986–1987 season with so many new girl products appearing on the market. Girls are thought to respond to "cute and cuddly" and apparently watch, in vast numbers, *Kissyfur, The Wuzzles, The Care Bears, Pound Puppies,* and *Muppet Babies.* The cheap syndicated shows, on the other hand, have captured the boy-product market with shows like *He-Man and the Masters of the Universe* and *Inhumanoids. Pee-wee's Playhouse,* however, attempts to be a cross-over show, not only appealing to viewers of different ages but to children of opposite sexes. The fast-forward speed of *Pee-wee's Playhouse* is intended to capture the fidgety attention of little boys, and its endearing characters the sentimental devotion of little girls. But there is much more here than a grab-bag attempt to appeal to both boys and girls. *Pee-wee's Playhouse* offers something that elicits the fascinated attention of all small children. We could call it terror, the terror of sexuality, of sexual difference, and we are back again to infantile sexual investigation and even the uncanny. *Pee-wee's Playhouse* forgoes the easy channeling of children's sexual identification into either mastery for the boys (*He-Man and Masters of the Universe*) or permanent regression for the girls (*Kissyfur, The Wuzzles*). Instead, the program suggests that the question of sexual difference is highly problematic and possibly never entirely settled. CBS's vice-president of children's programing has said that the network is trying to attract people to its Saturday morning line-up "who have succeeded in bringing *fantasy* to children in books, movies, or whatever."[8] Although the CBS executive does not expand upon what she or the network means by "fantasy," psychoanalytic theory tells us that unconscious fantasy typically and generically involves a strong component of the scary, and what is scary for children is more often than not the questions posed by sexuality, and the children's own highly fraught relation to sexual knowledge. That CBS is indeed aiming toward programs that are edgier and more frightening than *Kissyfur,* yet which do not emphasize triumphant mastery like *Inhumanoids,* can be seen in their choice of Chris Columbus, who wrote the very nasty and quite terrifying *Gremlins* for Steven Spielberg, to script *Galaxy High.* CBS has also announced that

Maurice Sendak, the author of *Where the Wild Things Are*, may develop a show soon.[9] It should be said, though, that CBS's interest in conceiving more innovative programing for children is probably due, more than anything else, to the fact that the ratings for the syndicated cartoon shows based on toys have plunged precipitously, by about 60%, indicating that there may be a market for newer kinds of shows.[10] But in any case, CBS was willing to take a chance on its "great weird hope,"[11] Pee-wee Herman.

What do I mean by saying that CBS took a chance on Pee-wee Herman (and now I am back to the question of what CBS *knows*)? It was not only the fact that the show would have the only live actors on Saturday morning television, or that each episode was clearly going to cost more to produce than an animated show (the first season's episodes averaged $325,000 each and employed 150 artists and technicians).[12] The risk for CBS was the challenge of transforming a sexually risqué work of performance art into a children's television program. *The Pee-wee Herman Show*, a very adult take-off on children's shows, was successfully staged in two Los Angeles theaters before being made into an HBO special. It was fully scatological (the secret word was "latrine"), and entirely sadistic and voyeuristic. There are jokes about weenies, doggy doo, underwear, open flies, vaginal smells, anal intercourse, masturbation, and sexually transmitted diseases, among others. And Jambi was already the raging queen in a box that we still see on the Playhouse. CBS wanted Broadcast Arts to do a show for them, but needed a character on which to base it. They chose Pee-wee Herman, and according to the head of Broadcast Arts, asked the innovative production company to come up with a children's show, making only two stipulations. Pee-wee Herman should not be shown coming out of the bathroom trailing a piece of toilet paper stuck to his shoe, nor should he stick pencils in potatoes. Both were done in the first season. Stephen Oakes believes that CBS is fully aware of the gay references in the Saturday morning show, but says that the network has never mentioned them to Reubens or the producers. As the show went along, CBS had, in fact, only two objections, based on objections they thought were sure to come from parents groups. First, they were concerned about the "secret word," because not only are children watching the show supposed to "scream real loud" when they hear it on the show, they are told to do so all day long, whenever they hear the word. Since the secret words are frequently uttered ones like "this," "there," "okay," "time," or "day,"

the network executives feared that the effects of the show would spill over into the entire day, causing parental stress. Second, they objected to the attempt to rejuvenate the fifties game "Winky Dink" in the Connect-the-Dots sequence of the show. The idea was to sell clear, flexible plastic sheets at a franchise like McDonald's that children would attach to the TV screen and play Connect-the-Dots with special crayons that would also be supplied. Parents groups did not like the idea because they foresaw some kids playing Connect-the-Dots without the plastic sheet. They were also worried about the children being exposed to radiation from the television set since the game required them to be right next to it. The secret word stayed but the new "Winky Dink" was cancelled.

What is surprising in all these negotiations is that CBS never questioned or censored the show's presentation of sexuality, including its clear allusions to homosexuality. I earlier suggested that the CBS executives, like the prepubescent children who make up the majority of the target audience, simply do not take in those sexual references. Admittedly, this is unlikely, since those executives are sure to be sophisticated adults, tuned in to what "the public wants," which means that there must be other reasons for the network's sudden binge of tolerance. Surely CBS *knows*, but somehow feels that things are controllable, that the sexual meanings circulated by the show will somehow be contained.

Perhaps too much has been made of the homosexual subtext in *Pee-wee's Playhouse*. I say this even though most critics have scrupulously avoided any mention of Pee-wee's sexual orientation (variously describing Pee-wee as adolescent, androgynous, polymorphously perverse, or just "weird"), or bring it up only in order to put it aside. As an article in *Film Comment* said, "if Pee-wee has to have an inordinate number of handsome young men on the show, that's his business."[13] Although the allusions to gay culture are there, it is not enough merely to point them out. Bryan Bruce does a very good job of it, however, in his *CineAction* article, "Pee-wee Herman: the Homosexual Subtext."[14] Bruce gives a list of the many "disguised allusions to a gay sensibility in both the show and the film [*Pee-wee's Big Adventure*]" (4). He says that it is not just that there are a lot of handsome men on the show, "it's rather that each represents a specific gay male icon, prominent fantasy figures in homosexual pornography (although in the context of the Playhouse made human and friendly), including the sailor (Captain Carl), the black cowboy (Cowboy Curtis), and the muscular, scantily clad lifeguard (Tito), not to mention the escaped con (Mickey) in *Pee-wee's Big Adventure*" (5). In the film we see explicit references to gay fantasy in two instances of drag, once when Pee-wee disguises himself as Mickey's girlfriend to get them through a police roadblock (he forgets to change back into his boy clothes after they are out of danger) and again when Pee-wee makes a brief appearance as a nun near the end of the film. Bruce says the nun, in particular, is a dead giveaway in its appeal to the irreverent gay camp aesthetic (5).

It is precisely this last point about the "irreverent gay camp aesthetic" that needs to be brought more into focus. Perhaps with *Pee-wee's Playhouse* it is not a case of "disguised allusions," or latent meanings put there in the text to be discerned by a knowing gay following, but rather of an overall aesthetic, *a camp sensibility*, one in which everything is entirely on the surface. And if this camp sensibility has become so pervasive in our culture that it is no longer automatically equated with homosexuality, but has become available to a much wider set of artistic and social meanings, then this could help to explain the network's acquiescence to the Playhouse's sexual antics. It is only "troglodytes who . . . confuse camp with homosexual," claims Mark Booth in *Camp*, his definitive study of the subject, which challenges the received idea, first aired by Christopher Isherwood and then popularized by Susan Sontag, that camp originated in homosexual cliques of the thirties.[15] Booth instead traces the origins of the camp sensibility back to the nineteenth century, to the dandyism of Beau Brummell and Oscar Wilde, then even further back, to the artifices of Restoration comedy, and finally to the seventeenth century, to the elaborate dressing up and showing off of Louis XIV's Versailles, seen by later camp figures as a sort of camp Eden. Camp behavior, costume, language, and attitudes were taken up and extended in British pop, American Warholian pop, hippie exotica, punk, and most recently, in the postmodern predilection for quotation and pastiche. To say that camp cannot be equated with homosexuality is not to deny that gays have been the marginal group to make the greatest *use* of a camp sensibility now widely available to every producer and consumer of popular culture.

What are the characteristics of the modern "uses of camp"?[16] For Booth, camp is distinguished by artificiality, stylization, theatricality, naïveté, sexual ambiguity, tackiness, poor taste, and stylishness. The *sources* of camp are city life, pluralism, style, and learning (that is, possessing enough knowledge to be self-conscious). The *targets* of camp are conventional morality, good taste, marriage and family, suburbia, sports, and business. Booth sums up his description of camp and the camp persona thus: "All his life, the camp person remains a naughty child checking his elders" (57). Pee-wee Herman is, indeed, a naughty child checking his elders; but more to the point is the way the show *puts camp to work* as part of an overall strategy to playfully subvert the conventions of both sexuality and consumerism.

Camp, as an "operation of taste"[17] is everywhere apparent in the Playhouse. Booth claims that the most common manifestation of camp erudition over the past two centuries has been the habit of collecting. Beau Brummell, Robert de Montesquiou, and Boni de Castellane all had a passion for collecting. The epitome of the camp collector, however, was William Beckford, who built for himself an immense hideaway mixing Gothic, Oriental, and Spanish styles. Inside this folly he amassed a huge collection of furniture, books, and paintings, a place William Hazlitt described as "a cathedral turned into a toy shop" (51). Pee-wee's Playhouse too is a mad collector's dream: mixing periods (the forties, fifties, and sixties); styles ("modern," "German Expressionist," "Tex-Mex," "early Easter Island," "neo-Aztec,"); and trashy retro objects, both kitsch and camp. The periods, styles, and objects are, of course, not at all arbitrarily chosen: they have been selected for parodic recycling because they have their origins in what must have been the childhood and adolescence of the "real" Pee-wee Herman, the thirty-five-year-old Paul Reubens. Camp as cultural memory, resurrected for subversive ends, not to mention fun. Both the subversiveness and the fun lie in the way camp finds beauty in the seeming bizarre or outrageous, in the way it discovers the worthiness of something that is supposedly without value, here the debris of mass consumer culture.

But camp also has subversive fun with recycling and celebrating the kitschiest of sexual roles. We have seen how the show lovingly presents the icons of gay male pornography. And the Playhouse's ideas about femininity are equally pop: Miss Yvonne is the Burlesque Queen of camp theater, her femininity exaggerated into a parody of itself; the obese Mrs. Steve is the Divine stand-in, played by Shirley Stoler of Leonard Kastle's *The Honeymoon Killers*; and in the second season, Mrs. René is a sixties swinger decked out in mini-skirt and go-go boots. In camp, though, every sexual role can be satirized and celebrated, including the popular image of the homosexual.[18] Pee-wee's mincing step, affected gestures, exaggerated speech, obvious makeup, and extreme fastidiousness are constant reminders of this popular image. It is an image most sharply brought into focus when Pee-wee plays interior decorator in the first show of the second season, as he renovates the Playhouse. Ricardo, the Spanish-speaking soccer player, and Cowboy Curtis can only look on and roll their eyes as Pee-wee takes "ages" to decide where to place a chair.

It is, of course, inevitable that marriage, that haven in a heterosexual world, should come in for ridicule here. Pee-wee's stock response to the question of whether he likes something is, "Yes, but I wouldn't want to marry it!" But in the second season, during a mixed-sex slumber party at the Playhouse, Pee-wee does marry something he likes. Too excited to fall asleep, the pajama-clad guests decide to make a snack. Someone asks Pee-wee if he likes the snack and he gives his usual snappy comeback. This time, however, he has second thoughts. "But why not?," he asks slyly. With a quick cut we find ourselves in the middle of a wedding ceremony in which Pee-wee takes as his beautiful bride . . . a bowl of fruit salad!

In advocating the dissolution of hard and inflexible sexual identities and moral rules, camp also pleads for an attitude of tolerance, for an acceptance of difference, a plea whose pathos often tips over into sentimentality. John Waters has advanced this plea for acceptance by reconceiving one of camp's most dubious characters, the extremely fat woman. In *Hairspray*, even though Divine still *verges* on repulsiveness, both she and, especially, her daughter, played by Ricky Lake, are presented in an entirely sympathetic light and are, in fact, the lovable heroines of the film. (*Pee-wee's Playhouse*, fattist to the core, still has a ways to go here: Mrs. Steve is nasty and stupid, Mrs. René is a ditz.) In this plea for tolerance or acceptance, however, the camp figure typically exhibits a bitter wit, a form of "gay angst," the sadness of those who have internalized straight society's opinion of them.[19] But the Pee-wee persona seems to offer a new version of camp subjectivity because one finds in him no inner pathos, no inner struggle, no problem of feeling abnormal or wanting to hide it. Pee-wee's comic mode has most often been compared to that of Jerry Lewis in the way the two so spectacularly hystericize the male body. The difference, though, is that when Pee-wee turns into a woman, or oscillates between male and female, this transformation is not accompanied by any anxiety, as it always is with Lewis.[20] Perhaps this oscillation without anxiety represents a new, postmodernist stage of camp subjectivity, one distin-

guished by a capacity for zipping through sexual roles that is as fast and unremarkable as zapping through the channels.

Even before *Hairspray*, though, *Pee-wee's Playhouse* was already using camp to plead for the acceptance of racial difference as well as sexual difference (sexual difference, that is, in the sense of the variety of nonstandard or minority sexualities). One of the first and most immediate impressions of the show is the easygoing way it mixes races and ethnicities. For example, when Miss Yvonne asks Cowboy Curtis for a date, it is never mentioned (or in typical TV fashion made into an "issue" or "problem" to be addressed or resolved) that she is white and he is black. In the second season much is made of Pee-wee's efforts to learn Spanish from Ricardo. Often Ricardo's lines are not translated, thus acknowledging the Hispanic children in the audience who will get them anyway. One important way the show deals with racial difference is to make it one among many differences (ethnic, sexual, cross-cultural), all of which are to be mixed together and appreciated rather than condemned: Cowboy Curtis, for example, is black, male, a cowboy, and a gay pornographic icon. And in the Playhouse gang, one of the "real" little kids is Cher, an Asian girl dressed as Pocohontas. Although multiplying and celebrating "differences" can risk leveling or vitiating crucial political categories of difference, I would argue that here, in the context of Saturday morning television, the Playhouse's dizzying presentation of myriad differences, accompanied by a constant plea for tolerance, shows a sharp understanding of how one might go about reordering (attitudes toward) difference, even under the gaze of the masters of the television universe.

The culmination of all of this campy play with difference occurs in one episode in which all questions of racial and sexual difference are projected onto a more spectacular difference, that between humans and aliens. The camp passion for the horror/sf genre is well-known. In "Camp and the Gay Sensibility," Jack Babuscio argues that the horror genre, in particular, is susceptible to a gay interpretation.[21] Tourneur's *Cat People*, for example, could be seen as a film about the inner drives that threaten a person's equilibrium and way of life; Mamoulian's *Dr. Jekyll and Mr. Hyde*, about coping with pressures to conform and adapt; Siegal's *Invasion of the Body Snatchers*, about the masking of "abnormality" behind a facade of "normality," and so on. Thus it seems only appropriate that the Playhouse should one day be invaded by a monster from outer space, green of course, who is basically one big eye on a stalk that hops around. But after feeding the monster a sub-

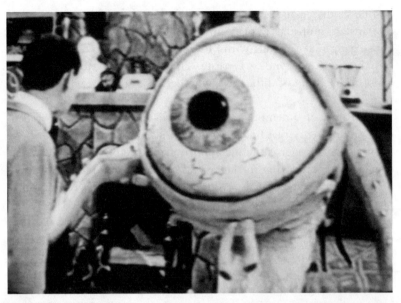

marine sandwich and getting to know it (Jambi grants Pee-wee's wish to translate monster-language into English), Pee-wee and the Playhouse gang make friends with "Roger," as he asks to be called, who soon becomes a Playhouse favorite. The moral of the story, of course, is not to be afraid of difference, whether it be sexual, racial, or interplanetary.

But Roger also demonstrates the coexistence of the two perspectives on difference that I have argued are at the core of the show. As a giant eyeball, Roger is the metaphorical and metonymical equivalent of what is threatened in the fantasy of castration (an unconscious fear of difference), yet he is also "our new friend Roger" from another planet (a social and conscious wish for acceptance of difference). Roger's pivotal role in mediating the show's two perspectives on difference is especially marked in the second season. Although he does not return to the Playhouse, except for a brief appearance at the slumber party, his huge bloodshot eyeball is embedded in Pee-wee's new helmet that he dons at the end of each episode before waving good-bye to his friends and riding off on his scooter. Here, in the figure of Roger, we can see how the Playhouse manages to bring together all the possible conscious and unconscious valences that can be given to the familiar and the unfamiliar, the homey and the unhomey, the like-me and the not-like-me. "Roger" is uncanny camp.

Although I have argued that *Pee-wee's Playhouse* plays to both children and adults, it is obvious that those two levels of address are not and cannot be seen as entirely separate. Rather, the interest of this show lies in the way it re-presents masculinity and male homosexuality right at the edge of the territory of the child, that morally quarantined and protected area. It is almost as if the show "recognizes" that as long as infantile sexuality remains conceptually off limits, it will be impossible to rethink sexual roles and sexed identities, masculine or otherwise. This is because the adult fantasy of childhood simplicity and happiness is a founding fantasy, one that offers the possibility of innocence to those who need to retain the idea of innocence itself. As long as this fantasy remains unexamined, so too will the fantasy of masculinity.

FEMINISM AND PEDAGOGY

La Chinoise *(Jean-Luc Godard, 1967)*.

NINE

Teaching in Your Sleep: Feminism and Psychoanalysis

THE APRIL 5, 1979, ISSUE of *The New York Review of Books* carried this letter from a reader:

Richard Wollheim ends his informative and challenging article on Jacques Lacan with a polemical aside that leaves me puzzled. He writes: "Lacan's ideas and Lacan's style, yoked in an indissoluble union, represent an invasive tyranny. And it is by a hideous irony that this tyranny should find its recruits among groups that have nothing in common except the sense that they lack a theory worthy of their cause or calling: feminists, *cinéastes*, professors of literature."

Would Professor Wollheim care to explain on what evidence he includes feminists in this list? Could he give the names of any individual women or women's groups, here or in France, that have become Lacan's "recruits"? I would certainly be curious to learn how Lacanian theory and feminism manage to coexist.

In his reply Richard Wollheim gives substance to his assertion of the existence of such an unholy alliance by listing several feminist authors and projects that indeed attempt to claim or forge a healthy working relation between feminism and Lacanian psychoanalysis. What this exchange serves to indicate in its mutual bafflement is the depth of the present inability to understand what possible interest feminism could have in psychoanalysis, particularly the Lacanian version of it. After all, haven't feminists themselves, from Betty Friedan to Mary Daly, typically ranged psychoanalysts in the category of men whose job it is to manage and adjust women's minds and bodies in accordance with strictly male standards? And don't feminists frequently expect psychoanalytic theory, in its notorious use of concepts like penis envy and the relative "weakness" of the feminine superego, to exemplify the worst kind of "scientific" rationalization of women's supposedly inherent inferiority? And wasn't it Jacques Lacan who took more than a little rhetorical pleasure in his notorious suggestion that "The woman does not exist" (*La femme n'existe pas*)?

These are some of the symptoms of a general incomprehension that must be met head-on in teaching a course on feminism and psychoanalysis. Yet students readily sign up for such courses. Why? One reason is the renewed academic interest in psychoanalysis (particularly apparent since the time of the *New York Review of Books* letter) that has manifested itself in a flood of conferences, working groups, and special issues of journals on psychoanalytic theory. A second reason is the genuine recognition of the intensity and quality of the work that has come out of the feminist rapprochement with psychoanalysis. Juliet Mitchell's *Psychoanalysis and Feminism* (1974),[1] for example, the first contemporary argument for the feminist use of psychoanalytic theory as a conceptual tool for analyzing the vicissitudes of sexual difference, has been extremely influential and continues to be widely read. But these are positive reasons for taking a course on feminism and psychoanalysis, and students can just as frequently enroll for more negative ones, such as the wish, for example, to validate an already firmly held belief in the fundamental theoretical and political incompatibility of the two areas. In what follows, I want to discuss some of the problems involved in teaching feminism and psychoanalysis *together*. I will not approach these problems directly, say through relating anecdotes of my teaching experiences or offering pedagogical tips, but rather more obliquely, through considering the relation of both feminism and psychoanalysis to *knowledge* and *authority*, an understanding of which seems to me essential to anything one could say about pedagogy. In *The Interpretation of Dreams* Freud said, "When in the course of a piece of scientific work we come upon a problem which is difficult to solve, it is often a good plan to take up a second problem along with the original one—just as it is easier to crack two nuts together rather than each separately."[2] Two tough nuts to crack, then, feminism and psychoanalysis, each in its relation to what might be called an ethics of teaching.

An Analytical Pedagogy?

Psychoanalysis has always had a particularly tenuous and highly fraught relation to pedagogy. Freud himself said very little on the matter, considering teaching to be one of the "impossible professions" (along with governing and healing) and later confessing his ultimate indifference: "I'm leaving all that to Anna,"[3] was his attitude. To the perennial question of whether the couch can come to the aid of the blackboard, a recent respondent answers with a strong negative: for Catherine Millot, a French Lacanian analyst and author of *Freud, Antipédagogue*,[4] psychoanalysis and pedagogy are *antithetical*: "It seems to me that Freud's own reserve [on the subject of teaching] has its basis in the radical opposition between the analytical process and the pedagogical process" (127). Millot argues that the discoveries of psychoanalysis represent an acute challenge to the assumption that pedagogy can be a science of education. What, then, is the nature of the antithesis? One way to sum it up would be to say that education works on the ego whereas psychoanalysis works on the unconscious. Or that teaching aims to reinforce repression (for social and cultural ends) while psychoanalysis tries to eliminate it as the source of the patient's suffering. The respective methods are no less opposed. Indeed we could say that there is a fundamental structural contradiction in education which makes it impossible to found an analytical pedagogy. The teacher's main pedagogical tool, for example, is the kind of identification known as transference; in "Reflections on Schoolboy Psychology,"[5] Freud offers a striking example of the unconscious and total respect that we accord our teachers:

> As you walked through the streets of Vienna—already a gray-beard and weighed down by all the cares of family life—you might come unexpectedly on some well-preserved, elderly gentleman, and would greet him humbly almost, because you had recognized him as one of your former schoolmasters. But afterwards, you would stop and reflect: "Was that really he? or only someone deceptively like him? How youthful he looks! And how old you yourself have grown! *Can it be possible that the men who used to stand for us as types of adulthood were so little older than we were?*" (241)

Freud proceeds to describe how these teachers become our "substitute fathers" upon whom we fix all the youthful and passionate emotions that were once associated with our parents. Lacan, following Freud, emphasizes that transference, or "the acting out of the reality of the unconscious," can take place only when there is somewhere *a subject supposed to know*.[6] He goes on to stress the direct correspondence between the question of knowledge and the question of love: "Transference *is* love . . . I insist: it is love directed toward, addressed to, knowledge."[7] Teaching proceeds by way of seduction; the student wants to learn because he or she loves the teacher insofar as he or she presumes that the teacher *knows*. Hence the fundamental dilemma in teaching I have already referred to—the teacher, to be effective, to be a teacher at all, must fully assume the mantle of the subject supposed to know. To relinquish that imaginary position would be to lose the most important pedagogical tool of all. Psychoanalysis, on the other hand, proceeds in large part through the *analysis of the transference*, its goal being the analysand's understanding of the illusory status of the subject supposed to know, and the fraudulence of absolute or complete knowledge. Whereas analysis asks the patient finally to recognize the reality of his or her own unconscious desires, the educational process requires that the student's desires be those of the teacher, that is, that the student's superego be modeled on that of the teacher. (This same process is manifest in psychoanalytic treatment based on an ego psychology in which the end of analysis is not the destruction of the transference but the final identification of the analysand with the analyst's superego.) In addition to the fact that education cannot take place without transference, the teacher has another reason for not wanting to give up this identificatory power over the students, and that is his or her own narcissistic satisfaction in seeing the students gradually coming to want what he or she wants "for" them. Seen in this light, education is on the side of narcissism and the imaginary, the ideal and "illusion."

Perhaps the difficulty of combining psychoanalysis and education can be seen most strikingly in Anna Freud's version of child analysis-cum-childhood education. She says that it is necessary to *use* the transference to ensure the formation of a parental-type attachment between child and analyst in order to open the door to suggestion. Child analysis, here construed as a kind of analytical education, is thus the opposite of adult analysis because the analyst reinforces the superego while dealing with the drives.

But what about the numerous attempts to reform pedagogy through radical means, many of which claim to found their principles in psychoanalytic insights? Do not these reformist efforts seek to circumvent the very problems we have just been discussing? Millot gives one particularly telling example of a radical educational practice which proposes putting the teacher in the position of the analyst.[8] She cites an exchange which took place between A. S. Neill and one of his students at Summerhill: "Teach me something, I'm bored stiff," demands a little girl who had done no schoolwork in weeks. "Righto!," Neill enthusiastically responds, "What do you want to learn?" "I don't know," she says. "And I don't either," he replies, and walks away. Millot is interested in this conversation because she believes that Neill is doing something psychoanalytically intelligent in his refusal to respond to the girl's demand to tell her what to desire. In analytic treatment such a refusal would serve to leave that demand hanging, so to speak, in the highly charged space between analyst and analysand, so that it could be recognized and seen for what it is (a demand for love, for the desire of the other). Millot, however, makes it quite clear that the teacher is *not* like the analyst, that the teacher is not a smooth mirror in which the student-subject can see the reflected structure of its own demand and desire. This is because the student can always sense the hidden demands of the teacher or parent. The student, like the child with the parent, is almost *clairvoyant* when it comes to understanding the desire of the Other and how best narcissistically to mirror what the Other desires. In A. S. Neill's case, the refusal to respond to the girl's demand clearly hides a demand of his own—that the child, in canonical Summerhill fashion, be autonomous and act according to her own desires. Analytically speaking, the child is already alienated with respect to both language and the desire of its parents. Neill's refusal enacts a comparable alienation in its obfuscation of his demand. All of this leads Millot to the conclusion that the role of the analyst and the teacher cannot be embodied in one and the same person because psychoanalysis and education are fundamentally opposed in their entirely different relations to *knowledge* and *authority*.

Lacan himself scarcely conceals his contempt for the "discourse of the university," assigning it a place between the "discourse of the master" and the "discourse of the hysteric."[9] He characterizes the "discourse of the university" not only by its neglect of the signifier and its obsession with discourse constituted as knowledge, but also by its tendency to ignore questions of subjectivity in favor of knowledge as the ultimate object of desire. But is Freud's and Lacan's highly visible pessimism about the psychoanalytic contribution to education everything that we can learn from them on this matter? In her discerning essay on "Psychoanalysis and Education: Teaching Terminable and Interminable,"[10] Shoshana Felman strongly disagrees with what she sees as Catherine Millot's "reductive conception" (24) of psychoanalytic thinking about pedagogy. Millot, like many others, is mistaken in re-

ferring "exclusively to Lacan's or Freud's explicit *statements* about pedagogy, and thus fails to see the illocutionary force, the didactic function of the *utterance* as opposed to the mere content of the statement"
(24). Felman goes on to say that

> invariably, all existing psychoanalytically-inspired theories of pedagogy
> fail to address the question of the pedagogical speech-act of Freud
> himself, or of Lacan himself: what can be learnt about pedagogy not just
> from their theories (which only fragmentarily and indirectly deal with
> the issue of education) but from their way of *teaching* it, from their own
> practice as teachers, from their own pedagogical performance. (24)

Reading off from the respective teaching *styles* of Freud and Lacan
(both of whom she sees as exemplary teachers because they thought of
themselves as *students*: Freud of his own unconscious, and Lacan of
Freud's writings), Felman redefines psychoanalysis as a pedagogical
experience in itself, as a process which provides access to knowledge
hitherto denied to consciousness and which therefore affords a lesson
in cognition as well as miscognition. Consequently, what is needed is
not a conscious *application* of the psychoanalytic process but rather an
understanding of its *implications* for teaching. Psychoanalysis, as a
means of access to "information hitherto *unlearnable*" (27), demands a
new mode of learning, if only because it involves a different temporal
experience of learning. It proceeds instead through "breakthroughs,
leaps, discontinuities, regressions and deferred action" (27), thus challenging "the traditional pedagogical belief in intellectual perfectibility,
the progressive view of learning as a simple one-way road from ignorance to knowledge" (27).

Conversely, the idea of the imperfectability of knowledge is based
on the assumption that the unconscious eludes intentionality and
meaning. As Lacan puts it, "Analysis appears on the scene to announce
that there is *knowledge which does not know itself.*"[11] "Ignorance" is not
a simple lack of knowledge but is, rather, understood as an integral
part of the very structure of knowledge. That is why Lacan opens his
seminar entitled *Encore* by announcing that "I am here only to analyze
my own 'I don't want to know anything about it' " (*"je n'en veux rien
savoir"* — 9). Thus the material of analysis (or of teaching) is that which
is not remembered, what will not be memorized. Ignorance is not a passive state but an active *excluding from consciousness* (that is, repression)
whatever it does not want to know. "Teaching, like analysis, has to
deal not so much with *lack* of knowledge as with *resistances* to knowl-

edge" (30), and an analytically informed pedagogy would have to come to terms with what Lacan called "the passion for ignorance" (110). This refusal, then, is not so much a refusal of information as a refusal to acknowledge *one's own implication* in that information. For Felman, the truly revolutionary insight—from the lesson of Freud's and Lacan's rhetorical styles—consists in showing the ways in which *ignorance itself can teach us something*. But this is an insight with consequences for teachers as well as students, because as Lacan said, "There is no true teaching other than the teaching which succeeds in provoking in those who listen an insistence—this desire to know which can only emerge when they themselves have *taken the measure of ignorance as such*—of ignorance inasmuch as it is, as such, fertile—in the one who teaches as well."[12] Teaching is not therefore the transmission of ready-made knowledge, but the creation of a "new condition of knowledge—the creation of an original learning-disposition" (31). "What I teach you," says Lacan, "does nothing other than express the *condition* thanks to which what Freud says is possible" (368).

As we have seen, Millot's strongest doubts about the possibility of a psychoanalytically informed pedagogy are rooted in her fundamental mistrust of the pedagogical need to *use* the transference relation to maintain the student's belief in the teacher's knowledge and authority. Neither the teacher nor the teaching institution can afford to question, much less subvert, this belief. Felman, however, argues that the transference relation *can* be put into question and, furthermore, that this *must* be done if any real learning (as opposed to mere indoctrination) is to take place. Taking her lesson again from Lacan, she shows that psychoanalytic learning (which constantly serves as her pedagogical model) is always *dialogic*: "No knowledge," writes Lacan, "can be supported or transported by one alone."[13] In the analytical situation, the analyst listens to and is taught by the analysand's unconscious: "It is by structurally occupying the position of the analysand's unconscious, and by thus making himself a *student of the patient's knowledge*, that the analyst becomes the teacher—makes the patient learn what would otherwise remain forever inaccessible to him" (33). For learning to take place there must always be an Other. Knowledge is what is already there, but always in the Other. Thus it cannot be said that the teacher (or the student) *contains* knowledge, but that it comes about in the intersection of "two partially unconscious speeches which both say more than they know" (33). If we follow out the implications of this unique pedagogical process, the clear-cut opposition between analyst and analysand or between teacher and student disappears. What we finally come to understand is both the psychical necessity and the actual contingency of these shifting and interchangeable positions. The student becomes a teacher when he or she realizes that it is impossible to know everything, that to be a teacher one must never stop being a student. And the teacher can teach nothing other than the *way he or she learns*. For Felman, then, psychoanalytic teaching is pedagogically unique in that it is inherently and interminably self-critical. It is a didactic mode of "self-subversive self-reflection" (39).

In comparing these two arguments—Millot's and Felman's—one pessimistically refuting the idea of an analytical pedagogy and the other polemically claiming psychoanalysis as the only pedagogical practice worthy of the name, we have seen both the problems and the possibilities of a psychoanalytically orientated pedagogy. Keeping in mind the kinds of issues that have been raised concerning the psychoanalytic understanding of knowledge and authority, let us now turn to feminism in its equally precarious relation to institutionalized learning.

A Feminist Pedagogy?

Just as Freud felt compelled to pose the question, "Should psychoanalysis be taught at the university?"[14] feminists have wondered if feminism could be taught within the traditional institutions of education. (Freud answered his own question by asserting that the university stood only to gain by the inclusion in its curriculum of the teaching of psychoanalysis; psychoanalysis, however, could dispense entirely with the university without any loss to itself.) In "Teaching Feminist Theory,"[15] Paula Treichler's comprehensive survey of feminist attitudes toward teaching feminist theory, as well as their methods, it is immediately apparent that few feminists see the relation of feminism and traditional pedagogy as an entirely unproblematic one, while they are in essential agreement that feminist teaching methods must accommodate or reflect the political givens of feminism. With respect to feminism's problematic relation to the university, feminists seem to share Freud's cast of mind: they believe that the university can greatly benefit from incorporating feminism into the curriculum but are more dubious about what feminism receives in turn from its new-found academicization. Their doubts, as outlined in Treichler's essay, understandably include the debilitating effects of the continuing entrenched sexism of the university, the loss of feminist theory's political radicalness through the attempt to ensure its academic respectability, and the creation of an "elite" of feminist scholars who take their research cues from the university rather than the movement. But beyond these doubts looms an even larger danger in the incompatibility of feminist *ways of teaching* with the more typical pedagogical requirements of exclusiveness, authority, and hierarchy. It is in particular the feminist commitment to "making the personal political" that poses the greatest difficulties for "normal" pedagogical practices. Applying the lessons of the kind of consciousness-raising that grew up with the movement, feminist pedagogy seeks "to restore personal observation and interpretation as trustworthy sources of information about the world" (69). Further, it is often held that feminist theory and its research methods will bring about a new epistemology, one which will challenge the subject/object dichotomies endemic to the "discourse of the university." To give an idea of what these rather general ideas would mean to the feminist classroom, I will cite, as Treichler does, Marilyn J. Boxer's summary of feminism's alternative techniques:

> The double purpose of women's studies—to expose and redress the oppression of women—was reflected in widespread attempts to restructure the classroom experience of students and faculty. Circular arrangements of chairs, periodic small-group sessions, use of first names for instructors as well as students, assignments that required journal keeping, "reflection papers," cooperative projects, and collective modes of teaching with student participation, all sought to transfer to women's studies the contemporary feminist criticism of authority and the validation of every woman's experience. These techniques borrowed from the women's movement also were designed to combat the institutional hierarchy and professional exclusiveness that had been used to shut out women. (69)

Let us now look more closely at the feminist perspective on knowledge and authority implied in the very specific pedagogical goals and methods listed above. Since the issue of power and its hierarchized distribution has been of paramount concern to feminists, we shall turn first to the question of authority. The pedagogical techniques typically adopted in the feminist classroom, "use of first names for instructors as well as students," or "collective modes of teaching with student participation," for example, clearly aim toward a dispersal or even elimination of authority. The risk, of course, in aiming at or claiming the eradication of power relations is that the force and pervasiveness of those relations may be overlooked, "out of sight, out of mind." But can the feminist classroom afford to lose sight of the extreme power of the transferential relation, of the narcissism underlying the demands of both students and teachers, or the basically eroticized nature of learning (the constant appeal for recognition)? I do not want to offer a "wild analysis" of the feminist classroom, but I would like to point to some of the contradictory demands around authority which can be seen there.

A very straightforward example might be found in the role of the teacher in the feminist classroom. Ideally, she carries out a very deliberate self-undermining of her own authority by refusing to be an "authority" at all, or by insisting that the validation of knowledge issue not from her acquired grasp of the material but from the students' own experiences as women and through a collective working-through of the issues raised. Another demand, often just as conscious even when recognized as contradictory, conflicts with the demand that she relinquish her authority. The woman who is a feminist teacher is expected at the very least to be an exemplary feminist, if not a "role model." Much of the effectiveness of the teaching in fact lies in the students' acceptance of her as an appropriate representative of feminism. The teacher, in turn, wants and expects the students to be "like" her insofar as she would rather that they turn out to be feminists than not. Given feminism's tendency toward factionalism, it would also be difficult for her not to want the students to accept her idea of feminism (no matter how determinably pluralistic she attempts to be) as feminism *tout court*.

Feminism, then, like psychoanalysis, is characterized by its willful reliance on nonauthoritative knowledge. (The difficulty of separating authority and knowledge is suggested in the spectacle of the discursive ease with which my argument runs one into the other.) Psychoanalysis has recourse to dreams, slips, jokes, and other revelatory "errors" of speech and psyche, while feminism looks beyond the "scientific" certitudes about femininity to what can be learned instead from the personal observations and experiences of women. Psychoanalysis and feminism also have similar ideas about the ambiguous *site* of knowledge. In the analytic situation, as we have seen, knowledge is not contained in the Other, but in the interplay of two partially unconscious speeches, each of which does not (alone) know what it is saying. For feminism, knowledge is likewise unlocalizable, resulting from a collective endeavor which involves retrieving one's own feelings and experiences, and comparing them with those of other women, while working through the material under discussion. There are however some important differences. Whereas Freud declared psychoanalysis to be "interminable," feminism, as a political project, necessarily hopes for some sort of termination (a state of achieved sexual equality where feminism would no longer be necessary). Like certain forms of revisionist psychoanalysis (usually the American variety) feminism believes that it cannot function unless it offers the promise of a "cure" (of sexism, of the historical oppression of women). It must therefore promote the possibility of a progressive acquisition of knowledge the mastery of which (when linked to activism) would result in a solution to women's oppression. There is nothing wrong with this idea: it is an absolutely necessary one for any movement seeking to bring about a radical transformation of existing relations (knowledge *is* power).

It is important to recognize, though, that the feminist emphasis on educational democracy, instrumental knowledge, and a common-sense understanding of the world has familiar echoes in the tradition of a distinctively American pedagogy. (We should also remind ourselves that the feminist classroom is not an isolated enclave but very much part of the university and hence of the state apparatus, no matter how intentionally "alternative" it might be.) John Dewey and others proposed a broad program of American education that stressed the democratic broadening of the constituency and questioned the usefulness of abstractions that may have no useful consequences. The American classroom is therefore geared toward practicality and "learning by doing." In recent years it has become a common enough claim that the advent of mass culture and the instrumental model of American pedagogy have colluded in producing students who are enslaved to the "concrete" and capable only of the most literal kind of thinking. Reality is dissolved into objecthood; empiricism claims the classroom as its laboratory.[16] Even if one believes that some kind of conceptual or critical thinking still occasionally occurs in the American classroom, the feminist classroom, can, ironically, look like the perfect embodiment of a Deweyesque instrumentalism in its demand for practical knowledge stemming from observation and experience rather than useless ("male") abstraction.

Feminism and Psychoanalysis Together?

Is it, then, on the question of empiricism that psychoanalytic and feminist pedagogy are most at odds? As Felman suggested, the didactic mode of psychoanalysis is one of "self-subversive self-reflection." This formula means that the analysand is required not only to recall and speak about past experiences (or dreams or fantasies) but also to *interpret* that speech to see what else might be hidden or contained there. "Experience" is not then a phenomenal reality simply to be retrieved and made "conscious" through language. Rather, the speech that the analysand uses to report or relate that experience is the material for analysis, much more so than the experience "itself." Was it not, indeed, the increasing emphasis in Freud's work on the importance of fantasy to our psychical lives that challenged the very notion of experience "itself?" In his analysis of the Wolf Man, for example, Freud questions whether the events that the Wolf Man recalls (various sexual scenes) ever took place. (He goes on to say, however, that it is not necessary for an event to have occurred for it to have an existence in concrete retrospective effects.) Feminism, by contrast, cannot afford to question either the reality of the woman's experience or the conscious credibility of her speech. This is because feminism's struggle is waged precisely against the historical denial of the value of women's experience as well as the refusal to believe that women are capable of giving a coherent account of that experience.

Clearly it is ironic that feminism should have come to be so closely aligned with empiricism, because feminist thinking, like psychoanalytic theory, constitutes one of the most crucial historical (and political) challenges to empiricism. Feminism shares with psychoanalysis a strong commitment to exposing the "naturally" given or socially self-evident forms of everyday life and language. Through its attention to symptoms, slips of the tongue, and dreams, psychoanalysis radically puts into question empiricism's reliance on observation and experience. Feminism, too, seeks to penetrate beneath the surface of observable phenomena and question not only the presumption of women's "natural" qualities but also the way in which the social system rationalizes those qualities into structures of inequality (sexual division of labor, gender-based wage scales, etc.). The greatest obstacles to the social changes that could be wrought by feminism are in fact those entrenched ideas that are based on "common sense," or that which is "obvious" or "natural" about women.

In a recent article, "Femininity and its Discontents," Jacqueline Rose offers an example of anti-empiricist thinking that shows important links between feminism and psychoanalysis.[17] She first discusses recent work by feminist historians[18] that demonstrates how social policy decisions (such as the Contagious Diseases Act of the 1860s) base themselves on specific qualitative categories of femininity—diseased, degenerate, hysterical, etc.; such women are then claimed to be in need of incarceration, regulation, reproductive restraints, etc. These categories are thus constructed on the basis of that which is "obvious" or "self-evident" about women's nature or anatomy (for example, fragility, underdeveloped sense of morality, sexual promiscuity, or an innate tendency toward hysteria). Rose goes on to argue that Freud's contribution to the study of hysteria helped to undermine these social categories of the "visible" which were so detrimental to women. Freud's earliest work on hysteria was under Charcot at the Salpetrière Clinic in Paris, a hospital for women who were considered to be the dregs of society. Charcot's achievement was to rescue hysterics from the closed category of sexual malingerers and to see their condition as a specific and acknowledged disease. The problem with Charcot's approach, however, was that he believed that hysteria was a degenerate, hereditary disease as well as a particular "type" of deviant behavior that was visible to the eye (thus the thousands of notorious Salpetrière photographs of women frozen into "hysterical" poses). Freud's intervention was two-fold. First, he questioned the idea that one could recognize a hysteric simply by looking at her body and the visible evidence of her symptoms. Second, he argued that the unconscious mental processes that he himself discovered while studying hysteria (displacement, repression, etc.) were to be found in every adult. Freud's approach thus challenged the fixed perception of hysteria as a mode of classifying certain degenerate and isolated individuals, and shifted this category into the center of everybody's psychic experience. Freud's discoveries, of course, are based on assumptions about the fundamental discontinuity of psychic life, assumptions that led him to posit the existence of the unconscious. The difficulty of teaching feminism and psychoanalysis together is that they have the same project of exposing the ideologies of "common sense" and the "visible" only insofar as feminism accepts the idea of the unconscious and

seeks to engage in a similar effort of "self-subversive self-reflection."
(A discussion of how the latter is and is not like feminist "consciousness-raising" would be too long to include here.) To accept the idea of
the unconscious, however, brings with it what many feminists view as
unwanted epistemological baggage: the hypotheses of the instability
of language and identity, the narcissism underlying all human relations, permanent psychical conflict, infantile sexuality, the pervasiveness and strength of transferential relations, and the links between intellectual activity and infantile sexual investigation, among others. As
Rose reminds us, psychoanalysis is clearly not a "utopianism of the
psyche" (18).

Ultimately, however, the greatest obstacle to bringing feminism
and psychoanalysis together on any common ground, pedagogical or
otherwise, is the very different relation each has to the question of
"identity." To be either a movement or a discipline, feminism *must*
presuppose the category "woman." Although the content of this category may be variously construed according to the aims of the analysis—for example, "victim" of a transhistorical male dominance or
"author" of a creative work giving voice to women's concerns—a
"feminine identity" has to be presumed even when (necessarily) citing
the given historical varieties of "woman," individual women, etc. It is
politically necessary to claim that there is a class or group of humans
("women") that is universally oppressed (by "men," "patriarchy,"
etc.) because no movement can constitute itself without notions of
identity and commonality. This clear need, however, conflicts sharply
with the refusal of psychoanalysis theoretically to posit a specifically
feminine (or masculine) identity. As Freud put it: "In conformity with
its peculiar nature, psychoanalysis does not try to describe what a
woman is—that would be a task it could scarcely perform—but sets
about enquiring how she comes into being."[19] Psychoanalysis does
not accept that "men and women, males and females, *exist*" (Juliet
Mitchell),[20] but rather seeks to describe and analyze the human laws
which determine sexual difference. The most striking formulation of
psychoanalysis's commitment to anti-essentialism can be found in
Jacques Lacan's statement that "The woman does not exist" (*La femme
n'existe pas*). Lacan does not mean by this that there are no real women
in the world but rather that there is no universal feminine essence, and
that what we take to be femininity is only a fantasmatic construction
used to support *the very idea of identity as complete and continuous with
itself* (the fantasy of wholeness and free access to one's "self"). The dis-

tance between the very different theoretical and political needs of psychoanalysis and feminism on the question of identity is perhaps best summed up in the contrast between the notorious bravura of "The woman does not exist" and Sojourner Truth's effectively polemical "Ain't I a woman?"[21] We have here, in my rather outrageous juxtaposition of Jacques Lacan and Sojourner Truth, two ideas or strategies that are vitally important to feminism, yet which appear completely at odds. Feminism, like psychoanalysis, must argue against the historical claim that all women are in essence alike, or that femininity is something that is self-evident, because it knows very well the kinds of stereotyped qualities that are invariably attributed to this feminine essence, and always to the detriment of women. It is, however, sometimes politically expedient to make the personal claim that one is a woman, and it is an assertion that can have immediate and concrete political effects. Sojourner Truth's famous declaration disguised as a question, "Ain't I a woman?" was a speech given in response to those who, in fact, refused to say that she was a woman because they refused to include black women in the category of womanhood. Sojourner Truth's femininity or womanness was not at all self-evident to many of those listening to her memorable speech: it was something for which she had to fight, and the establishment of that identity was crucial to her political struggle. Is there, then, any way out of this impasse of radically opposed ideas about the necessity or nonnecessity of an "identity"?

One of the paradoxes of contemporary feminism has been the strength of its assertion of an identity for women at precisely the historical moment when such accounts of individual subjectivity are being radically called into question by Lacan, Althusser, Derrida, and Foucault, among others. But in these new accounts of identity and individual subjectivity, feminism may discover ways to rethink the question of identity that not only acknowledge the absolute political necessity of *an identity* for women (a political one) but also maintains the equal necessity of examining "identity" (or "femininity") as an epistemological, metaphysical, or ideological category. These new accounts often argue that each individual comprises several "identities." One's identity for example as a legal subject does not always coincide with one's identity as a sexual or medical subject. Each individual "exists" only as a nexus of various and *sometimes contradictory* subjectivities which are legislated or assumed, either consciously or unconsciously. This allows us to support a more complex working definition of subjectivity as well as a firmer understanding of the conflicts and contradictions at work in our social and psychical makeup. Like the psychoanalytical emphasis on the importance of the unconscious and fantasy in our lives, this approach goes beyond those easy claims for conscious, controlled, or deliberate political action. But in its acknowledged political success and longstanding pledge to the idea that "the personal is political," it is perhaps feminism that can most productively incorporate these newer and more complex notions of subjectivity without succumbing to any political fatalism.

Another way to avoid the absolute opposition between an empirical subject and a psychical subject, and again to argue for a notion of multiple identities, is to acknowledge that political struggles (here, specifically, women's struggles) develop on all fronts (economic, ideological, political). These conditions often require the preservation, for longer or shorter periods, of presuppositions (like "woman" or "femininity") that will have to be questioned later or from someplace other than the point of actual, daily confrontation. It has to be accepted, moreover, that these presuppositions must and will be challenged because they are ideas that belong so solidly to the structures that are under attack: "Woman" or "Femininity" as the major allegory of Truth in western discourse, or as the fantasmatic other of its supposed complement, "masculinity."[22] It is psychoanalysis, of course, which first proposed the concept of the "split subject" (a subject divided against itself in its conflicting desires and conflictual responses to demands) that has become so crucial to these newer approaches to the question of subjectivity. Although there is an obvious tension or difference between the notions of identity found in psychoanalysis and feminism, it is through teaching them together that we can begin to fully determine what might now be gained from acknowledging or incorporating these more complex ideas about subjectivity at the very moment that feminism continues its necessary effort to forge a new identity for women.

In my discussion of the problems of teaching feminism and psychoanalysis together, I have neglected the difficulties that are specific to teaching psychoanalysis in relation to a progressive political movement such as feminism *in America today*. There are some very real and important reasons why American feminism has rejected psychoanalysis, reasons that can help us to understand why we do not have in America the kind of serious debate about feminism and psychoanalysis that is presently taking place in other countries like England and

France; perhaps, for the same reasons, American students experience difficulties in grasping the relation between feminism and psychoanalysis. In its move to America, psychoanalysis underwent both a theoretical retreat from the more radical of Freud's discoveries as well as an atrophication of its own institutional structures. The turn toward an adjustment-oriented ego psychology and the medicalization of the profession, with the consequent exclusion of women, was largely the result of the conservatism forced upon the emigré analysts (many of whom had been very active in European leftist politics) seeking respectability in an America that valued "professionalism" above all else.[23] Psychoanalysis in this country is an admittedly conservative institution. In Britain, by contrast, psychoanalysis is still considered socially and professionally "marginal," and since (following Freud's suggestion) analysts are not required to be doctors, there are many lay practitioners. In addition, much of the most important psychoanalytic work in England has been carried out by women like Anna Freud, Melanie Klein, Joan Rivière, Susan Isaacs, Paula Heimann, and, more recently, Juliet Mitchell.[24] French psychoanalysis has, of course, been marked by the iconoclastic presence of Lacan's anti-institutionalism, which encouraged would-be analysts to decide for themselves when they were ready to practice, and whose teachings have been readily assimilated to leftist politics.[25] Similarly, the names of certain women analysts are central to French psychoanalytic theory and its politics — Julia Kristeva, Catherine Clément, Luce Irigaray, Michèle Montrelay, and Eugènie Lemoine-Luccioni, among others. Thus in a very practical way it is important in a course on feminism and psychoanalysis to get across to the students the idea that "psychoanalysis" is not a homogeneous institution, nor does it exist solely in the politically and culturally impoverished version of it familiar to us in America, which has been so rightfully criticized by feminists.

In looking at the intertwined pedagogical and theoretical difficulties of teaching a course on feminism and psychoanalysis, I hope I have shown not only that it is *not* an "impossible" task, but also that teaching them together is perhaps the most productive way of teaching either feminism or psychoanalysis on its own. It is not a question of what feminism holds out for psychoanalysis or what psychoanalysis has to offer feminism, but how each invites the other to examine its relation to knowledge and authority as well as its understanding of identity and sexual difference.

NOTES

Notes

Preface

1. Joan W. Scott, "Gender: A Useful Category of Historical Analysis," *The American Historical Review* vol. 91, no. 5 (December 1986) 1056. Other useful recent discussions of the term "gender" as an analytic category include: Francine Wattman Frank and Paula A. Treichler, "Scholarship, Feminism, and Language Change" (section on "Sex and Gender"), introduction to the MLA's forthcoming *Language, Gender and Professional Writing: Theoretical Approaches and Guidelines for Nonsexist Usage*; Jane Flax, "Postmodernism and Gender Relations in Feminist Theory," *Signs* vol. 12, no. 4 (1987); and Linda Alcoff, "Cultural Feminism versus Post-Structuralism: The Identity Crisis in Feminist Theory," *Signs* vol. 13, no. 3 (1988).

2. Teresa de Lauretis, *Technologies of Gender* (Bloomington: Indiana University Press, 1987).

3. Michèle Barrett, "Ideology and the Cultural Production of Gender," *Feminist Criticism and Social Change: Sex, Class and Race in Literature and Culture*, eds. Judith Newton and Deborah Rosenfelt (New York and London: Methuen, 1985) 65–85.

4. A claim made by de Lauretis, for example, in *Technologies of Gender*: 2.

5. See note 1 for reference.

6. Jacqueline Rose, "Femininity and its Discontents," *Sexuality in the Field of Vision* (London: Verso, 1986) 101.

7. In feminist writing on psychoanalysis it is Jacqueline Rose who has most emphasized the extreme difficulty of taking up and maintaining a sexual identity at all. See especially, "Feminine Sexuality: Jacques Lacan and the *école freudienne*," *Sexuality in the Field of Vision*.

8. Laura Kipnis, "Feminism: The Political Conscience of Postmodernism?", *Universal Abandon? The Politics of Postmodernism*, ed. Andrew Ross (Minneapolis: University of Minnesota Press, 1988).

9. See, for example, Judith Walkowitz, *Prostitution and Victorian Society: Women, Class and the State* (Cambridge: Cambridge University Press, 1980); Barbara Taylor, *Eve and the New Jerusalem* (London: Virago, 1984); or, for a very strange twist on the hegemonic imbalance of oppression, complicity, and resistance as it concerns women, see Claudia Koonz, *Mothers in the Fatherland: Women, the Family and Nazi Politics* (New York: St. Martin's Press, 1987).

10. Rosalind Delmar, "What is Feminism?", *What is Feminism?*, eds. Juliet Mitchell and Ann Oakley (Oxford: Basil Blackwell, 1986) 28.

11. That the impossibility or failure of a natural unity of all women can be made into a positive politics of strategically created alliances is most forcefully presented in the

185

work of Ernesto Laclau and Chantal Mouffe. See *Hegemony and Socialist Strategy: Towards a Radical Democratic Politics* (London: Verso, 1985). This point is taken up and discussed in the interview with the editors of *m/f*, Parveen Adams and Elizabeth Cowie, in *m/f* nos. 11–12 (the "Last Issue," 1986).

12. See, for example, Homi Bhabha's use of the psychoanalytic account of paranoia to describe the subjective mechanisms of colonial authority, in "Sly Civility," *October* no. 34 (Fall 1985) 71–80. And in his essay "What Does the Black Man Want?" he explicates Frantz Fanon's use of psychoanalysis "in articulating the problem of colonial cultural alienation in the psychoanalytic language of demand and desire." *New Formations* no. 1 (Spring 1987) 118–24. This essay also appears as an introduction to Fanon's *Black Skin, White Masks* (London: Pluto, 1986).

CHAPTER 1. *The Avant-Garde and Its Imaginary*

1. Christian Metz, "Le signifiant imaginaire," *Communications* no. 23 (May 1975), translated by Ben Brewster, under the title "The Imaginary Signifier," *Screen* vol. 16, no. 2 (Summer 1975); Thierry Kuntzel, "Le travail du film, 2," *Communications* no. 23 (May 1975), "Savoir, pouvoir, voir," *Ça Cinéma* nos. 7–8 (May 1975); Jean-Louis Baudry, "Cinéma: effets idéologiques produits par l'appareil de base," *Cinéthique* nos. 7–8 (1970), trans. Alan Williams, *Film Quarterly* vol. 27, no. 2 (Winter 1974–75); "Le dispositif: approches métapsychologiques de l'impression de réalité," *Communications* no. 23 (May 1975), trans. Bertrand Augst and Jean Andrews, "The Apparatus," *Camera Obscura* no. 1 (Dec. 1976); Raymond Bellour, "Le cinéma et l'hypnose," unpublished lectures presented in his seminar at the Centre Universitaire Américain du Cinéma, Paris, Spring 1977.

2. Malcolm Le Grice, *Abstract Film and Beyond* (London: Studio Vista, 1977); Peter Gidal, *Structural Film Anthology* (London: British Film Institute, 1976). Deke Dusinberre's article "St. George in the Forest," *Afterimage* no. 6 (Summer 1976) offers a good overview of the different strains of the English avant-garde. According to Dusinberre, the writings of Gidal and Le Grice would not be representative of the whole English avant-garde, and he even claims that "the theoretical ambitions of those filmmakers who write about film (Gidal, Le Grice) lead to contributions which tend to complicate and/or obfuscate the immediate issues" (17). However, many of their premises are taken up throughout the English Co-op movement. For example, see the first issue (Feb. 1977) of the English journal *Readings*, edited by Annabel Nicolson and Paul Burwell.

3. Throughout *Abstract Film and Beyond* "abstract" and "formal" are used somewhat interchangeably. In the first part of the book Le Grice uses the term "abstract," "very much as it has come to be generally applied to the visual arts, implying 'non-representational'." But in chapter three he gives it a more general meaning: "Abstract implies the separation of qualities, aspects or generalizations from particular interests," that is abstract art as analytic work which "seeks to avoid representation in favor of non-referential elements" (32). Thus a representational film (in the photographic sense) could contain some "abstract" tendencies. Le Grice says that if it were not for the common use of "abstract," "concrete" would be better.

4. I realize that there is often a discrepancy between the theoretical writings of these filmmakers and the actual effects of their films. They do, however, consider their theoretical writings and their theoretical film-work to be homologous (but not identical); and the films are generated from their theoretical presuppositions. My interest here is to analyze the limits and the possibilities of those presuppositions for offering a theoretical matrix for a radical film practice.

5. Anne Cottringer's "On Peter Gidal's Theory and Definition of Structural/Materialist Film" discusses Gidal's use of the concept "materialism." *Afterimage* no. 6

(Summer 1976): 86–95. See also Ben Brewster's review of *Structural Film Anthology, Screen* vol. 17, no. 4 (Winter 1976–77): 117–20.

6. Peter Gidal, "Interview with Hollis Frampton," *Structural Film Anthology* 71.

7. Catherine Clément has given a very concise overview of the imaginary and symbolic in Lacan's system:

> The imaginary, the symbolic and the real constitute the *structure of the subject* in Lacan's system. We will give two formulations of it, both representing what Lacan calls diagram L. The diagram in question divides the subject (S) into four points that represent the instances that determine it: O, the Other; o' or I, the Ego; o, the other of the other, but under the irreducible form of the partial object of desire (object o). Thus the diagram in its simplified form ("D'une question préliminaire à tout traitement possible de la psychose," *Ecrits*, 1966):

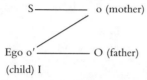

> This structure, which allows us to disintricate the axes of the real, the symbolic and the imaginary, must be placed in relation to the Oedipus complex, such as Freud formulated it, as a *triangle*: the father, the mother and the infant-subject between the two, for whom all the difficulty of being consists in situating himself between the two parental figures. The whole history of the Oedipus complex occurs in this see-sawing between the figures of the mother and the father; the "liquidation" of the Oedipus complex signifies, in a symbolic fashion, the entry into life, the end of infancy, the stabilization of identification. The structure of the subject as described by Lacan takes up these three terms, but transforms them in adding a fourth term: the subject himself, neither father, nor infant, nor mother, but the structure made up of these three terms. The Other is the place of Law, of cultural order. It is the place of the father which gives this law its particular figure; the partial object, called "little o," is the place of impossible unsatisfying desire, of the giant body of the mother before the separation, of her body, then, forbidden by the Law; it is very much the place of the mother, total and partial at the same time, impossible to attain; finally, the o', the place of the infant, which depends upon the other two places. There remains the subject. It is on the side of the real, whose entry into play appears as its being excluded from the structure, or rather *foreclosed*: present and determinant, but nonapparent and repressed, no longer there. The play of signifiers is the meeting of the two axes, imaginary and symbolic: the imaginary, between the place of the Ego and the place of the object of desire; the symbolic, between the Other and the absent subject of the combination. Thus is made precise the respective situations of the two instances; the symbolic is the order that establishes the subject in language, in *its* language, that of its father, of his father; the imaginary is that which reflects desire in the image that the subject has of himself. On the side of the imaginary is variety, diversity, the multiplicity of objects of desire in one's life; on the side of the symbolic is unicity, determination, the structuration of time. The imaginary, which comes to be hooked onto the panoply of the symbolic, lets itself be represented through the metaphor of *accessories*: objects of disguises, "the set of imaginary figures," figures of theater; meanwhile the symbolic, in the panoply, represents the support to which the variables of the subject attach themselves. (*La Psychanalyse*, eds. Catherine Clément, François Gantheret, Bernard Mérigot (Paris: Larousse, 1976): 50.)

The imaginary is the order of perception, whereas the symbolic is the discursive order. Serge Leclaire explains the relation of the Imaginary to the Symbolic and the Real in this way:

The experience of the Real presupposes the simultaneous use of two correlative functions, the Imaginary function and the Symbolic function. That is Imaginary which, like shadows, has no existence of its own, and yet whoseabsence, in the light of life, cannot be conceived; that which, without power of distinction inundates singularity and thus escapes any truly rational grasp. That is Imaginary which is irremediably opposed or which is indistinctly confused, without any dialectical movement; the dream is Imaginary . . . just as long as it is not interpreted. . . . No symbol can do without Imaginary support. ("A la recherche des principles d'une psychothérapie des psychoses," *L'Evolution Psychiatrique* (1958): 377– 411.)

Anthony Wilden adds to his above translation of Leclaire's text:

The topographical regression of "dream thoughts" to images in the dream might be described as a process of the Symbolic becoming Imaginary. (*The Language of the Self: The Function of Language in Psychoanalysis*, translations from Jacques Lacan with notes and commentary (Dell, 1968): 92.)

8. Translations are mine throughout the essay unless otherwise noted.

9. Melanie Klein, "Infantile Anxiety Situations Reflected in a Work of Art and in the Creative Impulse" (1929), *Contributions to Psychoanalysis* (London: Hogarth Press): 227–35.

10. *Christian Metz, Le signifiant imaginaire: Psychanalyse et cinéma* (Paris: Editions 10/18, 1977): 177–371.

11. Stephen Heath, "Narrative Space," *Screen*, vol. 17, no. 3 (Autumn 1976): 68–112.

12. See note 1 for references.

13. See note 1 for references. For a useful introduction to Baudry's work, see Bertrand Augst, "The Apparatus: An Introduction," *Camera Obscura* no. 1 (Dec. 1976): 97–101.

14. Sigmund Freud, *The Interpretation of Dreams* (New York: Avon Books, 1965): 526.

15. Beaumont Newhall, *The History of Photography* (New York: Museum of Modern Art Press, 1965).

16. Piera Aulagnier-Spairani, "Le 'désir de savoir' dans ses rapports à la transgression," *L'inconscient* no. 1 (January 1967): 109–25.

17. There are also ideological reasons for this emphasis in Le Grice and Gidal. Gidal takes the Althusserian dichotomy between ideology and science even further than Althusser himself in his belief in the possibility of a pure (i.e., non-ideological) scientific theory and a pure practice of that theory. Le Grice's problematic notion of "knowledge" arises from an idealist theory of history as progressive evolution (his book charts an inevitable "tendency" with its achievements, regressions, and successes in the direction of a greater abstraction and rationality) and a belief in technology (science) as a neutral and objective tool in helping to move from an outmoded form of consciousness to a more radical (more "aware") form of consciousness.

18. Jacques Lacan, *Le séminaire XI: Les quatre concepts fondamentaux de la psychoanalyse* (Paris: Seuil, 1973): 65–109.

19. Ricciotto Canudo, "L'usine aux images," *L'art du cinéma*, ed. Pierre L'Herminier (Paris: Seghers, 1960).

20. This work was presented in his seminar at the Centre Universitaire Américain du Cinéma, Paris, Spring 1977.

21. Jacques Lacan, "Le stade du miroir comme formateur de la fonction de Je," *Ecrits* (Paris: Seuil, 1966): 93–100. Translated as "The Mirror-Phase as Formative of the Function of the I," *New Left Review* no. 51 (Sept.–Oct. 1968): 71– 77.

22. Jacques Lacan, "Du regard comme objet petit *a*," *Le séminaire XI: Les quatre concepts fondamentaux de la psychanalyse* (Paris: Seuil, 1973): 65–109.

23. There is a tendency toward a kind of pseudo-scientism in much recent avant-garde work, in which the artists make references to various areas of experimental research to legitimate their work. This tactic is a false solution to the minimalist problem of attempting to go beyond an author-oriented aesthetic by replacing subjectivity with the "objectivity" of science. One of the problems with this tendency is that one cannot be sure that the present state of psychophysiological research could even permit distinguishing neatly between these different levels (conscious, preconscious, unconscious) or be able to determine if a certain "psychological reaction" was a *direct* consequence of certain "physical actions."

24. Lacan's explication of "object small o" with the example of the *fort-da* game (from *Le séminaire XI*, 60):

> This spool is not the mother reduced to a little ball . . . it is a little something of the subject which is detached from him while still being very much a part of him. This is the place to say, with Aristotle's imitation, that man thinks with his object. It is with his object that the infant leaps the boundaries of his domain now transformed into holes, shafts, and with which he commences his incantation. If it is true that the signifier is the first mark of the subject, how not to recognize here—from the single fact that this game is accompanied by one of the first oppositions to appear—that the object to which this opposition is applied in the act, the spool, is what we designate as the subject. To this object, we will give to it, finally, its name in the Lacanian algebra—small o.

25. Of course, for Lacan, if the look is taken in the same dialectic as the unconscious, then vision too is organized in relation to the insufficiency which is the castration complex. In this article I will not go into the problematic status of castration as *the* lack which retrospectively gives symbolic significance to all the other experiences of loss.

26. Metz, "The Imaginary Signifier," section III. 4, "On the idealist theory of the cinema": 54–56.

27. Julia Kristeva, "Le sujet en procès: le langage poétique," *L'identité*, eds. Julia Kristeva et al. (Paris: Grasset & Fasquelle, 1977): 238.

28. Kristeva: 238.

29. The background for this discussion of fetishism in relation to film was first formulated in a paper I wrote with Sandy Flitterman for Thierry Kuntzel's "Travail du film" seminar at the Centre Universitaire Américain du Cinéma, Paris, November 1976.

30. Guy Rosolato, "Difficultés à surmonter pour une esthétique psychoanalytique," *Essais sur le Symbolique* (Paris: Gallimard, 1965): 121–28.

31. However precarious the subject's control of that experience might actually be, as Jacqueline Rose points out in "The Imaginary—the Insufficient Signifier" (seminar paper, British Film Institute Education Advisory Service, Nov. 1975). She cites Lacan for his discussion of the potential reversibility of this situation: the subject can always be seized by the object of his own look, thus becoming the *object* of representation.

32. Metz, "The Imaginary Signifier": 15.

33. Roland Barthes, "En sortant du cinéma," *Communications* no. 23 (May 1975): 107.

34. Stephen Heath, "Narrative Space": 109.

CHAPTER 2. The Avant-Garde: Histories and Theories

1. Marilyn Singer, ed., *A History of the American Avant-Garde Cinema* (The American Federation of the Arts, 1976).

2. Christian Metz, "The Imaginary Signifier," trans. Ben Brewster, *Screen* vol. 16, no. 2 (Summer 1985): 24.

3. P. Adams Sitney, ed., *The Essential Cinema: Essays on the Films in the Collection of Anthology Film Archives* (New York: New York University Press and Anthology Film Archives, 1975). A 130-page bibliography of the films in the Anthology collection is included as an appendix.

4. Annette Michelson, "Toward Snow," *Artforum* (June 1971): 30.

5. Michelson 32.

6. Maurice Merleau-Ponty, "The Film and the New Psychology," *Sense and Nonsense* (Evanston: Northwestern University Press, 1964): 48–59.

7. P. Adams Sitney, however, makes a provocative link between phenomenology in cinema and American experimental film as a grand Romantic metaphor in his study of the "visionary" film, a type of film which he sees as predominant throughout the history of the American avant-garde. *Visionary Film: The American Avant-Garde* (New York: Oxford University Press, 1974): 422.

8. Maurice Merleau-Ponty, *Phénoménologie de la perception* (Paris: Gallimard, 1945): ii.

9. See, for example, "*Le défilement*: A View in Close-up," *Camera Obscura* no. 2 (1978): 51–65.

10. See also on p. 55 Metz's description of the resemblance between the subject of phenomenology and cinema: "The '*there is*' of phenomenology proper (philosophical phenomenology) as an ontic revelation to a perceiving-subject (= "perceptual *cogito*"), to a subject for which alone there can be anything, has close and precise affinities with the inauguration of the cinematic signifier in the ego as I have tried to define it, with the spectator falling back on himself as a pure instance of perception, the whole of the perceived being 'over the way'."

11. Michael Snow, Catalog of the 1967 Knokke-le-Zoute Film Festival.

CHAPTER 3. "A Certain Refusal of Difference": Feminism and Film Theory

1. Jacqueline Rose, *The Cinema in the Eighties: Proceedings of the Meeting* (Venice: Edizioni "La Biennale di Venezia," 1980): 24.

2. Claire Johnston, "Dorothy Arzner: Critical Strategies," and Pam Cook, "Approaching the Work of Dorothy Arzner," *The Work of Dorothy Arzner: Towards a Feminist Cinema*, ed. Claire Johnston (London: British Film Institute, 1975); Pam Cook and Claire Johnston, "The Place of Woman in the Cinema of Raoul Walsh," *Raoul Walsh*, ed. Phil Hardy (Edinburgh: Edinburgh Film Festival Publication, 1974).

3. Johnston, "Dorothy Arzner": 4.

4. Laura Mulvey, "Visual Pleasure and Narrative Cinema," *Screen* vol. 16, no. 3 (Autumn 1975): 6–18.

5. Selected articles on the textual analysis of film: Raymond Bellour, "Le blocage symbolique" (on *North by Northwest*), *Communications* (special issue on psychoanalysis and cinema) no. 23 (1975): 235–350; Thierry Kuntzel, "The Film-Work, 2" (on *The Most Dangerous Game*), *Camera Obscura* no. 5 (Spring 1980): 7–68; Stephen Heath, "Film and System: Terms of Analysis: (on *Touch of Evil*), *Screen* vol. 15, no. 1 (Spring 1975): 7–77, and no. 2 (Summer 1975): 91–113. For an incisive criticism of the "rupture thesis" in Claire Johnston's film analyses from the point of view of the work on the textual analysis of film, see Janet Bergstrom, "Rereading the Work of Claire Johnston," *Camera Obscura* nos. 3–4 (Summer 1979): 21–31.

6. There is, however, a notable difference of emphasis in Bellour and Heath's textual analyses. Bellour insists throughout his work on the classical film's striking ability to

"resolve" itself, primarily through what he calls the "repetition-resolution" effect. Heath, while adding considerably to the argument for the aim of classical film toward achieving "homeostasis" through the resolution of textual contradictions, prefers to characterize this tendency as an illusionistic effect of the economy of classical film rather than a fact of its textual organization. For Heath, following Barthes, believes that there is always an excess that escapes any narrative system, a loss that is nonetheless fundamental to the movement or narrative progression of the film. He is also concerned to show how the woman in the film comes to represent, through the problem of defining and containing her sexuality, the contradictions and difficulties of the textual system itself.

7. Janet Bergstrom, "Enunciation and Sexual Difference," *Camera Obscura* nos. 3–4 (Summer 1979): 47.

8. Janet Bergstrom, "Alternation, Segmentation, Hypnosis: Interview with Raymond Bellour," *Camera Obscura* nos. 3–4 (Summer 1979): 97.

9. Rose, *Cinema in the Eighties*: 24.

10. Jacqueline Rose, "Paranoia and the Film System," *Screen* vol. 17, no. 4 (Winter 1976–77): 85–104.

11. Raymond Bellour, "*Les Oiseaux*: analyse d'une séquence," *Cahiers du Cinéma* no. 219 (October 1969). A translation, "*The Birds*: Analysis of a Sequence," is available in mimeographed form from the British Film Institute Education Advisory Service.

12. Bellour, "Le blocage symbolique." See note 5 for full reference.

13. Raymond Bellour, "Psychosis, Neurosis, Perversion," *Camera Obscura* nos. 3–4 (Summer 1979): 105–32.

14. Bergstrom, "Alternation, Segmentation, Hypnosis": 93.

15. Bergstrom, "Enunciation and Sexual Difference."

16. Sigmund Freud, " 'A child is being beaten': A Contribution to the Study of the Origin of Sexual Perversions" (1919), *The Standard Edition of the Complete Psychological Works of Sigmund Freud*, ed. James Strachey (London: The Hogarth Press and the Institute of Psychoanalysis, 1958), vol. 17: 186.

17. Bergstrom, "Enunciation and Sexual Difference": 57–58.

18. Mary Ann Doane, "*Caught* and *Rebecca*: The Inscription of Femininity as Absence," *enclitic* vol. 5, no. 2 (Fall 1981); 6, no. 1 (Spring 1982). Similar to Doane's attempt to give an account of films where the problems specific to feminine sexuality predominate is Laura Mulvey's "Afterthoughts on 'Visual Pleasure and Narrative Cinema' Inspired by *Duel in the Sun*," *Framework* vol. 6, no. 15–17 (1981). In this "postscript" to her influential article, Mulvey questions her own earlier idea that the modes of cinematic pleasure and identification of Hollywood film impose a masculine point of view on the spectator. She now argues that the female spectator is much more than a simply alienated one. She demonstrates her point by discussing films in which a central female protagonist struggles and finally fails to achieve a stable feminine identity (e.g., Pearl as a tomboy in *Duel in the Sun*). This struggle mirrors that of the female spectator in her attempt to find a stable feminine identity, based as her sexuality is in the perpetual possibility of regression to the phallic phase. She concludes that the female spectator is a transvestite, an idea that can be interestingly compared to Mary Ann Doane's notion of femininity as "masquerade" (see note 19).

19. Mary Ann Doane, "Film and the Masquerade—Theorising the Female Spectator," *Screen* vol. 23, nos. 3–4 (September–October 1982): 74–87.

20. I have not mentioned in this article the important feminist critiques of the theories of the "apparatus" which are complementary to the work on point of view, identification, and narrative discussed here. For a discussion of these critiques, see my "Feminism, Film Theory and the Bachelor Machines" in chapter 4 of this volume.

21. For a discussion of enunciation and point of view in the films of Chantal Akerman, see Janet Bergstrom, *"Jeanne Dielman, 23 Quai du Commerce, 1080 Bruxelles," Camera Obscura* no. 2 (Fall 1977): 114–21; Janet Bergstrom, "The Avant-Garde: Histories and Theories" (Part II), *Screen* vol. 19, no. 3 (Autumn 1978): 126–27.

22. Janet Bergstrom, "Yvonne Rainer: An Introduction," *Camera Obscura* no. 1 (Fall 1976): 62.

23. My comments here are based upon Elisabeth Lyon's discussion of fantasy, desire, and sexual difference in *India Song*, "The Cinema of Lol V. Stein," *Camera Obscura* no. 6 (Fall 1980): 7–41. Joan Copjec describes how repetition works very differently from Bellour's description of it in classical film in *India Song* and its "remake," *Son nom de Venise dans Calcutta désert*, in *"India Song/Son nom de Venise dans Calcutta désert*: The Compulsion to Repeat," *October* no. 17 (Summer 1981): 37–52.

CHAPTER 4. *Feminism, Film Theory, and the Bachelor Machines*

1. Michel Carrouges, *Les Machines Célibataires* (Paris: Le Chêne, 1954); see also the catalog with essays on the "Bachelor Machines" exhibition of 1973 appeared in 1975, *Les Machines Célibataires*, eds. Jean Clair and Harald Szeemann (Venice: Alfieri, 1975).

2. Sigmund Freud, *The Origins of Psycho-Analysis: Letters to Wilhelm Fliess, Drafts and Notes 1877–1902*, eds. *Marie Bonaparte, Anna Freud, and Ernst Kris, trans. Eric Mosbacher and James Strachey (New York: Basic Books, 1954), Letter 32 (10–20–95).*

3. Jacques Derrida, "Freud and the Scene of Writing," trans. Jeffrey Mehlman, *Yale French Studies* no. 48 (1972): 117.

4. Clair and Szeemann: 94; the Michel de Certeau essay is titled "Arts de Mourir: Ecritures anti-mystiques."

5. Jean-Louis Baudry, "Ideological Effects of the Basic Cinematographic Apparatus," trans. Alan Williams, *Film Quarterly* vol. 27, no. 2 (Winter 1974–75): 39–47; "The Apparatus: Metapsychological Approaches to the Impression of Reality in the Cinema," trans. Jean Andrews and Bertrand Augst, *Camera Obscura* no. 1 (Fall 1976): 104–26; Christian Metz, "The Imaginary Signifier," trans. Ben Brewster, *The Imaginary Signifier* (Bloomington: Indiana University Press, 1982): 3–87.

6. Janet Bergstrom, "Alternation, Segmentation, Hypnosis: Interview with Raymond Bellour," *Camera Obscura* nos. 3–4 (Summer 1979): 89.

7. Janet Bergstrom, "Enunciation and Sexual Difference," *Camera Obscura* nos. 3–4 (Summer 1979): 55.

8. Stephen Heath, "Narrative Space," *Screen* vol. 17, no. 3 (Autumn 1976): 99.

9. Sigmund Freud, *The Interpretation of Dreams*, in *The Standard Edition of the Complete Psychological Works of Sigmund Freud*, ed. and trans. James Strachey (London: The Hogarth Press and the Institute of Psychoanalysis, 1958), vol. 5: 356.

10. For a recent discussion of the vicissitudes of the "woman question" in Marxism and "feminine sexuality" in psychoanalysis, see Rosalind Coward, *Patriarchal Precedents* (London: Routledge and Kegan Paul, 1983).

11. Heath, 107.

12. Derrida, 117.

13. Jacqueline Rose, conference presentation in *The Cinema in the Eighties: Proceedings of the Meeting* (Venice: Edizioni "La Biennale di Venezia," 1980): 24.

14. Jacqueline Rose, "The Imaginary," *The Talking Cure: Essays in Psychoanalysis and Language*, ed. Colin MacCabe (London and Basingstoke: Macmillan, 1981): 132–61; "The Cinematic Apparatus: Problems in Current Theory," *The Cinematic Apparatus*, eds. Teresa de Lauretis and Stephen Heath (New York: St. Martin's Press, 1980): 172–86.

15. Jacques Lacan, translated by Alan Sheridan as "Of the Gaze as *Objet Petit a*," *The Four Fundamental Concepts of Psychoanalysis* (New York W. W. Norton & Co., 1981): 67–119.

16. Lacan, 153; translation slightly modified.

17. Rose, "The Imaginary": 154.

18. Rose, "The Cinematic Apparatus": 174.

19. Metz, 79.

20. See Metz's discussion of disavowal and fetishism, 69–78.

21. Rose, "The Cinematic Apparatus": 175.

22. Rose, "The Cinematic Apparatus": 175.

23. Joan Copjec, "The Anxiety of the Influencing Machine," *October* no. 23 (Winter 1982): 43–59.

24. Copjec, 57.

25. Freud, *The Interpretation of Dreams*: 541.

26. Joan Copjec, "*India Song/Son nom de Venise dans Calcutta désert*: The Compulsion to Repeat," *October* no. 17 (Summer 1981): 37–52.

27. Metz, 19.

28. Raymond Bellour, "Cine-Repetitions," *Screen* vol. 20, no. 2 (Summer 1979).

29. Metz, 19.

30. Bergstrom, "Alternation, Segmentation, Hypnosis": 81– 82.

31. Lacan, "Tuché and Automaton," *The Four Fundamental Concepts*: 62.

32. Lacan, "Tuché and Automaton": 62.

33. Mary Ann Doane, "Woman's Stake: Filming the Female Body," *October* no. 17 (Summer 1981): 23–36.

34. Joan Copjec, "*India Song*" (see note 26 for complete reference).

35. Sigmund Freud, "On Narcissism: An Introduction," *Standard Edition*, vol. 14: 88.

36. Stephen Heath, "Difference," *Screen* vol. 19, no. 3 (Autumn 1978): 99.

37. Jean Laplanche, *Life and Death in Psychoanalysis*, trans. Jeffrey Mehlman (Baltimore and London: Johns Hopkins University Press, 1976).

38. Julia Kristeva, "Motherhood According to Giovanni Bellini," *Desire in Language* (New York: Columbia University Press, 1980); Michèle Montrelay, "Inquiry into Femininity," *m/f* no. 1 (1978); Luce Irigaray, "That Sex Which Is Not One," trans. R. Albury and Meaghan Morris (Darlington: Feral Publications, 1978). For discussions of this work see, for example, Beverley Brown and Parveen Adams, "The Feminine Body and Feminist Politics," *m/f* no. 3 (1979); Claire Pajaczkowska, "Introduction to Kristeva," *m/f* nos. 5 & 6 (1981); Mary Ann Doane, "Woman's Stake: Filming the Female Body," *October* no. 17 (Summer 1981).

39. My discussion of the narcissism/phallus model is indebted to Jacqueline Rose's introduction to *Feminine Sexuality: Jacques Lacan and the Ecole Freudienne*, eds. Juliet Mitchell and Jacqueline Rose, trans. Jacqueline Rose (London and Basingstoke: Macmillan, 1982).

40. For a recent discussion of the psychoanalytic account of the "mother" see "*L'Ane* dossier—the mother in the unconscious," trans. Ben Brewster, *m/f* no. 8 (1982). Essays by Marie-Hélène Brousse-Delancoe, Marie-Christine Hamon, Dominique Calfon, Bernard Fonty, Eric Laurent. See also in the same issue Parveen Adams, "Mothering."

41. For example see Elisabeth Lyon, "The Cinema of Lol V. Stein," *Camera Obscura* no. 6 (Fall 1980): 7–41; Janet Bergstrom, "Enunciation and Sexual Difference," *Camera Obscura* nos. 3–4 (Summer 1979), especially 56–58; Elizabeth Cowie, "Fantasia," *m/f* no. 9 (1984): 71–104.

42. Jean Laplanche and J.-B. Pontalis, "Fantasy and the Origins of Sexuality," *The International Journal of Psycho-Analysis* 49 (1968).

43. Elisabeth Lyon's formulation of Laplanche and Pontalis's description of "primal fantasies" in "The Cinema of Lol V. Stein" 12.

CHAPTER 5. *Pornography, Eroticism* (*on* Every Man for Himself)

1. This essay was written as a complement to two other essays on *Sauve qui peut (la vie)* by Janet Bergstrom and Elisabeth Lyon. We each chose to write something on the film in lieu of an editorial for the special issue of *Camera Obscura*, nos. 8–9–10, on the film and television work of Jean-Luc Godard. The Bergstrom and Lyon articles, as well as Raymond Bellour's short essay in the same issue, "I Am an Image," also discuss the idealization of women in the film and the aggression against them that this produces.

CHAPTER 6. *Les Enfants de la Patrie* (*on* France/Tour/Detour/Two Children)

1. Colin MacCabe with Mick Eaton and Laura Mulvey, *Godard: Images, Sounds, Politics* (London and Basingstoke: MacMillan and the British Film Institute, 1980): 104.

2. Sonimage's 1978 trip to Mozambique at the invitation of the People's Republic would appear to be an interesting exception to Godard and Miéville's concern with the French family. In fact, this project too was concerned with the nature and quality of images to be imported from "elsewhere," as well as the kinds of images the people of Mozambique should produce to represent themselves to others. See Jean-Luc Godard, "Rapport sur le voyage no 2A de la Société Sonimage au Mozambique," in the special issue of *Cahiers du Cinéma* edited by Godard, no. 300 (May 1979).

3. All citations from dialogue in *France/tour/détour/deux enfants* and *Six fois deux* are taken from transcripts provided by the British Film Institute to accompany the videotapes. They are distributed in Great Britain by the BFI, but are not subtitled or dubbed. *France/tour/détour/deux enfants*, trans. Tom Milne and Gilbert Adair; *Six fois deux*, trans. Jill Forbes. The transcripts are © the British Film Institute Film and Video Library.

4. Phillipe Ariès, *Centuries of Childhood* (Harmondsworth: Peregrine Books, 1979).

5. Michel Foucault, *Discipline and Punish: The Birth of the Prison*, trans. Alan Sheridan (Harmondsworth: Peregrine Books, 1979), see especially III.1, "Docile Bodies."

6. Foucault, 149.

7. St. Augustine, *De Magistro*, trans. George G. Leckie (London: D. Appleton-Century Co., 1938).

8. This verbal play recalls the word association test given to the little boy and the old man in *Le Gai Savoir*.

9. Raymond Williams, *Television: Technology and Cultural Form* (New York: Schocken Books, 1975).

10. Williams, 131.

11. For example, see Jean-Luc Godard, *Introduction à une véritable histoire du cinéma* (Paris: Editions Albatros, 1980): 147.

12. Godard, *Introduction*: 112–13.

13. Statement made by Godard at the conference on "The Arts and Audio-visual Languages," sponsored by the Institut National de l'Audiovisuel (INA) and the University of Pennsylvania, June 5–11, La Napoule, France.

14. Godard, conference on "The Arts and Audio-visual Languages."

15. Godard, *Introduction*: 46.

16. MacCabe, 103.

17. Stephen Heath and Gillian Skirrow, "Television: A World in Action," *Screen* vol. 18, no. 2 (Summer 1977): 7–59.

18. Heath and Skirrow, 29.

19. Heath and Skirrow, 46.

20. Heath and Skirrow, 44; see also the discussion 57–59, television as "the produc-tion-reproduction of the novelistic."

21. See Roland Barthes, "The Family of Man," *Mythologies*, trans. Annette Lavers (New York: Hill and Wang, 1972).

22. MacCabe, 139.

23. Heath and Skirrow, 46.

24. MacCabe, 46.

25. Godard, *Introduction*: 47.

26. For an example of Foucault's prison/school comparison taken to its most ex-treme, see the Italian architect Aldo Rossi's elementary school at Fagnano Olona (1972–76). Its design reproduces the space of a prison and a concentration camp in order to make a statement about the authoritarian structure of schools. Discussed in Dan Gra-ham, "Not Post-Modernism: History as Against Historicism, European Archetypal Vernacular in Relation to American Commerical Vernacular, and the City as Opposed to the Individual Building," *Artforum*, vol. 20, no. 4 (December 1981).

27. For this position see MacCabe, 103. He criticizes Godard because in *Numéro Deux*, "the woman just becomes a metaphor instead of being the real subject of the film." (See also 99.)

28. Raymond Bellour, "I Am an Image" (on *Sauve qui peut (la vie)*), *Camera Obscura* nos. 8–9–10: 120.

29. In Colin MacCabe's interview with Godard in *Godard: Images, Sounds, Politics* on the subject of his television programs, the following exchange takes place:

MacCabe: It's almost as if you're saying that the structures of television are so rotten that there's nothing you can do . . .

Godard: Yes. Make movies.

30. Heath and Skirrow, 56: "It should be added that, before the fact of drama or of any other particular form, watching television in itself is a requirement of socialization ex-actly insofar as it represents the proposition of the intelligible, the conception of the lim-its of communicating."

31. Interview with Jean-Luc Godard, *Cahiers du Cinéma* no. 138 (Dec. 1962). In *God-ard on Godard*, ed. and trans. Tom Milne (New York: The Viking Press, 1972): 191.

32. MacCabe, 156.

33. Godard appears to take very seriously the possibility of using film or video for "research": "I proposed to CNRS [the French national research foundation] a film project to solve once and for all the problem of cancer. We would only have to look at it . . . one has to look at things, one should look and keep on looking. The cinema could use other similar means, such as the electron microscope, it could work like a computer. . . . They didn't even respond. They can't imagine that a filmmaker could say, 'I'm go-ing to help you solve . . . indeed make great advances on the problem of cancer.' That has always been my problem. . . . " "Propos Rompus," a transcription of Godard's comments at the Avignon Festival, July 1980, in *Cahiers du Cinéma* no. 316 (Oct. 1980), 13.

CHAPTER 7. Time Travel, Primal Scene, and the Critical Dystopia (on The Terminator *and* La Jetée)

1. Fredric Jameson, "Progress Versus Utopia; or Can We Imagine the Future?," *Sci-ence Fiction Studies* 9 (1982).

2. Stanislaw Lem, "Cosmology and Science Fiction," trans. Franz Rottenstein, *Science Fiction Studies* 4 (1977): 109.

3. Randall Frakes and Bill Wisher, *The Terminator* (a novel based on the screenplay by James Cameron with Gale Anne Hurd) (New York: Bantam Books, 1984).

4. I have recently been told that this scene was filmed but ended up on the cutting-room floor. One of the producers was given one of the roles and played it so badly that the scene was unsalvageable.

5. See Jessie L. Weston, *From Ritual to Romance: An Account of the Holy Grail from Ancient Ritual to Christian Symbol* (Cambridge: Cambridge University Press, 1920): 42–48.

6. For a full and very interesting discussion of the political dimensions of the cyborg, see Donna Harraway, "A Manifesto for Cyborgs: Science, Technology, and Socialist Feminism in the 1980s," *Socialist Review* no. 80 (March– April, 1985).

7. Useful essays on time travel and its paradoxes include Stanislaw Lem, "The Time-Travel Story and Related Matters of SF Structuring," *Science Fiction Studies* 1 (1974); Monte Cook, "Tips for Time Travel," *Philosophers Look at Science Fiction* (Chicago: Nelson-Hall, 1982); and David Lewis, "The Paradoxes of Time Travel," *Thought Probes*, eds. Fred D. Miller, Jr. and Nicholas D. Smith (New Jersey: Prentice Hall, Inc., 1981).

8. Sigmund Freud, "The Paths to the Formation of Symptoms," *The Standard Edition of the Complete Psychological Works of Sigmund Freud*, ed. James Strachey (London: The Hogarth Press and the Institute of Psychoanalysis, 1958) vol. 16, 370.

9. See, among others, Elisabeth Lyon, "The Cinema of Lol V. Stein," *Camera Obscura* no. 6 (1980); Elizabeth Cowie, "Fantasia," *m/f* no. 9 (1984); and Steve Neale, "Sexual Difference in Cinema," *Sexual Difference* (special issue of *The Oxford Literary Review* 8, nos. 1–2 (1986)).

10. For the best formulation of this idea, see Joan Copjec, "*India Song/Son nom de Venise dans Calcutta désert*: The Compulsion to Repeat," *October* 17 (Summer 1981).

11. Brian Henderson, "The Searchers: An American Dilemma," *Film Quarterly* 34, no. 2 (Winter 1980–1981); reprinted in *Movies and Methods* Vol. II, ed. Bill Nichols (Berkeley: University of California Press, 1985).

12. There are, of course, important exceptions to this standard narrative logic, as Jacqueline Rose has shown, for example, in her analysis of *The Birds*, in which Mitch's "successful" attainment of a masculine and paternal identity comes at the price of regression and catatonia for Melanie ("Paranoia and the Film System," *Screen* 17, no. 4 (Winter 1976–1977)).

13. Depending upon the way science fiction is read or seen or *used*, it can offer other versions of difference as well. Samuel R. Delany says that as a little boy growing up in Harlem, he understood Isaac Asimov's robot stories to be about racial difference. Thus he thought the three laws of robotics spelled out the proper rules of behavior for a good black man to follow with his white superiors. (Talk given at Writers and Books, Rochester N.Y., Dec. 7, 1987.)

14. Raymond Bellour, "Un jour, la castration," *L'Arc*, special issue on Alexandre Dumas, no. 71 (1978).

15. This wholly unremarkable series seems surprisingly capable of taking on a great deal of cultural resonance in its radical presentation of "difference." Andrew Kopkind (*The Nation* 243, no. 17, Nov. 22, 1986) reports that *V* is currently one of the most popular shows in South Africa. He speculates that the show's success lies in the unconsciously ironic, allegorical reading that it allows. Kopkind cites the newspaper description of the week's episode (broadcast on the state controlled television channel):

TV 4: 9:03. "Visitor's Choice." The Resistance Stages a daring attack at a convention of Visitor Commanders where Diana intends to show off the ultimate device in processing humans for food.

Robit Hairman in *The Voice* (Jan. 13, 1987) also reports on the cult that has grown up around *V* in South Africa because of the allegorical readings that escaped the government censors. Before the series was over, anti-government forces were spraying slogans from the series on walls in Johannesburg and Soweto, and T-shirts with a large V painted on front and back became a feature on the streets: "*V* joined the mythology of the resistance."

There are also at least two fanzines devoted to *V*, the newest of which, *The Resistance Chronicles*, describes its first issue in terms that evoke infantile sexual investigation:

This volume will contain the answers to the following burning questions—Why is that blue Chevy with the fogged-up windows rocking back and forth??? How does Chris Farber feel about virtue . . . and boobs? What color underwear does Ham Tyler wear? What do Ham and Chris keep in their medicine cabinet? Plus a musical *V* parody, "We're off to See the Lizard. . . . "

Description taken from *Datazine* no. 44 (Oct.–Nov. 1986).

16. Danny Peary reports this in his interview with Sigourney Weaver, "Playing Ripley in *Alien*," *OMNI's Screen Flights/ Screen Fantasies: The Future According to Science Fiction Cinema*, ed. Danny Peary (Garden City, N.Y.: Doubleday & Co., 1984): 162.

17. Mark Rose, *Alien Encounters: Anatomy of Science Fiction* (Cambridge, Mass.: Harvard University Press, 1981): 99.

18. My discussion of primal-scene fantasy in *Le Jetée* is indebted to Thierry Kuntzel's lectures on that topic in his 1975–1976 seminar at the American University Center for Film Studies in Paris.

19. Ned Lukacher's formulation of the primal-scene fantasy in *Primal Scenes: Literature, Philosophy, Psychoanalysis* (Ithaca: Cornell University Press, 1986): 42. This book contains the best recent discussion of the structure of the primal-scene fantasy.

20. In his lectures on *La Jetée* at the American University Center for Film Studies.

21. The distinction made by Roland Barthes in "Rhetoric of the Image," trans. Stephen Heath (New York: Hill and Wang, 1977): 45.

22. Jacques Lacan, *Ecrits: A Selection* (New York: W. W. Norton and Co., 1977): 141. A distinction cited by Lukacher, 43.

CHAPTER 8. The Cabinet of Dr. Pee-wee: Consumerism and Sexual Terror

1. Sigmund Freud, *Three Essays on Sexuality, The Standard Edition of the Complete Psychological Works of Sigmund Freud* (hereafter referred to as *S.E.*), ed. James Strachey (London: The Hogarth Press and The Institute of Psychoanalysis, 1962), vol. 6: 195.

2. Squire D. Rushnell, quoted by Matt Roush, "Pee-wee pops up on fall's lineup," *USA Today* (Sept. 9, 1986): 1D–2D.

3. Sigmund Freud, "The 'Uncanny'," *S.E.*, vol. 17: 219–52.

4. Sigmund Freud, "The Dissolution of the Oedipus Complex," *S.E.*, vol. 19: 175.

5. On Broadcast Arts, see *Millimeter* (September 1986), section on "Special F/X": 107–10; *Advertising Age* (May 13, 1985): 4; *On Location* (June 1982): 1.

6. I am very grateful to Stephen Oakes for answering my many questions about *Pee-wee's Playhouse*. I particularly appreciate the response he gave to this paper when it was presented as a talk at a conference on television at Johns Hopkins University, organized by the Graduate Student Representative Organization on Mar. 7, 1987.

7. Margy Rochlin, "Pee-wee Herman" (interview), *Interview* (July 1987): 49.

8. Judy Price quoted by Roush, "Pee-wee pops up on fall's lineup": 2D.

9. Judy Price quoted by Roush, "Pee-wee pops up on fall's lineup": 2D.

10. David Diamond, "Is the Toy Business Taking Over Kids' TV?," *TV Guide* (June 13, 1987): 8. Also pushing CBS to look for newer kinds of children's programing is the growing strength of the movement to reregulate children's television in response to the consequences of the Reagan administration's radical deregulation policies.

11. Roush, 2D.

12. Figures reported by Diana Loevy, "Morning Becomes Eccentric," *Channels* (Oct. 1986): 71.

13. Jack Barth, "Pee-wee TV," *Film Comment* vol. 22, no. 6 (Nov.–Dec. 1986): 79.

14. Bryan Bruce, "Pee Wee Herman: The Homosexual Subtext," *CineAction* no. 9 (Summer 1987): 3–6.

15. Mark Booth, *Camp* (London: Quartet Books, 1983).

16. Andrew Ross, "Uses of Camp," in *No Respect: American Intellectuals and Popular Culture*, forthcoming from Routledge, Chapman and Hall.

17. Ross, "Uses of Camp."

18. Booth, 20: "In camp culture, the popular image of the homosexual, like the popular image of the feminine woman, is mimicked as a type of the marginal."

19. Jack Basbucio, "Camp and the Gay Sensibility," *Gays and Film*, ed. Richard Dyer (New York: New York Zoetrope, 1984) 47–48.

20. A comparison made by Joe McElhaney in his paper "I Know I Am But What Is He?: Looking at Pee-wee Herman," presented on the Lesbian/Gay Male Reception panel at the 1986 meeting of the Society for Cinema Studies.

21. Basbucio, 43.

CHAPTER 9. *Teaching in Your Sleep: Feminism and Psychoanalysis*

1. Juliet Mitchell, *Psychoanalysis and Feminism* (New York: Vintage Books, 1975).

2. Sigmund Freud, *The Interpretation of Dreams*, in *The Standard Edition of the Complete Psychological Works of Sigmund Freud* (hereafter abbreviated S.E.), ed. James Strachey (London: The Hogarth Press and The Institute of Psychoanalysis, 1962), vol. 5: 135–36.

3. Sigmund Freud, "Explanations and Applications," *New Introductory Lectures on Psychoanalysis, S.E.* vol. 22: 146–47: "[With respect to] the application of psychoanalysis to education . . . I am glad that I am at least able to say that my daughter, Anna Freud, has made this study her life-work and has in that way compensated for my neglect."

4. Catherine Millot, *Freud, Anti-Pédagogue* (Paris: Editions du Seuil, 1979).

5. Sigmund Freud, "Some Reflections on Schoolboy Psychology," *S.E.* vol. 13: 241–44.

6. Jacques Lacan, *The Four Fundamental Concepts of Psychoanalysis* (New York: W. W. Norton, 1981): 174–267.

7. Jacques Lacan, *Scilicet* V: 16.

8. Millot, 162.

9. For a concise discussion of Lacan's "four discourses," which were introduced in his 1969–70 seminar, *L'envers de la psychanalyse* (XVIII), see Jacqueline Rose, *Feminine Sexuality: Jacques Lacan and the Ecole Freudienne*, eds. Juliet Mitchell and Jacqueline Rose (London: Macmillan, 1982): 160–61.

10. Shoshana Felman, "Psychoanalysis and Education: Teaching Terminable and Interminable," *Yale French Studies* 63 (1982): 21–44.

11. Jacques Lacan, Seminar XX, *Encore* (Paris: Editions du Seuil, 1975): 88.

12. Jacques Lacan, Seminar II, *Le moi dans le théorie de Freud et dans la technique de la psychanalyse* (Paris: Editions du Seuil, 1978): 242.

13. Lacan, *Scilicet* I: 59.

14. "Should Psychoanalysis Be Taught at the University?" is the original title of a paper Freud published in a Hungarian translation. The *S.E.* title is "On the Teaching of Psychoanalysis in Universities," vol. 17: 171–73.

15. Paula Treichler, "Teaching Feminist Theory," *Theory in the Classroom*, ed. Cary Nelson (Urbana and Chicago: University of Illinois Press, 1986): 57–128. For another comprehensive survey of feminist pedagogical theory and techniques see *Learning Our Way: Essays in Feminist Education*, eds. Charlotte Bunch and Sandra Pollack (Trumansburg, N.Y.: The Crossing Press, 1983).

16. For example, see Stanley Aronowitz's "Mass Culture and the Eclipse of Reason," *The Crisis in Historical Materialism* (New York: Praeger, 1981).

17. Jacqueline Rose, "Femininity and its Discontents," *Feminist Review* 14 (Summer 1983): 5–21. My discussion of the feminist alliance with anti-empiricism is indebted to Rose's argument in this essay.

18. For example, Carol Dyhouse, *Girls Growing Up in Late Victorian England* (London: Routledge and Kegan Paul, 1981) and Judith Walkowitz, *Prostitution and Victorian Society: Women, Class and the State* (Cambridge: Cambridge University Press, 1980).

19. Sigmund Freud, "Femininity," *S.E.* vol. 22: 116.

20. Juliet Mitchell, "Feminine Sexuality": 23. As opposed to Kleinian and non-Kleinian object-relations theorists for whom "the distinction between the sexes is not the result of a division but a fact that is already given, men and women, males and females, *exist.*"

21. Sojourner Truth's famous speech can be found in *Ain't I a Woman?*, Bell Hooks (Boston: South End Press, 1981).

22. Clearly a Derridean formulation of the "multiple identities" solution.

23. For a history of the political consequences of the American "professionalization" of psychoanalysis see Russell Jacoby, *The Repression of Psychoanalysis: Otto Fenichel and the Political Freudians* (New York: Basic Books, 1983).

24. An important point made by Rose in "Femininity and Its Discontents" 6.

25. See Sherry Turkle, *Psychoanalytic Politics: Freud's French Revolution* (Cambridge, Mass.: The MIT Press, 1981).

INDEX

Index

Prepared by Robin Jackson

Constance Penley is associate professor of English and film studies at the University of Rochester. She has also taught at the University of California, Berkeley, the San Francisco Art Institute, and the University of Illinois. Penley received her Ph.D. in rhetoric from the University of California and studied in Paris at the Centre Universitaire Américain de Cinéma and the Ecole des Hautes Etudes en Sciences Sociales. A co-editor of Camera Obscura *since 1974, she has also served in an editorial capacity on the journals* Women and Film, *and* m/f, *and as editor of the book* Feminism and Film Theory *(1988). Her articles and reviews have appeared in* Camera Obscura, m/f, Jump Cut, Women and Film, *and* Screen.